ROBERT LOUIS STEVENSON

VOL. XV

THE AMATEUR EMIGRANT
ACROSS THE PLAINS ❧ THE
SILVERADO SQUATTERS ❧ ❧

" Far away were hilltops like little islands."

Drawn by S. W. VAN SCHAICK.

THE TRAVELS AND ESSAYS OF ROBERT LOUIS STEVENSON

THE AMATEUR EMIGRANT ❧ ❧ ACROSS THE PLAINS ❧ THE SILVERADO SQUATTERS ❧

PUBLISHED IN NEW YORK BY CHARLES SCRIBNER'S SONS ❧ ❧ 1895 ❧

CONTENTS

CONTENTS

THE AMATEUR EMIGRANT
From the Clyde to Sandy Hook

ACROSS THE PLAINS
WITH OTHER MEMORIES AND ESSAYS

CONTENTS

THE SILVERADO SQUATTERS

BOOK I

IN THE VALLEY

BOOK II

WITH THE CHILDREN OF ISRAEL

THE AMATEUR EMIGRANT

FROM THE CLYDE TO SANDY HOOK

TO

ROBERT ALAN MOWBRAY STEVENSON

OUR friendship was not only founded before we were
born by a community of blood, but is in itself near
as old as my life. It began with our early ages, and,
like a history, has been continued to the present
time. Although we may not be old in the world,
we are old to each other, having so long been inti-
mates. We are now widely separated, a great sea
and continent intervening; but memory, like care,
mounts into iron ships and rides post behind the
horseman. Neither time nor space nor enmity can
conquer old affection; and as I dedicate these
sketches, it is not to you only, but to all in the old
country, that I send the greeting of my heart.

R. L. S.

1879.

THE AMATEUR EMIGRANT

THE SECOND CABIN

I FIRST encountered my fellow-passengers on the Broomielaw in Glasgow. Thence we descended the Clyde in no familiar spirit, but looking askance on each other as on possible enemies. A few Scandinavians, who had already grown acquainted on the North Sea, were friendly and voluble over their long pipes; but among English speakers distance and suspicion reigned supreme. The sun was soon overclouded, the wind freshened and grew sharp as we continued to descend the widening estuary; and with the falling temperature the gloom among the passengers increased. Two of the women wept. Any one who had come aboard might have supposed we were all absconding from the law. There was scarce a word interchanged, and no common sentiment but that of cold united us, until at length, having touched at Greenock, a pointing arm and a rush to the starboard now announced that our ocean steamer was in sight. There she lay in mid-river, at the tail of the Bank, her sea-signal flying: a wall of bulwark, a street of white deck-houses, an aspiring forest of spars, larger than a church, and soon to be as populous as many an incorporated town in the land to which she was to bear us.

I was not, in truth, a steerage passenger. Although anxious to see the worst of emigrant life, I had some work to finish on the voyage, and was advised to go by the second cabin, where at least I should have a table at command. The advice was excellent; but to understand the choice, and what I gained, some outline of the internal disposition of the ship will first be necessary. In her very nose is Steerage No. 1, down two pair of stairs. A little abaft, another companion, labelled Steerage No. 2 and 3, gives admission to three galleries, two running forward towards Steerage No. 1, and the third aft towards the engines. The starboard forward gallery is the second cabin. Away abaft the engines and below the officers' cabins, to complete our survey of the vessel, there is yet a third nest of steerages, labelled 4 and 5. The second cabin, to return, is thus a modified oasis in the very heart of the steerages. Through the thin partition you can hear the steerage passengers being sick, the rattle of tin dishes as they sit at meals, the varied accents in which they converse, the crying of their children terrified by this new experience, or the clean flat smack of the parental hand in chastisement.

There are, however, many advantages for the inhabitant of this strip. He does not require to bring his own bedding or dishes, but finds berths and a table completely if somewhat roughly furnished. He enjoys a distinct superiority in diet; but this, strange to say, differs not only on different ships, but on the same ship according as her head is to the east or west. In my own experience, the principal difference between our table and that of the true steerage passenger was the table itself, and the crockery plates from which we ate. But lest I should show myself ungrateful, let me recapitulate every advantage. At breakfast, we had a choice between tea and coffee for beverage; a choice not easy to make, the two were so surprisingly alike. I found that I could sleep after the coffee and lay awake after the tea, which is proof conclusive of some chemical disparity; and even by the palate I could distinguish a smack of snuff in the former from a flavour of boiling and dish-cloths in the second. As a matter of fact, I have seen passengers, after many sips, still doubting which had been supplied them. In the way of eatables at the same meal we were gloriously favoured; for in addition to porridge, which was common to all, we had Irish stew, sometimes a bit of fish, and sometimes rissoles. The dinner of soup, roast fresh beef, boiled salt junk, and potatoes, was, I believe, exactly common to the steerage and the second cabin; only I have heard it rumoured that our potatoes were of a superior brand; and twice a week, on pudding-days, instead of duff, we had a saddle-bag filled with currants under the name of a plum-pudding. At tea we were served with some broken meat from the saloon; sometimes in the comparatively elegant form of spare patties or rissoles; but as a general thing, mere chicken-bones and flakes of fish, neither hot nor cold. If these were not the scrapings of plates their looks belied them sorely; yet we were all too hungry to be proud, and fell to these leavings greedily. These, the bread, which was excellent, and the soup and porridge

3

which were both good, formed my whole diet throughout the voyage; so that except for the broken meat and
the convenience of a table I might as well have been in
the steerage outright. Had they given me porridge again
in the evening, I should have been perfectly contented
with the fare. As it was, with a few biscuits and some
whisky and water before turning in, I kept my body
going and my spirits up to the mark.

The last particular in which the second cabin passenger remarkably stands ahead of his brother of the steerage is one altogether of sentiment. In the steerage there
are males and females; in the second cabin ladies and
gentlemen. For some time after I came aboard I thought
I was only a male; but in the course of a voyage of discovery between decks, I came on a brass plate, and
learned that I was still a gentleman. Nobody knew it,
of course. I was lost in the crowd of males and females,
and rigorously confined to the same quarter of the deck.
Who could tell whether I housed on the port or starboard side of steerage No. 2 and 3? And it was only
there that my superiority became practical; everywhere
else I was incognito, moving among my inferiors with
simplicity, not so much as a swagger to indicate that I
was a gentleman after all, and had broken meat to tea.
Still, I was like one with a patent of nobility in a drawer
at home; and when I felt out of spirits I could go down
and refresh myself with a look of that brass plate.

For all these advantages I paid but two guineas. Six
guineas is the steerage fare; eight that by the second
cabin; and when you remember that the steerage passenger must supply bedding and dishes, and, in five
cases out of ten, either brings some dainties with him,

or privately pays the steward for extra rations, the difference in price becomes almost nominal. Air comparatively fit to breathe, food comparatively varied, and the satisfaction of being still privately a gentleman, may thus be had almost for the asking. Two of my fellow-passengers in the second cabin had already made the passage by the cheaper fare, and declared it was an experiment not to be repeated. As I go on to tell about my steerage friends, the reader will perceive that they were not alone in their opinion. Out of ten with whom I was more or less intimate, I am sure not fewer than five vowed, if they returned, to travel second cabin; and all who had left their wives behind them assured me they would go without the comfort of their presence until they could afford to bring them by saloon.

Our party in the second cabin was not perhaps the most interesting on board. Perhaps even in the saloon there was as much good-will and character. Yet it had some elements of curiosity. There was a mixed group of Swedes, Danes, and Norsemen, one of whom, generally known by the name of "Johnny," in spite of his own protests, greatly diverted us by his clever, cross-country efforts to speak English, and became on the strength of that an universal favourite — it takes so little in this world of shipboard to create a popularity. There was, besides, a Scots mason, known from his favourite dish as "Irish Stew," three or four nondescript Scots, a fine young Irishman, O'Reilly, and a pair of young men who deserve a special word of condemnation. One of them was Scots; the other claimed to be American; admitted, after some fencing, that he was born in England; and ultimately proved to be an Irishman born and

5

nurtured, but ashamed to own his country. He had a sister on board, whom he faithfully neglected throughout the voyage, though she was not only sick, but much his senior, and had nursed and cared for him in childhood. In appearance he was like an imbecile Henry the Third of France. The Scotsman, though perhaps as big an ass, was not so dead of heart; and I have only bracketed them together because they were fast friends, and disgraced themselves equally by their conduct at the table.

Next, to turn to topics more agreeable, we had a newly married couple, devoted to each other, with a pleasant story of how they had first seen each other years ago at a preparatory school, and that very afternoon he had carried her books home for her. I do not know if this story will be plain to Southern readers; but to me it recalls many a school idyll, with wrathful swains of eight and nine confronting each other stride-legs, flushed with jealousy; for to carry home a young lady's books was both a delicate attention and a privilege.

Then there was an old lady, or indeed I am not sure that she was as much old as antiquated and strangely out of place, who had left her husband, and was travelling all the way to Kansas by herself. We had to take her own word that she was married; for it was sorely contradicted by the testimony of her appearance. Nature seemed to have sanctified her for the single state; even the colour of her hair was incompatible with matrimony, and her husband, I thought, should be a man of saintly spirit and phantasmal bodily presence. She was ill, poor thing; her soul turned from the viands; the dirty table-cloth shocked her like an impropriety; and the whole

6

strength of her endeavour was bent upon keeping her watch true to Glasgow time till she should reach New York. They had heard reports, her husband and she, of some unwarrantable disparity of hours between these two cities; and with a spirit commendably scientific, had seized on this occasion to put them to the proof. It was a good thing for the old lady; for she passed much leisure time in studying the watch. Once, when prostrated by sickness, she let it run down. It was inscribed on her harmless mind in letters of adamant that the hands of a watch must never be turned backwards; and so it behoved her to lie in wait for the exact moment ere she started it again. When she imagined this was about due, she sought out one of the young second-cabin Scotsmen, who was embarked on the same experiment as herself and had hitherto been less neglectful. She was in quest of two o'clock; and when she learned it was already seven on the shores of Clyde, she lifted up her voice and cried "Gravy!" I had not heard this innocent expletive since I was a young child; and I suppose it must have been the same with the other Scotsmen present, for we all laughed our fill.

Last but not least, I come to my excellent friend Mr. Jones. It would be difficult to say whether I was his right-hand man, or he mine, during the voyage. Thus at table I carved, while he only scooped gravy; but at our concerts, of which more anon, he was the president who called up performers to sing, and I but his messenger who ran his errands and pleaded privately with the over-modest. I knew I liked Mr. Jones from the moment I saw him. I thought him by his face to be Scottish; nor could his accent undeceive me. For as

7

there is a *lingua franca* of many tongues on the moles
and in the feluccas of the Mediterranean, so there is a
free or common accent among English-speaking men
who follow the sea. They catch a twang in a New
England port; from a cockney skipper, even a Scotsman sometimes learns to drop an *h;* a word of a dialect
is picked up from another hand in the forecastle; until
often the result is undecipherable, and you have to ask
for the man's place of birth. So it was with Mr. Jones.
I thought him a Scotsman who had been long to sea;
and yet he was from Wales, and had been most of his
life a blacksmith at an inland forge; a few years in
America and half a score of ocean voyages having suf-
ficed to modify his speech into the common pattern.
By his own account he was both strong and skilful in
his trade. A few years back, he had been married and
after a fashion a rich man; now the wife was dead and
the money gone. But his was the nature that looks
forward, and goes on from one year to another and
through all the extremities of fortune undismayed; and
if the sky were to fall to-morrow, I should look to see
Jones, the day following, perched on a step-ladder and
getting things to rights. He was always hovering
round inventions like a bee over a flower, and lived in
a dream of patents. He had with him a patent medicine, for instance, the composition of which he had
bought years ago for five dollars from an American
peddler, and sold the other day for a hundred pounds
(I think it was) to an English apothecary. It was called
Golden Oil, cured all maladies without exception; and
I am bound to say that I partook of it myself with good
results. It is a character of the man that he was not

only perpetually dosing himself with Golden Oil, but wherever there was a head aching or a finger cut, there would be Jones with his bottle.

If he had one taste more strongly than another, it was to study character. Many an hour have we two walked upon the deck dissecting our neighbours in a spirit that was too purely scientific to be called unkind; whenever a quaint or human trait slipped out in conversation, you might have seen Jones and me exchanging glances; and we could hardly go to bed in comfort till we had exchanged notes and discussed the day's experience. We were then like a couple of anglers comparing a day's kill. But the fish we angled for were of a metaphysical species, and we angled as often as not in one another's baskets. Once, in the midst of a serious talk, each found there was a scrutinising eye upon himself; I own I paused in embarrassment at this double detection; but Jones, with a better civility, broke into a peal of unaffected laughter, and declared, what was the truth, that there was a pair of us indeed.

EARLY IMPRESSIONS

WE steamed out of the Clyde on Thursday night, and early on the Friday forenoon we took in our last batch of emigrants at Lough Foyle, in Ireland, and said farewell to Europe. The company was now complete, and began to draw together, by inscrutable magnetisms, upon the decks. There were Scots and Irish in plenty, a few English, a few Americans, a good handful of Scandinavians, a German or two, and one Russian; all now belonging for ten days to one small iron country on the deep.

As I walked the deck and looked round upon my fellow-passengers, thus curiously assorted from all northern Europe, I began for the first time to understand the nature of emigration. Day by day throughout the passage, and thenceforward across all the States, and on to the shores of the Pacific, this knowledge grew more clear and melancholy. Emigration, from a word of the most cheerful import, came to sound most dismally in my ear. There is nothing more agreeable to picture and nothing more pathetic to behold. The abstract idea, as conceived at home, is hopeful and adventurous. A young man, you fancy, scorning restraints and helpers, issues forth into life, that great battle, to fight for his own hand.

The most pleasant stories of ambition, of difficulties overcome, and of ultimate success, are but as episodes to this great epic of self-help. The epic is composed of individual heroisms; it stands to them as the victorious war which subdued an empire stands to the personal act of bravery which spiked a single cannon and was adequately rewarded with a medal. For in emigration the young men enter direct and by the shipload on their heritage of work; empty continents swarm, as at the bo'sun's whistle, with industrious hands, and whole new empires are domesticated to the service of man.

This is the closet picture, and is found, on trial, to consist mostly of embellishments. The more I saw of my fellow-passengers, the less I was tempted to the lyric note. Comparatively few of the men were below thirty; many were married, and encumbered with families; not a few were already up in years; and this itself was out of tune with my imaginations, for the ideal emigrant should certainly be young. Again, I thought he should offer to the eye some bold type of humanity, with bluff or hawk-like features, and the stamp of an eager and pushing disposition. Now those around me were for the most part quiet, orderly, obedient citizens, family men broken by adversity, elderly youths who had failed to place themselves in life, and people who had seen better days. Mildness was the prevailing character; mild mirth and mild endurance. In a word, I was not taking part in an impetuous and conquering sally, such as swept over Mexico or Siberia, but found myself, like Marmion, "in the lost battle, borne down by the flying."

Labouring mankind had in the last years, and throughout Great Britain, sustained a prolonged and crushing

series of defeats. I had heard vaguely of these reverses;
of whole streets of houses standing deserted by the
Tyne, the cellar-doors broken and removed for firewood;
of homeless men loitering at the street-corners of Glasgow with their chests beside them; of closed factories,
useless strikes, and starving girls. But I had never
taken them home to me or represented these distresses
livingly to my imagination. A turn of the market may
be a calamity as disastrous as the French retreat from
Moscow; but it hardly lends itself to lively treatment,
and makes a trifling figure in the morning papers. We
may struggle as we please, we are not born economists.
The individual is more affecting than the mass. It is by
the scenic accidents, and the appeal to the carnal eye,
that for the most part we grasp the significance of trage-
dies. Thus it was only now, when I found myself involved in the rout, that I began to appreciate how sharp
had been the battle. We were a company of the rejected; the drunken, the incompetent, the weak, the
prodigal, all who had been unable to prevail against circumstances in the one land, were now fleeing pitifully
to another; and though one or two might still succeed,
all had already failed. We were a shipful of failures, the
broken men of England. Yet it must not be supposed
that these people exhibited depression. The scene, on
the contrary, was cheerful. Not a tear was shed on
board the vessel. All were full of hope for the future,
and showed an inclination to innocent gaiety. Some
were heard to sing, and all began to scrape acquaintance
with small jests and ready laughter.

The children found each other out like dogs, and ran
about the decks scraping acquaintance after their fash-

ion also. "What do you call your mither?" I heard one ask. "Mawmaw," was the reply, indicating, I fancy, a shade of difference in the social scale. When people pass each other on the high seas of life at so early an age, the contact is but slight, and the relation more like what we may imagine to be the friendship of flies than that of men; it is so quickly joined, so easily dissolved, so open in its communications and so devoid of deeper human qualities. The children, I observed, were all in a band, and as thick as thieves at a fair, while their elders were still ceremoniously manœuvring on the outskirts of acquaintance. The sea, the ship, and the seamen were soon as familiar as home to these half-conscious little ones. It was odd to hear them, throughout the voyage, employ shore words to designate portions of the vessel. "Go' 'way doon to yon dyke," I heard one say, probably meaning the bulwark. I often had my heart in my mouth, watching them climb into the shrouds or on the rails, while the ship went swinging through the waves; and I admired and envied the courage of their mothers, who sat by in the sun and looked on with composure at these perilous feats. "He 'll maybe be a sailor," I heard one remark; "now 's the time to learn." I had been on the point of running forward to interfere, but stood back at that, reproved. Very few in the more delicate classes have the nerve to look upon the peril of one dear to them; but the life of poorer folk, where necessity is so much more immediate and imperious, braces even a mother to this extreme of endurance. And perhaps, after all, it is better that the lad should break his neck than that you should break his spirit.

13

And since I am here on the chapter of the children, I
must mention one little fellow, whose family belonged
to Steerage No. 4 and 5, and who, wherever he went,
was like a strain of music round the ship. He was an
ugly, merry, unbreeched child of three, his lint-white
hair in a tangle, his face smeared with suet and treacle;
but he ran to and fro with so natural a step, and fell and
picked himself up again with such grace and good-
humour, that he might fairly be called beautiful when he
was in motion. To meet him, crowing with laughter
and beating an accompaniment to his own mirth with
a tin spoon upon a tin cup, was to meet a little triumph
of the human species. Even when his mother and the
rest of his family lay sick and prostrate around him, he
sat upright in their midst and sang aloud in the pleasant
heartlessness of infancy.

Throughout the Friday, intimacy among us men made
but a few advances. We discussed the probable duration of the voyage, we exchanged pieces of information,
naming our trades, what we hoped to find in the new
world, or what we were fleeing from in the old; and,
above all, we condoled together over the food and the
vileness of the steerage. One or two had been so near
famine that you may say they had run into the ship with
the devil at their heels; and to these all seemed for the
best in the best of possible steamers. But the majority
were hugely discontented. Coming as they did from a
country in so low a state as Great Britain, many of them
from Glasgow, which commercially speaking was as
good as dead, and many having long been out of work,
I was surprised to find them so dainty in their notions.
I myself lived almost exclusively on bread, porridge,

and soup, precisely as it was supplied to them, and found it, if not luxurious, at least sufficient. But these working men were loud in their outcries. It was not "food for human beings," it was "only fit for pigs," it was "a disgrace." Many of them lived almost entirely upon biscuit, others on their own private supplies, and some paid extra for better rations from the ship. This marvellously changed my notion of the degree of luxury habitual to the artisan. I was prepared to hear him grumble, for grumbling is the traveller's pastime; but I was not prepared to find him turn away from a diet which was palatable to myself. Words I should have disregarded, or taken with a liberal allowance; but when a man prefers dry biscuit there can be no question of the sincerity of his disgust.

With one of their complaints I could most heartily sympathise. A single night of the steerage had filled them with horror. I had myself suffered, even in my decent second-cabin berth, from the lack of air; and as the night promised to be fine and quiet, I determined to sleep on deck, and advised all who complained of their quarters to follow my example. I daresay a dozen of others agreed to do so, and I thought we should have been quite a party. Yet, when I brought up my rug about seven bells, there was no one to be seen but the watch. That chimerical terror of good night-air, which makes men close their windows, list their doors, and seal themselves up with their own poisonous exhalations, had sent all these healthy workmen down below. One would think we had been brought up in a fever country; yet in England the most malarious districts are in the bedchambers.

I felt saddened at this defection, and yet half-pleased to have the night so quietly to myself. The wind had hauled a little ahead on the starboard bow, and was dry but chilly. I found a shelter near the fire-hole, and made myself snug for the night. The ship moved over the uneven sea with a gentle and cradling movement. The ponderous, organic labours of the engine in her bowels occupied the mind, and prepared it for slumber. From time to time a heavier lurch would disturb me as I lay, and recall me to the obscure borders of consciousness; or I heard, as it were through a veil, the clear note of the clapper on the brass and the beautiful sea-cry, "All's well!" I know nothing, whether for poetry or music, that can surpass the effect of these two syllables in the darkness of a night at sea.

The day dawned fairly enough, and during the early part we had some pleasant hours to improve acquaintance in the open air; but towards nightfall the wind freshened, the rain began to fall, and the sea rose so high that it was difficult to keep one's footing on the deck. I have spoken of our concerts. We were indeed a musical ship's company, and cheered our way into exile with the fiddle, the accordion, and the songs of all nations. Good, bad, or indifferent — Scottish, English, Irish, Russian, German or Norse, — the songs were received with generous applause. Once or twice, a recitation, very spiritedly rendered in a powerful Scottish accent, varied the proceedings; and once we sought in vain to dance a quadrille, eight men of us together, to the music of the violin. The performers were all humorous, frisky fellows, who loved to cut capers in private life; but as soon as they were arranged for the dance, they conducted themselves like so many mutes at a funeral. I have never seen decorum pushed so far; and as this was not expected, the quadrille was soon whistled down, and the dancers departed under a cloud. Eight Frenchmen, even eight Englishmen from another rank of society, would have dared to make some fun for themselves and the spectators; but the working man, when sober, takes an extreme and even melancholy view of personal deportment. A fifth-form schoolboy is not more careful of dignity. He dares not be comical; his fun must escape from him unprepared, and above all, it must be unaccompanied by any physical demonstration. I like his society under most circumstances, but let me never again join with him in public gambols.

But the impulse to sing was strong, and triumphed over modesty and even the inclemencies of sea and sky. On this rough Saturday night, we got together by the main deck-house, in a place sheltered from the wind and rain. Some clinging to a ladder which led to the hurricane deck, and the rest knitting arms or taking hands, we made a ring to support the women in the violent lurching of the ship; and when we were thus disposed, sang to our hearts' content. Some of the songs were appropriate to the scene; others strikingly the reverse. Bastard doggrel of the music-hall, such as, "Around her splendid form, I weaved the magic circle," sounded bald, bleak, and pitifully silly. "We don't want to fight, but, by Jingo, if we do," was in some measure saved by the vigour and unanimity with which the chorus was thrown forth into the night. I observed a Platt-Deutsch mason, entirely innocent of English, adding heartily to the general effect. And perhaps the German mason is but a fair example of the sincerity with which the song was rendered; for nearly all with whom I conversed upon the subject were bitterly opposed to war, and attributed their own misfortunes, and frequently their own taste for whisky, to the campaigns in Zululand and Afghanistan.

Every now and again, however, some song that touched the pathos of our situation was given forth; and you could hear by the voices that took up the burden how the sentiment came home to each. "The Anchor's Weighed" was true for us. We were indeed "Rocked on the bosom of the stormy deep." How many of us could say with the singer, "I'm lonely to-night, love, without you," or "Go, some one, and tell them from me, to write me a letter from home!" And when was there a more appropriate moment for "Auld Lang Syne" than now, when the land, the friends, and the affections of that mingled but beloved time were fading and fleeing behind us in the vessel's wake? It pointed forward to the hour when these labours should be overpast, to the return voyage, and to many a meeting in the sanded inn, when those who had parted in the spring of youth should again drink a cup of kindness in their age. Had not Burns contemplated emigration, I scarce believe he would have found that note.

All Sunday the weather remained wild and cloudy; many were prostrated by sickness; only five sat down to tea in the second cabin, and two of these departed abruptly ere the meal was at an end. The Sabbath was observed strictly by the majority of the emigrants. I heard an old woman express her surprise that "the ship didna gae doon," as she saw some one pass her with a chess-board on the holy day. Some sang Scottish psalms. Many went to service, and in true Scottish fashion came back ill pleased with their divine. "I didna think he was an experienced preacher," said one girl to me.

It was a bleak, uncomfortable day; but at night, by six bells, although the wind had not yet moderated, the clouds were all wrecked and blown away behind the rim of the horizon, and the stars came out thickly over-head. I saw Venus burning as steadily and sweetly across this hurly-burly of the winds and waters as ever at home upon the summer woods. The engine pounded, the screw tossed out of the water with a roar, and shook the ship from end to end; the bows battled with loud reports against the billows: and as I stood in the lee-scuppers and looked up to where the funnel leaned out, over my head, vomiting smoke, and the black and monstrous topsails blotted, at each lurch, a different crop of stars, it seemed as if all this trouble were a thing of small account, and that just above the mast reigned peace unbroken and eternal.

STEERAGE SCENES

OUR companion (Steerage No. 2 and 3) was a favourite resort. Down one flight of stairs there was a comparatively large open space, the center occupied by a hatchway, which made a convenient seat for about twenty persons, while barrels, coils of rope, and the carpenter's bench afforded perches for perhaps as many more. The canteen, or steerage bar, was on one side of the stair; on the other, a no less attractive spot, the cabin of the indefatigable interpreter. I have seen people packed into this space like herrings in a barrel, and many merry evenings prolonged there until five bells, when the lights were ruthlessly extinguished and all must go to roost.

It had been rumoured since Friday that there was a fiddler aboard, who lay sick and unmelodious in Steerage No. 1; and on the Monday forenoon, as I came down the companion, I was saluted by something in Strathspey time. A white-faced Orpheus was cheerily playing to an audience of white-faced women. It was as much as he could do to play, and some of his hearers were scarce able to sit; yet they had crawled from their bunks at the first experimental flourish, and found better than medicine in the music. Some of the heaviest heads

20

began to nod in time, and a degree of animation looked from some of the palest eyes. Humanly speaking, it is a more important matter to play the fiddle, even badly, than to write huge works upon recondite subjects. What could Mr. Darwin have done for these sick women? But this fellow scraped away; and the world was positively a better place for all who heard him. We have yet to understand the economical value of these mere accomplishments. I told the fiddler he was a happy man, carrying happiness about with him in his fiddle-case, and he seemed alive to the fact.

"It is a privilege," I said. He thought a while upon the word, turning it over in his Scots head, and then answered with conviction, "Yes, a privilege."

That night I was summoned by "Merrily danced the Quaker's wife" into the companion of Steerage No. 4 and 5. This was, properly speaking, but a strip across a deck-house, lit by a sickly lantern which swung to and fro with the motion of the ship. Through the open slide-door we had a glimpse of a grey night sea, with patches of phosphorescent foam flying, swift as birds, into the wake, and the horizon rising and falling as the vessel rolled to the wind. In the center the companion ladder plunged down sheerly like an open pit. Below, on the first landing, and lighted by another lamp, lads and lasses danced, not more than three at a time for lack of space, in jigs and reels and hornpipes. Above, on either side, there was a recess railed with iron, perhaps two feet wide and four long, which stood for orchestra and seats of honour. In the one balcony, five slatternly Irish lasses sat woven in a comely group. In the other was posted Orpheus, his body, which was convulsively in motion, forming an odd contrast to his somnolent, imperturbable Scots face. His brother, a dark man with a vehement, interested countenance, who made a god of the fiddler, sat by with open mouth, drinking in the general admiration and throwing out remarks to kindle it.

"That's a bonny hornpipe now," he would say, "it's a great favourite with performers; they dance the sand dance to it." And he expounded the sand dance. Then suddenly, it would be a long "Hush!" with uplifted finger and glowing, supplicating eyes; "he's going to play ' Auld Robin Gray ' on one string!" And throughout this excruciating movement, — "On one string, that's on one string!" he kept crying. I would have given something myself that it had been on none; but the hearers were much awed. I called for a tune or two, and thus introduced myself to the notice of the brother, who directed his talk to me for some little while, keeping, I need hardly mention, true to his topic, like the seamen to the star. "He's grand of it," he said confidentially. "His master was a music-hall man." Indeed the music-hall man had left his mark, for our fiddler was ignorant of many of our best old airs; " Logie o' Buchan," for instance, he only knew as a quick, jigging figure in a set of quadrilles, and had never heard it called by name. Perhaps, after all, the brother was the more interesting performer of the two. I have spoken with him afterwards repeatedly, and found him always the same quick, fiery bit of a man, not without brains; but he never showed to such advantage as when he was thus squiring the fiddler into public note. There is nothing more becoming than a genuine admiration; and it shares this

22

with love, that it does not become contemptible although misplaced.

The dancing was but feebly carried on. The space was almost impracticably small; and the Irish wenches combined the extreme of bashfulness about this innocent display with a surprising impudence and roughness of address. Most often, either the fiddle lifted up its voice unheeded, or only a couple of lads would be footing it and snapping fingers on the landing. And such was the eagerness of the brother to display all the acquirements of his idol, and such the sleepy indifference of the performer, that the tune would as often as not be changed, and the hornpipe expire into a ballad before the dancers had cut half a dozen shuffles.

In the meantime, however, the audience had been growing more and more numerous every moment; there was hardly standing-room round the top of the companion; and the strange instinct of the race moved some of the new-comers to close both the doors, so that the atmosphere grew insupportable. It was a good place, as the saying is, to leave.

The wind hauled ahead with a head sea. By ten at night heavy sprays were flying and drumming over the forecastle; the companion of Steerage No. 1 had to be closed, and the door of communication through the second cabin thrown open. Either from the convenience of the opportunity, or because we had already a number of acquaintances in that part of the ship, Mr. Jones and I paid it a late visit. Steerage No. 1 is shaped like an isosceles triangle, the sides opposite the equal angles bulging outward with the contour of the ship. It is lined with eight pens of sixteen bunks apiece, four bunks

23

below and four above on either side. At night the place is lit with two lanterns, one to each table. As the steamer beat on her way among the rough billows, the light passed through violent phases of change, and was thrown to and fro and up and down with startling swiftness. You were tempted to wonder, as you looked, how so thin a glimmer could control and disperse such solid blackness. When Jones and I entered we found a little company of our acquaintances seated together at the triangular foremost table. A more forlorn party, in more dismal circumstances, it would be hard to imagine. The motion here in the ship's nose was very violent; the uproar of the sea often overpoweringly loud. The yellow flicker of the lantern spun round and round and tossed the shadows in masses. The air was hot, but it struck a chill from its fœtor. From all round in the dark bunks, the scarcely human noises of the sick joined into a kind of farmyard chorus. In the midst, these five friends of mine were keeping up what heart they could in company. Singing was their refuge from discomfortable thoughts and sensations. One piped, in feeble tones, "Oh why left I my hame ?" which seemed a pertinent question in the circumstances. Another, from the invisible horrors of a pen where he lay dog-sick upon the upper shelf, found courage, in a blink of his sufferings, to give us several verses of the "Death of Nelson"; and it was odd and eerie to hear the chorus breathe feebly from all sorts of dark corners, and "this day has done his dooty" rise and fall and be taken up again in this dim *inferno*, to an accompaniment of plunging, hollow-sounding bows and the rattling spray-showers overhead.

All seemed unfit for conversation; a certain dizziness had interrupted the activity of their minds; and except to sing they were tongue-tied. There was present, however, one tall, powerful fellow of doubtful nationality, being neither quite Scotsman nor altogether Irish, but of surprising clearness of conviction on the highest problems. He had gone nearly beside himself on the Sunday, because of a general backwardness to indorse his definition of mind as "a living, thinking substance which cannot be felt, heard, or seen" — nor, I presume, although he failed to mention it, smelt. Now he came forward in a pause with another contribution to our culture.

"Just by way of change," said he, "I'll ask you a Scripture riddle. There's profit in them too," he added ungrammatically.

This was the riddle —

C and P
Did agree
To cut down C;
But C and P
Could not agree
Without the leave of G
All the people cried to see
The crueltie
Of C and P.

Harsh are the words of Mercury after the songs of Apollo! We were a long while over the problem, shaking our heads and gloomily wondering how a man could be such a fool; but at length he put us out of suspense and divulged the fact that C and P stood for Caiaphas and Pontius Pilate.

I think it must have been the riddle that settled us; but the motion and the close air likewise hurried our departure. We had not been gone long, we heard next morning, ere two or even three out of the five fell sick. We thought it little wonder on the whole, for the sea kept contrary all night. I now made my bed upon the second cabin floor, where, although I ran the risk of being stepped upon, I had a free current of air, more or less vitiated indeed, and running only from steerage to steerage, but at least not stagnant; and from this couch, as well as the usual sounds of a rough night at sea, the hateful coughing and retching of the sick and the sobs of children, I heard a man run wild with terror beseeching his friend for encouragement. "The ship's going down!" he cried with a thrill of agony. "The ship's going down!" he repeated, now in a blank whisper, now with his voice rising towards a sob; and his friend might reassure him, reason with him, joke at him — all was in vain, and the old cry came back, "The ship's going down!" There was something panicky and catching in the emotion of his tones; and I saw in a clear flash what an involved and hideous tragedy was a disaster to an emigrant ship. If this whole parishful of people came no more to land, into how many houses would the newspaper carry woe, and what a great part of the web of our corporate human life would be rent across for ever!

The next morning when I came on deck I found a new world indeed. The wind was fair; the sun mounted into a cloudless heaven; through great dark blue seas the ship cut a swath of curded foam. The horizon was dotted all day with companionable sails, and the sun shone pleasantly on the long, heaving deck.

We had many fine-weather diversions to beguile the time. There was a single chess-board and a single pack of cards. Sometimes as many as twenty of us would be playing dominoes for love. Feats of dexterity, puzzles for the intelligence, some arithmetical, some of the same order as the old problem of the fox and goose and cabbage, were always welcome; and the latter, I observed, more popular as well as more conspicuously well done than the former. We had a regular daily competition to guess the vessel's progress; and twelve o'clock, when the result was published in the wheel-house, came to be a moment of considerable interest. But the interest was unmixed. Not a bet was laid upon our guesses. From the Clyde to Sandy Hook I never heard a wager offered or taken. We had, besides, romps in plenty. Puss in the Corner, which we had rebaptized, in more manly style, Devil and four Corners, was my own favourite game; but there were many who preferred another, the humour of which was to box a person's ears until he found out who had cuffed him.

This Tuesday morning we were all delighted with the change of weather, and in the highest possible spirits. We got in a cluster like bees, sitting between each other's feet under lee of the deck-houses. Stories and laughter went around. The children climbed about the shrouds. White faces appeared for the first time, and began to take on colour from the wind. I was kept hard at work making cigarettes for one amateur after another, and my less than moderate skill was heartily admired. Lastly, down sat the fiddler in our midst and began to discourse his reels, and jigs, and

27

ballads, with now and then a voice or two to take up
the air and throw in the interest of human speech.

Through this merry and good-hearted scene there
came three cabin passengers, a gentleman and two
young ladies, picking their way with little gracious tit-
ters of indulgence, and a Lady-Bountiful air about nothing, which galled me to the quick. I have little of
the radical in social questions, and have always nourished an idea that one person was as good as another.
But I began to be troubled by this episode. It was as-
tonishing what insults these people managed to convey
by their presence. They seemed to throw their clothes
in our faces. Their eyes searched us all over for tatters
and incongruities. A laugh was ready at their lips; but
they were too well-mannered to indulge it in our hearing. Wait a bit, till they were all back in the saloon,
and then hear how wittily they would depict the manners of the steerage. We were in truth very innocently,
cheerfully, and sensibly engaged, and there was no
shadow of excuse for the swaying elegant superiority
with which these damsels passed among us, or for the
stiff and waggish glances of their squire. Not a word
was said; only when they were gone Mackay sullenly
damned their impudence under his breath; but we were
all conscious of an icy influence and a dead break in the
course of our enjoyment.

STEERAGE TYPES

WE had a fellow on board, an Irish-American, for all the world like a beggar in a print by Callot; one-eyed, with great, splay crow's-feet round the sockets; a knotty squab nose coming down over his mustache; a miraculous hat; a shirt that had been white, ay, ages long ago; an alpaca coat in its last sleeves; and, without hyperbole, no buttons to his trousers. Even in these rags and tatters, the man twinkled all over with impudence like a piece of sham jewellery; and I have heard him offer a situation to one of his fellow-passengers with the air of a lord. Nothing could overlie such a fellow; a kind of base success was written on his brow. He was then in his ill days; but I can imagine him in Congress with his mouth full of bombast and sawder. As we moved in the same circle, I was brought necessarily into his society. I do not think I ever heard him say anything that was true, kind, or interesting; but there was entertainment in the man's demeanour. You might call him a half-educated Irish Tigg.

Our Russian made a remarkable contrast to this impossible fellow. Rumours and legends were current in the steerages about his antecedents. Some said he was a Nihilist escaping; others set him down for a harmless spendthrift, who had squandered fifty thousand roubles, and whose father had now despatched him to America by way of penance. Either tale might flourish in security; there was no contradiction to be feared, for the hero spoke not one word of English. I got on with him lumberingly enough in broken German, and learnt from his own lips that he had been an apothecary. He carried the photograph of his betrothed in a pocket-book, and remarked that it did not do her justice. The cut of his head stood out from among the passengers with an air of startling strangeness. The first natural instinct was to take him for a desperado; but although the features, to our Western eyes, had a barbaric and unhomely cast, the eye both reassured and touched. It was large and very dark and soft, with an expression of dumb endurance, as if it had often looked on desperate circumstances and never looked on them without resolution.

He cried out when I used the word. "No, no," he said, "not resolution."

"The resolution to endure," I explained.

And then he shrugged his shoulders, and said, "*Ach, ja,*" with gusto, like a man who has been flattered in his favourite pretensions. Indeed, he was always hinting at some secret sorrow; and his life, he said, had been one of unusual trouble and anxiety; so the legends of the steerage may have represented at least some shadow of the truth. Once, and once only, he sang a song at our concerts; standing forth without embarrassment, his great stature somewhat humped, his long arms frequently extended, his Kalmuck head thrown backward. It was a suitable piece of music, as deep as a cow's bellow and wild like the White Sea. He was struck and charmed by the freedom and sociality of our manners. At home, he said, no one on a journey would speak to him, but those with whom he would not care to speak; thus unconsciously involving himself in the condemnation of his countrymen. But Russia was soon to be changed; the ice of the Neva was softening under the sun of civilization; the new ideas, *"wie eine feine Violine,"* were audible among the big empty drum notes of Imperial diplomacy; and he looked to see a great revival, though with a somewhat indistinct and childish hope.

We had a father and son who made a pair of Jacks-of-all-trades. It was the son who sang the "Death of Nelson" under such contrarious circumstances. He was by trade a shearer of ship plates; but he could touch the organ, had led two choirs, and played the flute and piccolo in a professional string band. His repertory of songs was, besides, inexhaustible, and ranged impartially from the very best to the very worst within his reach. Nor did he seem to make the least distinction between these extremes, but would cheerfully follow up "Tom Bowling" with "Around her splendid form."

The father, an old, cheery, small piece of manhood, could do everything connected with tinwork from one end of the process to the other, use almost every carpenter's tool, and make picture frames to boot. "I sat down with silver plate every Sunday," said he, "and pictures on the wall. I have made enough money to be rolling in my carriage. But, sir," looking at me unsteadily with his bright rheumy eyes, "I was troubled with a drunken wife." He took a hostile view of matrimony in consequence. "It's an old saying," he remarked: "God made 'em, and the devil he mixed 'em."

I think he was justified by his experience. It was a dreary story. He would bring home three pounds on Saturday, and on Monday all the clothes would be in pawn. Sick of the useless struggle, he gave up a paying contract, and contented himself with small and ill-paid jobs. "A bad job was as good as a good job for me," he said; "it all went the same way." Once the wife showed signs of amendment; she kept steady for weeks on end; it was again worth while to labour and to do one's best. The husband found a good situation some distance from home, and, to make a little upon every hand, started the wife in a cook-shop; the children were here and there, busy as mice; savings began to grow together in the bank, and the golden age of hope had returned again to that unhappy family. But one week my old acquaintance, getting earlier through with his work, came home on the Friday instead of the Saturday, and there was his wife to receive him reeling drunk. He "took and gave her a pair o' black eyes," for which I pardon him, nailed up the cook-shop door, gave up his situation, and resigned himself to a life of poverty, with the workhouse at the end. As the children came to their full age they fled the house, and established themselves in other countries; some did well, some not so well; but the father remained at home alone with his drunken wife, all his sound-hearted pluck and varied accomplishments depressed and negatived.

Was she dead now? or, after all these years, had he broken the chain, and run from home like a schoolboy? I could not discover which; but here at least he was out on the adventure, and still one of the bravest and most youthful men on board.

"Now, I suppose, I must put my old bones to work again," said he; "but I can do a turn yet."

And the son to whom he was going, I asked, was he not able to support him?

"Oh yes," he replied. "But I'm never happy without a job on hand. And I'm stout; I can eat a'most anything. You see no craze about me."

This tale of a drunken wife was paralleled on board by another of a drunken father. He was a capable man, with a good chance in life; but he had drunk up two thriving businesses like a bottle of sherry, and involved his sons along with him in ruin. Now they were on board with us, fleeing his disastrous neighbourhood.

Total abstinence, like all ascetical conclusions, is unfriendly to the most generous, cheerful, and human parts of man; but it could have adduced many instances and arguments from among our ship's company. I was one day conversing with a kind and happy Scotsman, running to fat and perspiration in the physical, but with a taste for poetry and a genial sense of fun. I had asked him his hopes in emigrating. They were like those of so many others, vague and unfounded; times were bad at home; they were said to have a turn for the better in the States; and a man could get on anywhere, he thought. That was precisely the weak point of his position; for if he could get on in America, why could he not do the same in Scotland? But I never had the courage to use that argument, though it was often on the tip of my tongue, and instead I agreed with him heartily, adding, with reckless originality, "If the man stuck to his work, and kept away from drink."

"Ah!" said he slowly, "the drink! You see, that's just my trouble."

He spoke with a simplicity that was touching, looking at me at the same time with something strange and timid in his eye, half-ashamed, half-sorry, like a good child who knows he should be beaten. You would have said he recognised a destiny to which he was born, and accepted the consequences mildly. Like the merchant Abudah, he was at the same time fleeing from his destiny and carrying it along with him, the whole at an expense of six guineas.

As far as I saw, drink, idleness, and incompetency were the three great causes of emigration, and for all of them, and drink first and foremost, this trick of getting transported overseas appears to me the silliest means of cure. You cannot run away from a weakness; you must some time fight it out or perish; and if that be so, why not now, and where you stand? *Cœlum non animam*. Change Glenlivat for Bourbon, and it is still whisky, only not so good. A sea-voyage will not give a man the nerve to put aside cheap pleasure; emigration has to be done before we climb the vessel; an aim in life is the only fortune worth the finding; and it is not to be found in foreign lands, but in the heart itself.

Speaking generally, there is no vice of this kind more contemptible than another; for each is but a result and outward sign of a soul tragically shipwrecked. In the majority of cases, cheap pleasure is resorted to by way of anodyne. The pleasure-seeker sets forth upon life with high and difficult ambitions; he meant to be nobly good and nobly happy, though at as little pains as possible to himself; and it is because all has failed in his

34

celestial enterprise that you now behold him rolling in
the garbage. Hence the comparative success of the tee-
total pledge; because to a man who had nothing it sets
at least a negative aim in life. Somewhat as prisoners
beguile their days by taming a spider, the reformed
drunkard makes an interest out of abstaining from in-
toxicating drinks, and may live for that negation. There
is something, at least, *not to be done* each day; and a
cold triumph awaits him every evening.

We had one on board with us, whom I have already
referred to under the name of Mackay, who seemed to
me not only a good instance of this failure in life of
which we have been speaking, but a good type of the
intelligence which here surrounded me. Physically he
was a small Scotsman, standing a little back as though
he were already carrying the elements of a corporation,
and his looks somewhat marred by the smallness of his
eyes. Mentally, he was endowed above the average.
There were but few subjects on which he could not
converse with understanding and a dash of wit; deliver-
ing himself slowly and with gusto, like a man who enjoyed his own sententiousness. He was a dry, quick,
pertinent debater, speaking with a small voice, and
swinging on his heels to launch and emphasise an argument. When he began a discussion, he could not bear
to leave it off, but would pick the subject to the bone,
without once relinquishing a point. An engineer by
trade, Mackay believed in the unlimited perfectibility of
all machines except the human machine. The latter he
gave up with ridicule for a compound of carrion and
perverse gases. He had an appetite for disconnected
facts which I can only compare to the savage taste for

beads. What is called information was indeed a passion
with the man, and he not only delighted to receive it,
but could pay you back in kind.

With all these capabilities, here was Mackay, already
no longer young, on his way to a new country, with no
prospects, no money, and but little hope. He was almost tedious in the cynical disclosures of his despair.
"The ship may go down for me," he would say, "now
or to-morrow. I have nothing to lose and nothing to
hope." And again: "I am sick of the whole damned
performance." He was, like the kind little man already
quoted, another so-called victim of the bottle. But
Mackay was miles from publishing his weakness to the
world; laid the blame of his failure on corrupt masters
and a corrupt State policy; and after he had been one
night overtaken and had played the buffoon in his cups,
sternly, though not without tact, suppressed all reference to his escapade. It was a treat to see him manage
this; the various jesters withered under his gaze, and you
were forced to recognise in him a certain steely force, and
a gift of command which might have ruled a senate.

In truth it was not whisky that had ruined him; he
was ruined long before for all good human purposes but
conversation. His eyes were sealed by a cheap, school-
book materialism. He could see nothing in the world
but money and steam-engines. He did not know what
you meant by the word happiness. He had forgotten
the simple emotions of childhood, and perhaps never
encountered the delights of youth. He believed in production, that useful figment of economy, as if it had
been real like laughter; and production, without prejudice to liquor, was his god and guide. One day he

took me to task — a novel cry to me — upon the over-payment of literature. Literary men, he said, were more highly paid than artisans; yet the artisan made threshing-machines and butter-churns, and the man of letters, except in the way of a few useful handbooks, made nothing worth the while. He produced a mere fancy article. Mackay's notion of a book was *Hoppus's Measurer*. Now in my time I have possessed and even studied that work; but if I were to be left to-morrow on Juan Fernandez, Hoppus's is not the book that I should choose for my companion volume.

I tried to fight the point with Mackay. I made him own that he had taken pleasure in reading books other-wise, to his view, insignificant; but he was too wary to advance a step beyond the admission. It was in vain for me to argue that here was pleasure ready-made and running from the spring, whereas his ploughs and but-ter-churns were but means and mechanisms to give men the necessary food and leisure before they start upon the search for pleasure; he jibbed and ran away from such conclusions. The thing was different, he declared, and nothing was serviceable but what had to do with food. "Eat, eat, eat!" he cried; "that's the bottom and the top." By an odd irony of circumstance, he grew so much interested in this discussion that he let the hour slip by unnoticed and had to go without his tea. He had enough sense and humour, indeed he had no lack of either, to have chuckled over this himself in private; and even to me he referred to it with the sha-dow of a smile.

Mackay was a hot bigot. He would not hear of re-ligion. I have seen him waste hours of time in argument with all sort of poor human creatures who understood neither him nor themselves, and he had had the boyishness to dissect and criticise even so small a matter as the riddler's definition of mind. He snorted aloud with zealotry and the lust for intellectual battle. Anything, whatever it was, that seemed to him likely to discourage the continued passionate production of corn and steam-engines he resented like a conspiracy against the people. Thus, when I put in the plea for literature, that it was only in good books, or in the society of the good, that a man could get help in his conduct, he declared I was in a different world from him. "Damn my conduct!" said he. "I have given it up for a bad job. My question is, "Can I drive a nail?" And he plainly looked upon me as one who was insidiously seeking to reduce the people's annual bellyful of corn and steam-engines.

It may be argued that these opinions spring from the defect of culture; that a narrow and pinching way of life not only exaggerates to a man the importance of material conditions, but indirectly, by denying him the necessary books and leisure, keeps his mind ignorant of larger thoughts; and that hence springs this overwhelming concern about diet, and hence the bald view of existence professed by Mackay. Had this been an English peasant the conclusion would be tenable. But Mackay had most of the elements of a liberal education. He had skirted metaphysical and mathematical studies. He had a thoughtful hold of what he knew, which would be exceptional among bankers. He had been brought up in the midst of hot-house piety, and told, with incongruous pride, the story of his own brother's deathbed

ecstasies. Yet he had somehow failed to fulfil himself,
and was adrift like a dead thing among external circumstances, without hope or lively preference or shaping
aim. And further, there seemed a tendency among
many of his fellows to fall into the same blank and unlovely opinions. One thing, indeed, is not to be learned
in Scotland, and that is the way to be happy, Yet that
is the whole of culture, and perhaps two-thirds of morality. Can it be that the Puritan school, by divorcing
a man from nature, by thinning out his instincts, and
setting a stamp of its disapproval on whole fields of
human activity and interest, leads at last directly to
material greed?

Nature is a good guide through life, and the love of
simple pleasures next, if not superior, to virtue; and we
had on board an Irishman who based his claim to the
widest and most affectionate popularity precisely upon
these two qualities, that he was natural and happy. He
boasted a fresh colour, a tight little figure, unquenchable
gaiety, and indefatigable good-will. His clothes puzzled
the diagnostic mind, until you heard he had been once a
private coachman, when they became eloquent and
seemed a part of his biography. His face contained the
rest, and, I fear, a prophecy of the future; the hawk's
nose above accorded so ill with the pink baby's mouth
below. His spirit and his pride belonged, you might
say, to the nose; while it was the general shiftlessness
expressed by the other that had thrown him from situation to situation, and at length on board the emigrant
ship. Barney ate, so to speak, nothing from the galley;
his own tea, butter and eggs supported him throughout the voyage; and about mealtime you might often

find him up to the elbows in amateur cookery. His was
the first voice heard singing among all the passengers;
he was the first who fell to dancing. From Loch Foyle
to Sandy Hook, there was not a piece of fun undertaken
but there was Barney in the midst.

You ought to have seen him when he stood up to sing
at our concerts — his tight little figure stepping to and
fro, and his feet shuffling to the air, his eyes seeking and
bestowing encouragement — and to have enjoyed the
bow, so nicely calculated between jest and earnest, between grace and clumsiness, with which he brought
each song to a conclusion. He was not only a great
favourite among ourselves, but his songs attracted the
lords of the saloon, who often leaned to hear him over
the rails of the hurricane-deck. He was somewhat
pleased, but not at all abashed by this attention; and
one night, in the midst of his famous performance of
"Billy Keogh," I saw him spin half round in a pirou-
ette and throw an audacious wink to an old gentleman
above.

This was the more characteristic, as, for all his daffing,
he was a modest and very polite little fellow among
ourselves.

He would not have hurt the feelings of a fly, nor
throughout the passage did he give a shadow of of-
ence; yet he was always, by his innocent freedoms and
love of fun, brought upon that narrow margin where
politeness must be natural to walk without a fall. He
was once seriously angry, and that in a grave, quiet
manner, because they supplied no fish on Friday; for
Barney was a conscientious Catholic. He had likewise
strict notions of refinement; and when, late one eve-

ning, after the women had retired, a young Scotsman struck up an indecent song, Barney's drab clothes were immediately missing from the group. His taste was for the society of gentlemen, of whom, with the reader's permission, there was no lack in our five steerages and second cabin; and he avoided the rough and positive with a girlish shrinking. Mackay, partly from his superior powers of mind, which rendered him incomprehensible, partly from his extreme opinions, was especially distasteful to the Irishman. I have seen him slink off with backward looks of terror and offended delicacy, while the other, in his witty, ugly way, had been professing hostility to God, and an extreme theatrical readiness to be shipwrecked on the spot. These utterances hurt the little coachman's modesty like a bad word.

THE SICK MAN

ONE night Jones, the young O'Reilly, and myself were walking arm-in-arm and briskly up and down the deck. Six bells had rung; a head-wind blew chill and fitful, the fog was closing in with a sprinkle of rain, and the fog-whistle had been turned on, and now divided time with its unwelcome outcries, loud like a bull, thrilling and intense like a mosquito. Even the watch lay somewhere snugly out of sight.

For some time we observed something lying black and huddled in the scuppers, which at last heaved a little and moaned aloud. We ran to the rails. An elderly man, but whether passenger or seaman it was impossible in the darkness to determine, lay grovelling on his belly in the wet scuppers, and kicking feebly with his outspread toes. We asked him what was amiss, and he replied incoherently, with a strange accent and in a voice unmanned by terror, that he had cramp in the stomach, that he had been ailing all day, had seen the doctor twice, and had walked the deck against fatigue till he was overmastered and had fallen where we found him.

Jones remained by his side, while O'Reilly and I hurried off to seek the doctor. We knocked in vain at the doctor's cabin; there came no reply; nor could we find any one to guide us. It was no time for delicacy; so we ran once more forward; and I, whipping up a ladder and touching my hat to the officer of the watch, addressed him as politely as I could:

"I beg your pardon, sir; but there is a man lying bad with cramp in the lee scuppers; and I can't find the doctor."

He looked at me peeringly in the darkness; and then, somewhat harshly, "Well, *I* can't leave the bridge, my man," said he.

"No, sir; but you can tell me what to do," I returned.

"Is it one of the crew ?" he asked.

"I believe him to be a fireman," I replied.

I daresay officers are much annoyed by complaints and alarmist information from their freight of human creatures; but certainly, whether it was the idea that the sick man was one of the crew, or from something conciliatory in my address, the officer in question was immediately relieved and mollified; and speaking in a voice much freer from constraint, advised me to find a steward and despatch him in quest of the doctor, who would now be in the smoking-room over his pipe.

One of the stewards was often enough to be found about this hour down our companion, Steerage No. 2 and 3; that was his smoking-room of a night. Let me call him Blackwood. O'Reilly and I rattled down the companion, breathing hurry; and in his shirt-sleeves and perched across the carpenter's bench upon one thigh, found Blackwood; a neat, bright, dapper, Glasgow-looking man, with a bead of an eye and a rank twang in his speech. I forget who was with him, but the pair

were enjoying a deliberate talk over their pipes. I dare
say he was tired with his day's work, and eminently
comfortable at that moment; and the truth is, I did not
stop to consider his feelings, but told my story in a
breath.

"Steward," said I, "there's a man lying bad with
cramp, and I can't find the doctor."

He turned upon me as pert as a sparrow, but with a
black look that is the prerogative of man; and taking
his pipe out of his mouth——

"That's none of my business," said he. "I don't
care."

I could have strangled the little ruffian where he sat.
The thought of his cabin civility and cabin tips filled me
with indignation. I glanced at O'Reilly; he was pale
and quivering, and looked like assault and battery,
every inch of him. But we had a better card than
violence.

"You will have to make it your business," said I,
"for I am sent to you by the officer on the bridge."

Blackwood was fairly tripped. He made no answer,
but put out his pipe, gave me one murderous look, and
set off upon his errand strolling. From that day forward, I should say, he improved to me in courtesy, as
though he had repented his evil speech and were anxious to leave a better impression.

When we got on deck again, Jones was still beside
the sick man; and two or three late stragglers had
gathered round and were offering suggestions. One
proposed to give the patient water, which was promptly
negatived. Another bade us hold him up; he himself
prayed to be let lie; but as it was at least as well to

keep him off the streaming decks, O'Reilly and I supported him between us. It was only by main force that we did so, and neither an easy nor an agreeable duty; for he fought in his paroxysms like a frightened child, and moaned miserably when he resigned himself to our control.

"O let me lie!" he pleaded. "I'll no' get better anyway." And then, with a moan that went to my heart, "O why did I come upon this miserable journey?"

I was reminded of the song which I had heard a little while before in the close, tossing steerage: "O why left I my hame?"

Meantime Jones, relieved of his immediate charge, had gone off to the galley, where we could see a light. There he found a belated cook scouring pans by the radiance of two lanterns, and one of these he sought to borrow. The scullion was backward. "Was it one of the crew?" he asked. And when Jones, smitten with my theory, had assured that it was a fireman, he reluctantly left his scouring and came towards us at an easy pace, with one of the lanterns swinging from his finger. The light, as it reached the spot, showed us an elderly man, thick-set, and grizzled with years; but the shifting and coarse shadows concealed from us the expression and even the design of his face.

So soon as the cook set eyes on him he gave a sort of whistle.

"*It's only a passenger!*" said he; and turning about, made, lantern and all, for the galley.

"He's a man anyway," cried Jones in indignation.

"Nobody said he was a woman," said a gruff voice, which I recognised for that of the bo's'un.

45

All this while there was no word of Blackwood or the doctor; and now the officer came to our side of the ship and asked, over the hurricane-deck rails, if the doctor were not yet come. We told him not.

"No?" he repeated with a breathing of anger; and we saw him hurry aft in person.

Ten minutes after the doctor made his appearance deliberately enough and examined our patient with the lantern. He made little of the case, had the man brought aft to the dispensary, dosed him, and sent him forward to his bunk. Two of his neighbours in the steerage had now come to our assistance, expressing loud sorrow that such "a fine cheery body" should be sick; and these, claiming a sort of possession, took him entirely under their own care. The drug had probably relieved him, for he struggled no more, and was led along plaintive and patient, but protesting. His heart recoiled at the thought of the steerage. "O let me lie down upon the bieldy side," he cried; "O dinna take me down!" And again: "O why did ever I come upon this miserable voyage?" And yet once more, with a gasp and a wailing prolongation of the fourth word: "I had no *call* to come." But there he was; and by the doctor's orders and the kind force of his two shipmates disappeared down the companion of Steerage No. 1 into the den allotted him.

At the foot of our own companion, just where I found Blackwood, Jones and the bo's'un were now engaged in talk. This last was a gruff, cruel-looking seaman, who must have passed near half a century upon the seas; square-headed, goat-bearded, with heavy blond eyebrows, and an eye without radiance, but inflexibly

steady and hard. I had not forgotten his rough speech;
but I remembered also that he had helped us about the
lantern; and now seeing him in conversation with Jones,
and being choked with indignation, I proceeded to blow
off my steam.

"Well," said I, "I make you my compliments upon
your steward," and furiously narrated what had happened.

"I've nothing to do with him," replied the bo's'un.
"They're all alike. They wouldn't mind if they saw
you all lying dead one upon the top of another."

This was enough. A very little humanity went a
long way with me after the experience of the evening. A sympathy grew up at once between the
bo's'un and myself; and that night, and during the
next few days, I learned to appreciate him better.
He was a remarkable type, and not at all the kind of
man you find in books. He had been at Sebastopol
under English colours; and again in a States ship,
"after the *Alabama,* and praying God we shouldn't
find her." He was a high Tory and a high Englishman.
No manufacturer could have held opinions more hostile
to the working man and his strikes. "The workmen,"
he said, "think nothing of their country. They think
of nothing but themselves. They're damned greedy,
selfish fellows." He would not hear of the decadence
of England. "They say they send us beef from America," he argued; "but who pays for it? All the money in the world's in England." The Royal Navy
was the best of possible services, according to him.
"Anyway the officers are gentlemen," said he; "and
you can't get hazed to death by a damned non-commis-

sioned ——— as you can in the army." Among nations, England was the first; then came France. He
respected the French navy and liked the French people;
and if he were forced to make a new choice in life, "by
God, he would try Frenchmen!" For all his looks and
rough, cold manners, I observed that children were
never frightened by him; they divined him at once to be
a friend; and one night when he had chalked his hand
and went about stealthily setting his mark on people's
clothes, it was incongruous to hear this formidable old
salt chuckling over his boyish monkey trick.

In the morning, my first thought was of the sick man.
I was afraid I should not recognise him, so baffling had
been the light of the lantern; and found myself unable
to decide if he were Scots, English, or Irish. He had
certainly employed north-country words and elisions;
but the accent and the pronunciation seemed unfamiliar
and incongruous in my ear.

To descend on an empty stomach into Steerage No.
1, was an adventure that required some nerve. The
stench was atrocious; each respiration tasted in the
throat like some horrible kind of cheese; and the
squalid aspect of the place was aggravated by so many
people worming themselves into their clothes in the
twilight of the bunks. You may guess if I was pleased,
not only for him, but for myself also, when I heard that
the sick man was better and had gone on deck.

The morning was raw and foggy, though the sun
suffused the fog with pink and amber; the fog-horn still
blew, stertorous and intermittent; and to add to the discomfort, the seamen were just beginning to wash down
the decks. But for a sick man this was heaven com-

pared to the steerage. I found him standing on the hot-
water pipe, just forward of the saloon deck house. He
was smaller than I had fancied, and plain-looking; but
his face was distinguished by strange and fascinating
eyes, limpid grey from a distance, but, when looked
into, full of changing colours and grains of gold. His
manners were mild and uncompromisingly plain; and
I soon saw that, when once started, he delighted to
talk. His accent and language had been formed in the
most natural way, since he was born in Ireland, had
lived a quarter of a century on the banks of Tyne, and
was married to a Scots wife. A fisherman in the season,
he had fished the east coast from Fisherrow to Whitby.
When the season was over, and the great boats, which
required extra hands, were once drawn up on shore till
the next spring, he worked as a labourer about chemical
furnaces, or along the wharves unloading vessels. In
this comparatively humble way of life he had gathered
a competence, and could speak of his comfortable house,
his hayfield, and his garden. On this ship, where so
many accomplished artisans were fleeing from starvation,
he was present on a pleasure trip to visit a brother in
New York.

Ere he started, he informed me, he had been warned
against the steerage and the steerage fare, and recommended to bring with him a ham and tea and a spice loaf.
But he laughed to scorn such counsels. " *I'm* not afraid,"
he had told his adviser; " *I'll* get on for ten days. I've
not been a fisherman for nothing." For it is no light
matter, as he reminded me, to be in an open boat, perhaps waist-deep with herrings, day breaking with a
scowl, and for miles on every hand lee-shores, unbroken,

iron-bound, surf-beat, with only here and there an anchorage where you dare not lie, or a harbour impossible to enter with the wind that blows. The life of a North Sea fisher is one long chapter of exposure and hard work and insufficient fare; and even if he makes land at some bleak fisher port, perhaps the season is bad or his boat has been unlucky, and after fifty hours' unsleeping vigilance and toil, not a shop will give him credit for a loaf of bread. Yet the steerage of the emigrant ship had been too vile for the endurance of a man thus rudely trained. He had scarce eaten since he came on board, until the day before, when his appetite was tempted by some excellent pea-soup. We were all much of the same mind on board, and beginning with myself, had dined upon pea-soup not wisely but too well; only with him the excess had been punished, perhaps because he was weakened by former abstinence, and his first meal had resulted in a cramp. He had determined to live henceforth on biscuit; and when, two months later, he should return to England, to make the passage by saloon. The second cabin, after due inquiry, he scouted as another edition of the steerage.

He spoke apologetically of his emotion when ill. "Ye see, I had no call to be here," said he; "and I thought it was by with me last night. I've a good house at home, and plenty to nurse me, and I had no real call to leave them." Speaking of the attentions he had received from his shipmates generally, "they were all so kind," he said, "that there's none to mention." And except in so far as I might share in this, he troubled me with no reference to my services.

But what affected me in the most lively manner was

50

the wealth of this day-labourer, paying a two months'
pleasure visit to the States, and preparing to return in
the saloon, and the new testimony rendered by his
story, not so much to the horrors of the steerage as to
the habitual comfort of the working classes. One foggy,
frosty December evening, I encountered on Liberton
Hill, near Edinburgh, an Irish labourer trudging homeward from the fields. Our roads lay together, and it
was natural that we should fall into talk. He was covered with mud; an inoffensive, ignorant creature, who
thought the Atlantic Cable was a secret contrivance of
the masters the better to oppress labouring mankind;
and I confess I was astonished to learn that he had
nearly three hundred pounds in the bank. But this
man had travelled over most of the world, and enjoyed
wonderful opportunities on some American railroad,
with two dollars a shift and double pay on Sunday
and at night; whereas my fellow-passenger had never
quitted Tyneside, and had made all that he possessed
in that same accursed, down-falling England, whence
skilled mechanics, engineers, millwrights, and carpenters
were fleeing as from the native country of starvation.

Fitly enough, we slid off on the subject of strikes and
wages and hard times. Being from the Tyne, and a
man who had gained and lost in his own pocket by
these fluctuations, he had much to say, and held strong
opinions on the subject. He spoke sharply of the masters, and, when I led him on, of the men also. The
masters had been selfish and obstructive; the men
selfish, silly, and light-headed. He rehearsed to me
the course of a meeting at which he had been present,
and the somewhat long discourse which he had there

pronounced, calling into question the wisdom and even the good faith of the Union delegates; and although he had escaped himself through flush times and starvation times with a handsomely provided purse, he had so little faith in either man or master, and so profound a terror for the unerring Nemesis of mercantile affairs, that he could think of no hope for our country outside of a sudden and complete political subversion. Down must go Lords and Church and Army; and capital, by some happy direction, must change hands from worse to better, or England stood condemned. Such principles, he said, were growing "like a seed."

From this mild, soft, domestic man, these words sounded unusually ominous and grave. I had heard enough revolutionary talk among my workmen fellow-passengers; but most of it was hot and turgid, and fell discredited from the lips of unsuccessful men. This man was calm; he had attained prosperity and ease; he disapproved the policy which had been pursued by labour in the past; and yet this was his panacea,— to rend the old country from end to end, and from top to bottom, and in clamour and civil discord remodel it with the hand of violence.

THE AMATEUR EMIGRANT

THE STOWAWAYS

ON the Sunday, among a party of men who were
talking in our companion, Steerage Nos. 2 and 3, we
remarked a new figure. He wore tweed clothes, well
enough made if not very fresh, and a plain smoking-cap.
His face was pale, with pale eyes, and spiritedly enough
designed; but though not yet thirty, a sort of black-
guardly degeneration had already overtaken his features.
The fine nose had grown fleshy towards the point, the
pale eyes were sunk in fat. His hands were strong and
elegant; his experience of life evidently varied; his
speech full of pith and verve; his manners forward, but
perfectly presentable. The lad who helped in the second cabin told me, in answer to a question, that he did
not know who he was, but thought, "by his way of
speaking, and because he was so polite, that he was
some one from the saloon."

I was not so sure, for to me there was something
equivocal in his air and bearing. He might have been,
I thought, the son of some good family who had fallen
early into dissipation and run from home. But, making
every allowance, how admirable was his talk! I wish
you could have heard him tell his own stories. They
were so swingingly set forth, in such dramatic language,

53

and illustrated here and there by such luminous bits of acting, that they could only lose in any reproduction. There were tales of the P. and O. Company, where he had been an officer; of the East Indies, where in former years he had lived lavishly; of the Royal Engineers, where he had served for a period; and of a dozen other sides of life, each introducing some vigorous thumb-nail portrait. He had the talk to himself that night, we were all so glad to listen. The best talkers usually address themselves to some particular society; there they are kings, elsewhere camp-followers, as a man may know Russian and yet be ignorant of Spanish; but this fellow had a frank, headlong power of style, and a broad, human choice of subject, that would have turned any circle in the world into a circle of hearers. He was a Homeric talker, plain, strong, and cheerful; and the things and the people of which he spoke became readily and clearly present to the minds of those who heard him. This, with a certain added colouring of rhetoric and rodomontade, must have been the style of Burns, who equally charmed the ears of duchesses and hostlers.

Yet freely and personally as he spoke, many points remained obscure in his narration. The Engineers, for instance, was a service which he praised highly; it is true there would be trouble with the sergeants; but then the officers were gentlemen, and his own, in particular, one among ten thousand. It sounded so far exactly like an episode in the rakish, topsy-turvy life of such an one as I had imagined. But then there came incidents more doubtful, which showed an almost impudent greed after gratuities, and a truly impudent disregard for truth. And then there was the tale of his departure. He had

wearied, it seems, of Woolwich, and one fine day, with
a companion, slipped up to London for a spree. I have
a suspicion that spree was meant to be a long one; but
God disposes all things; and one morning, near West-
minster Bridge, whom should he come across but the
very sergeant who had recruited him at first! What
followed? He himself indicated cavalierly that he had
then resigned. Let us put it so. But these resignations
are sometimes very trying.

At length, after having delighted us for hours, he took
himself away from the companion; and I could ask
Mackay who and what he was. "That?" said Mackay. "Why, that's one of the stowaways."

"No man," said the same authority, "who has had
anything to do with the sea, would ever think of paying for a passage." I give the statement as Mackay's,
without endorsement; yet I am tempted to believe that
it contains a grain of truth; and if you add that the man
shall be impudent and thievish, or else dead-broke, it
may even pass for a fair representation of the facts. We
gentlemen of England who live at home at ease have, I
suspect, very insufficient ideas on the subject. All the
world over, people are stowing away in coal-holes and
dark corners, and when ships are once out to sea, appearing again, begrimed and bashful, upon deck. The
career of these sea-tramps partakes largely of the adventurous. They may be poisoned by coal-gas, or die by
starvation in their place of concealment; or when found
they may be clapped at once and ignominiously into
irons, thus to be carried to their promised land, the port
of destination, and alas! brought back in the same way
to that from which they started, and there delivered over

to the magistrates and the seclusion of a county jail. Since I crossed the Atlantic, one miserable stowaway was found in a dying state among the fuel, uttered but a word or two, and departed for a farther country than America.

When the stowaway appears on deck, he has but one thing to pray for: that he be set to work, which is the price and sign of his forgiveness. After half an hour with a swab or a bucket, he feels himself as secure as if he had paid for his passage. It is not altogether a bad thing for the company, who get more or less efficient hands for nothing but a few plates of junk and duff; and every now and again find themselves better paid than by a whole family of cabin passengers. Not long ago, for instance, a packet was saved from nearly certain loss by the skill and courage of a stowaway engineer. As was no more than just, a handsome subscription rewarded him for his success; but even without such exceptional good fortune, as things stand in England and America, the stowaway will often make a good profit out of his adventure. Four engineers stowed away last summer on the same ship, the *Circassia;* and before two days after their arrival each of the four had found a comfortable berth. This was the most hopeful tale of emigration that I heard from first to last; and as you see, the luck was for stowaways.

My curiosity was much inflamed by what I heard; and the next morning, as I was making the round of the ship, I was delighted to find the ex-Royal Engineer engaged in washing down the white paint of a deck house. There was another fellow at work beside him, a lad not more than twenty, in the most miraculous tatters, his handsome face sown with grains of beauty and lighted up by expressive eyes. Four stowaways had been found aboard our ship before she left the Clyde, but these two had alone escaped the ignominy of being put ashore. Alick, my acquaintance of last night, was Scots by birth, and by trade a practical engineer; the other was from Devonshire, and had been to sea before the mast. Two people more unlike by training, character, and habits, it would be hard to imagine; yet here they were together, scrubbing paint.

Alick had held all sorts of good situations, and wasted many opportunities in life. I have heard him end a story with these words: "That was in my golden days, when I used finger-glasses." Situation after situation failed him; then followed the depression of trade, and for months he had hung round with other idlers, playing marbles all day in the West Park, and going home at night to tell his landlady how he had been seeking for a job. I believe this kind of existence was not unpleasant to Alick himself, and he might have long continued to enjoy idleness and a life on tick; but he had a comrade, let us call him Brown, who grew restive. This fellow was continually threatening to slip his cable for the States, and at last, one Wednesday, Glasgow was left widowed of her Brown. Some months afterwards, Alick met another old chum in Sauchiehall Street.

"By the by, Alick," said he, "I met a gentleman in New York who was asking for you."

"Who was that?" asked Alick.

"The new second engineer on board the *So-and-so,*" was the reply.

"Well, and who is he?"

"Brown, to be sure."

For Brown had been one of the fortunate quartette aboard the *Circassia*. If that was the way of it in the States, Alick thought it was high time to follow Brown's example. He spent his last day, as he put it, "reviewing the yeomanry," and the next morning says he to his landlady, "Mrs. X., I'll not take porridge to-day, please; I'll take some eggs."

"Why, have you found a job?" she asked, delighted.

"Well, yes," returned the perfidious Alick; "I think I'll start to-day."

And so, well lined with eggs, start he did, but for America. I am afraid that landlady has seen the last of him.

It was easy enough to get on board in the confusion that attends a vessel's departure; and in one of the dark corners of Steerage No. 1, flat in a bunk and with an empty stomach, Alick made the voyage from the Broomielaw to Greenock. That night, the ship's yeoman pulled him out by the heels and had him before the mate. Two other stowaways had already been found and sent ashore; but by this time darkness had fallen, they were out in the middle of the estuary, and the last steamer had left them till the morning.

"Take him to the forecastle and give him a meal," said the mate, "and see and pack him off the first thing to-morrow."

In the forecastle he had supper, a good night's rest, and breakfast; and was sitting placidly with a pipe, fancying all was over and the game up for good with that ship, when one of the sailors grumbled out an oath

at him, with a "What are you doing there?" and "Do
you call that hiding, anyway?" There was need of no
more; Alick was in another bunk before the day was
older. Shortly before the passengers arrived, the ship
was cursorily inspected. He heard the round come
down the companion and look into one pen after another, until they came within two of the one in which
he lay concealed. Into these last two they did not
enter, but merely glanced from without; and Alick
had no doubt that he was personally favoured in this
escape. It was the character of the man to attribute
nothing to luck and but little to kindness; whatever
happened to him he had earned in his own right amply;
favours came to him from his singular attraction and
adroitness, and misfortunes he had always accepted
with his eyes open. Half an hour after the searchers
had departed, the steerage began to fill with legitimate
passengers, and the worst of Alick's troubles was at an
end. He was soon making himself popular, smoking
other people's tobacco, and politely sharing their private stock of delicacies, and when night came he retired to his bunk beside the others with composure.

Next day by afternoon, Lough Foyle being already
far behind, and only the rough north-western hills of
Ireland within view, Alick appeared on deck to court
inquiry and decide his fate. As a matter of fact, he
was known to several on board, and even intimate
with one of the engineers; but it was plainly not the
etiquette of such occasions for the authorities to avow
their information. Every one professed surprise and
anger on his appearance, and he was led prisoner before the captain.

"What have you got to say for yourself?" inquired the captain.

"Not much," said Alick; "but when a man has been a long time out of a job, he will do things he would not under other circumstances."

"Are you willing to work?"

Alick swore he was burning to be useful.

"And what can you do?" asked the captain.

He replied composedly that he was a brass-fitter by trade.

"I think you will be better at engineering?" suggested the officer, with a shrewd look.

"No, sir," says Alick simply.—"There's few can beat me at a lie," was his engaging commentary to me as he recounted the affair.

"Have you been to sea?" again asked the captain.

"I've had a trip on a Clyde steamboat, sir, but no more," replied the unabashed Alick.

"Well, we must try and find some work for you," concluded the officer.

And hence we behold Alick, clear of the hot engine-room, lazily scraping paint and now and then taking a pull upon a sheet. "You leave me alone," was his deduction. "When I get talking to a man, I can get round him."

The other stowaway, whom I will call the Devonian —it was noticeable that neither of them told his name —had both been brought up and seen the world in a much smaller way. His father, a confectioner, died and was closely followed by his mother. His sisters had taken, I think, to dress-making. He himself had returned from sea about a year ago and gone to live with his brother, who kept the "George Hotel"—"it was not quite a real hotel," added the candid fellow—"and had a hired man to mind the horses." At first the Devonian was very welcome; but as time went on his brother not unnaturally grew cool towards him, and he began to find himself one too many at the "George Hotel." "I don't think brothers care much for you," he said, as a general reflection upon life. Hurt at this change, nearly penniless, and too proud to ask for more, he set off on foot and walked eighty miles to Weymouth, living on the journey as he could. He would have enlisted, but he was too small for the army and too old for the navy; and thought himself fortunate at last to find a berth on board a trading dandy. Somewhere in the Bristol Channel, the dandy sprung a leak and went down; and though the crew were picked up and brought ashore by fishermen, they found themselves with nothing but the clothes upon their back. His next engagement was scarcely better starred; for the ship proved so leaky, and frightened them all so heartily during a short passage through the Irish Sea, that the entire crew deserted and remained behind upon the quays of Belfast.

Evil days were now coming thick on the Devonian. He could find no berth in Belfast, and had to work a passage to Glasgow on a steamer. She reached the Broomielaw on a Wednesday: the Devonian had a bellyful that morning, laying in breakfast manfully to provide against the future, and set off along the quays to seek employment. But he was now not only penniless, his clothes had begun to fall in tatters; he had begun to have the look of a street Arab; and captains will have nothing to say to a ragamuffin; for in that trade, as in

61

all others, it is the coat that depicts the man. You may
hand, reef, and steer like an angel, but if you have a
hole in your trousers, it is like a millstone round your
neck. The Devonian lost heart at so many refusals.
He had not the impudence to beg; although, as he said,
"when I had money of my own, I always gave it."
It was only on Saturday morning, after three whole
days of starvation, that he asked a scone from a milk-
woman, who added of her own accord a glass of milk.
He had now made up his mind to stow away, not from
any desire to see America, but merely to obtain the
comfort of a place in the forecastle and a supply of
familiar sea-fare. He lived by begging, always from
milkwomen, and always scones and milk, and was not
once refused. It was vile wet weather, and he could
never have been dry. By night he walked the streets,
and by day slept upon Glasgow Green, and heard, in
the intervals of his dozing, the famous theologians of
the spot clear up intricate points of doctrine and appraise
the merits of the clergy. He had not much instruction;
he could "read bills on the street," but was "main bad
at writing"; yet these theologians seem to have impressed him with a genuine sense of amusement. Why
he did not go to the Sailor's Home I know not; I presume there is in Glasgow one of these institutions,
which are by far the happiest and the wisest effort of
contemporaneous charity; but I must stand to my author, as they say in old books, and relate the story as
I heard it. In the meantime, he had tried four times to
stow away in different vessels, and four times had been
discovered and handed back to starvation. The fifth
time was lucky; and you may judge if he were pleased

to be aboard ship again, at his old work, and with duff twice a week. He was, said Alick, "a devil for the duff." Or if devil was not the word, it was one if anything stronger.

The difference in the conduct of the two was remarkable. The Devonian was as willing as any paid hand, swarmed aloft among the first, pulled his natural weight and firmly upon a rope, and found work for himself when there was none to show him. Alick, on the other hand, was not only a skulker in the grain, but took a humourous and fine gentlemanly view of the transaction. He would speak to me by the hour in ostentatious idleness; and only if the bo's'un or a mate came by, fell-to languidly for just the necessary time till they were out of sight. "I'm not breaking my heart with it," he remarked.

Once there was a hatch to be opened near where he was stationed; he watched the preparations for a second or so suspiciously, and then, "Hullo," said he, "here's some real work coming—I'm off," and he was gone that moment. Again, calculating the six guinea passage-money, and the probable duration of the passage, he remarked pleasantly that he was getting six shillings a day for this job, "and it's pretty dear to the company at that." "They are making nothing by me," was another of his observations; "they're making something by that fellow." And he pointed to the Devonian, who was just then busy to the eyes.

The more you saw of Alick, the more, it must be owned, you learned to despise him. His natural talents were of no use either to himself or others; for his character had degenerated like his face, and become pulpy

63

and pretentious. Even his power of persuasion, which was certainly very surprising, stood in some danger of being lost or neutralised by over-confidence. He lied in an aggressive, brazen manner, like a pert criminal in the dock; and he was so vain of his own cleverness that he could not refrain from boasting, ten minutes after, of the very trick by which he had deceived you. "Why, now I have more money than when I came on board," he said one night, exhibiting a sixpence, "and yet I stood myself a bottle of beer before I went to bed yesterday. And as for tobacco, I have fifteen sticks of it." That was fairly successful indeed; yet a man of his superiority, and with a less obtrusive policy, might, who knows? have got the length of half a crown. A man who prides himself upon persuasion should learn the persuasive faculty of silence, above all as to his own misdeeds. It is only in the farce and for dramatic purposes that Scapin enlarges on his peculiar talents to the world at large.

Scapin is perhaps a good name for this clever, unfortunate Alick; for at the bottom of all his misconduct there was a guiding sense of humour that moved you to forgive him. It was more than half a jest that he conducted his existence. "Oh, man," he said to me once with unusual emotion, like a man thinking of his mistress, "I would give up anything for a lark."

It was in relation to his fellow-stowaway that Alick showed the best, or perhaps I should say the only good, points of his nature. "Mind you," he said suddenly, changing his tone, "mind you that's a good boy. He wouldn't tell you a lie. A lot of them think he is a scamp because his clothes are ragged, but he isn't; he's as good as gold." To hear him, you become aware that Alick himself had a taste for virtue. He thought his own idleness and the other's industry equally becoming. He was no more anxious to insure his own reputation as a liar than to uphold the truthfulness of his companion; and he seemed unaware of what was incongruous in his attitude, and was plainly sincere in both characters.

It was not surprising that he should take an interest in the Devonian, for the lad worshipped and served him in love and wonder. Busy as he was, he would find time to warn Alick of an approaching officer, or even to tell him that the coast was clear, and he might slip off and smoke a pipe in safety. "Tom," he once said to him, for that was the name which Alick ordered him to use, "if you don't like going to the galley, I'll go for you. You ain't used to this kind of thing, you ain't. But I'm a sailor; and I can understand the feelings of any fellow, I can." Again, he was hard up, and casting about for some tobacco, for he was not so liberally used in this respect as others perhaps less worthy, when Alick offered him the half of one of his fifteen sticks. I think, for my part, he might have increased the offer to a whole one, or perhaps a pair of them, and not lived to regret his liberality. But the Devonian refused. "No," he said, "you're a stowaway like me; I won't take it from you, I'll take it from some one who's not down on his luck."

It was notable in this generous lad that he was strongly under the influence of sex. If a woman passed near where he was working, his eyes lit up, his hand paused, and his mind wandered instantly to other thoughts. It was natural that he should exercise a fascination propor-

tionally strong upon women. He begged, you will remember, from women only, and was never refused.
Without wishing to explain away the charity of those
who helped him, I cannot but fancy he may have owed
a little to his handsome face, and to that quick, respon-
sive nature, formed for love, which speaks eloquently
through all disguises, and can stamp an impression in
ten minutes' talk or an exchange of glances. He was
the more dangerous in that he was far from bold, but
seemed to woo in spite of himself, and with a soft and
pleading eye. Ragged as he was, and many a scare-
crow is in that respect more comfortably furnished, even
on board he was not without some curious admirers.

There was a girl among the passengers, a tall, blonde,
handsome, strapping Irishwoman, with a wild, accom-
modating eye, whom Alick had dubbed Tommy, with
that transcendental appropriateness that defies analysis.
One day the Devonian was lying for warmth in the
upper stoke-hole, which stands open on the deck, when
Irish Tommy came past, very neatly attired, as was her
custom.

"Poor fellow," she said, stopping, "you haven't a
vest."

"No," he said; "I wish I 'ad."

Then she stood and gazed on him in silence, until, in
his embarrassment, for he knew not how to look under
this scrutiny, he pulled out his pipe and began to fill it
with tobacco.

"Do you want a match?" she asked. And before he
had time to reply, she ran off and presently returned
with more than one.

That was the beginning and the end, as far as our

passage is concerned, of what I will make bold to call
this love-affair. There are many relations which go on
to marriage and last during a lifetime, in which less human feeling is engaged than in this scene of five minutes
at the stoke-hole.

Rigidly speaking, this would end the chapter of the
stowaways; but in a larger sense of the word I have yet
more to add. Jones had discovered and pointed out to
me a young woman who was remarkable among her
fellows for a pleasing and interesting air. She was
poorly clad, to the verge, if not over the line, of disre-
spectability, with a ragged old jacket and a bit of a sealskin cap no bigger than your fist; but her eyes, her
whole expression, and her manner, even in ordinary
moments, told of a true womanly nature, capable of
love, anger, and devotion. She had a look, too, of refinement, like one who might have been a better lady
than most, had she been allowed the opportunity.
When alone she seemed preoccupied and sad; but she
was not often alone; there was usually by her side a
heavy, dull, gross man in rough clothes, chary of speech
and gesture — not from caution, but poverty of disposition; a man like a ditcher, unlovely and uninteresting;
whom she petted and tended and waited on with her
eyes as if he had been Amadis of Gaul. It was strange
to see this hulking fellow dog-sick, and this delicate,
sad woman caring for him. He seemed, from first to
last, insensible of her caresses and attentions, and she
seemed unconscious of his insensibility. The Irish husband, who sang his wife to sleep, and this Scottish girl
serving her Orson, were the two bits of human nature
that most appealed to me throughout the voyage.

On the Thursday before we arrived, the tickets were collected; and soon a rumour began to go round the vessel; and this girl, with her bit of sealskin cap, became the centre of whipering and pointed fingers. She also, it was said, was a stowaway of a sort; for she was on board with neither ticket nor money; and the man with whom she travelled was the father of a family, who had left wife and children to be hers. The ship's officers discouraged the story, which may therefore have been a story and no more; but it was believed in the steerage, and the poor girl had to encounter many curious eyes from that day forth.

PERSONAL EXPERIENCE AND REVIEW

TRAVEL is of two kinds; and this voyage of mine across the ocean combined both. "Out of my country and myself I go," sings the old poet: and I was not only travelling out of my country in latitude and longitude, but out of myself in diet, associates, and consideration. Part of the interest and a great deal of the amusement flowed, at least to me, from this novel situation in the world.

I found that I had what they call fallen in life with absolute success and verisimilitude. I was taken for a steerage passenger; no one seemed surprised that I should be so; and there was nothing but the brass plate between decks to remind me that I had once been a gentleman. In a former book, describing a former journey, I expressed some wonder that I could be readily and naturally taken for a pedlar, and explained the accident by the difference of language and manners between England and France. I must now take a humbler view; for here I was among my own countrymen, somewhat roughly clad, to be sure, but with every advantage of speech and manner; and I am bound to confess that I passed for nearly anything you please except an educated gentleman. The sailors called me "mate," the officers addressed me as "my man," my comrades accepted me without hesitation for a person of their own character and experience, but with some curious information. One, a mason himself, believed I was a mason; several, and among these at least one of the seamen, judged me to be a petty officer in the American navy; and I was so often set down for a practical engineer that at last I had not the heart to deny it. From all these guesses I drew one conclusion, which told against the insight of my companions. They might be close observers in their own way, and read the manners in the face; but it was plain that they did not extend their observation to the hands.

To the saloon passengers also I sustained my part without a hitch. It is true I came little in their way; but when we did encounter, there was no recognition in their eye, although I confess I sometimes courted it in silence. All these, my inferiors and equals, took me, like the transformed monarch in the story, for a mere common, human man. They gave me a hard, dead look, with the flesh about the eye kept unrelaxed.

With the women this surprised me less, as I had already experimented on the sex by going abroad through a suburban part of London simply attired in a sleeve-waistcoat. The result was curious. I then learned for the first time, and by the exhaustive process, how much attention ladies are accustomed to bestow on all male creatures of their own station; for, in my humble rig, each one who went by me caused me a certain shock of surprise and a sense of something wanting. In my normal circumstances, it appeared every young lady must have paid me some tribute of a glance; and though

I had often not detected it when it was given, I was well aware of its absence when it was withheld. My height seemed to decrease with every woman who passed me, for she passed me like a dog. This is one of my grounds for supposing that what are called the upper classes may sometimes produce a disagreeable impression in what are called the lower; and I wish some one would continue my experiment, and find out exactly at what stage of toilette a man becomes invisible to the well-regulated female eye.

Here on shipboard the matter was put to a more complete test; for, even with the addition of speech and manner, I passed among the ladies for precisely the average man of the steerage. It was one afternoon that I saw this demonstrated. A very plainly dressed woman was taken ill on deck. I think I had the luck to be present at every sudden seizure during all the passage; and on this occasion found myself in the place of importance, supporting the sufferer. There was not only a large crowd immediately around us, but a considerable knot of saloon passengers leaning over our heads from the hurricane-deck. One of these, an elderly managing woman, hailed me with counsels. Of course I had to reply; and as the talk went on, I began to discover that the whole group took me for the husband. I looked upon my new wife, poor creature, with mingled feelings; and I must own she had not even the appearance of the poorest class of city servant-maids, but looked more like a country wench who should have been employed at a roadside inn. Now was the time for me to go and study the brass plate.

To such of the officers as knew about me — the doctor, the purser, and the stewards — I appeared in the light of a broad joke. The fact that I spent the better part of my day in writing had gone abroad over the ship and tickled them all prodigiously. Whenever they met me they referred to my absurd occupation with familiarity and breadth of humorous intention. Their manner was well calculated to remind me of my fallen fortunes. You may be sincerely amused by the amateur literary efforts of a gentleman, but you scarce publish the feeling to his face. "Well!" they would say: "still writing?" And the smile would widen into a laugh. The purser came one day into the cabin, and, touched to the heart by my misguided industry, offered me some other kind of writing, "for which," he added pointedly, "you will be paid." This was nothing else than to copy out the list of passengers.

Another trick of mine which told against my reputation was my choice of roosting-place in an active draught upon the cabin floor. I was openly jeered and flouted for this eccentricity; and a considerable knot would sometimes gather at the door to see my last dispositions for the night. This was embarrassing, but I learned to support the trial with equanimity.

Indeed I may say that, upon the whole, my new position sat lightly and naturally upon my spirits. I accepted the consequences with readiness, and found them far from difficult to bear. The steerage conquered me; I conformed more and more to the type of the place, not only in manner but at heart, growing hostile to the officers and cabin passengers who looked down upon me, and day by day greedier for small delicacies. Such was the result, as I fancy, of a diet of bread and butter, soup and porridge. We think we have no sweet tooth as long as we are full to the brim of molasses; but a man must have sojourned in the workhouse before he boasts himself indifferent to dainties. Every evening, for instance, I was more and more preoccupied about our doubtful fare at tea. If it was delicate my heart was much lightened; if it was but broken fish I was proportionally downcast. The offer of a little jelly from a fellow-passenger more provident than myself caused a marked elevation in my spirits. And I would have gone to the ship's end and back again for an oyster or a chipped fruit.

In other ways I was content with my position. It seemed no disgrace to be confounded with my company; for I may as well declare at once I found their manners as gentle and becoming as those of any other class. I do not mean that my friends could have sat down without embarrassment and laughable disaster at the table of a duke. That does not imply an inferiority of breeding, but a difference of usage. Thus I flatter myself that I conducted myself well among my fellow-passengers; yet my most ambitious hope is not to have avoided faults, but to have committed as few as possible. I know too well that my tact is not the same as their tact, and that my habit of a different society constituted, not only no qualification, but a positive disability to move easily and becomingly in this. When Jones complimented me — because I "managed to behave very pleasantly" to my fellow-passengers, was how he put it — I could follow the thought in his mind, and knew his compliment to be such as we pay foreigners on their proficiency in English. I dare say this praise

was given me immediately on the back of some un-
pardonable solecism, which had led him to review my
conduct as a whole. We are all ready to laugh at the
ploughman among lords; we should consider also the
case of a lord among the ploughmen. I have seen a
lawyer in the house of a Hebridean fisherman; and I
know, but nothing will induce me to disclose, which of
these two was the better gentleman. Some of our finest
behaviour, though it looks well enough from the boxes,
may seem even brutal to the gallery. We boast too
often manners that are parochial rather than universal;
that, like a country wine, will not bear transportation
for a hundred miles, nor from the parlour to the kitchen.
To be a gentleman is to be one all the world over, and
in every relation and grade of society. It is a high calling, to which a man must first be born, and then devote
himself for life. And, unhappily, the manners of a certain so-called upper grade have a kind of currency, and
meet with a certain external acceptation throughout all
the others, and this tends to keep us well satisfied with
slight acquirements and the amateurish accomplishments
of a clique. But manners, like art, should be human and
central.

Some of my fellow-passengers, as I now moved among
them in a relation of equality, seemed to me excellent
gentlemen. They were not rough, nor hasty, nor dis-
putatious; debated pleasantly, differed kindly; were
helpful, gentle, patient, and placid. The type of manners was plain, and even heavy; there was little to
please the eye, but nothing to shock; and I thought
gentleness lay more nearly at the spring of behaviour
than in many more ornate and delicate societies. I say

delicate, where I cannot say refined; a thing may be fine, like ironwork, without being delicate, like lace. There was here less delicacy; the skin supported more callously the natural surface of events, the mind received more bravely the crude facts of human existence; but I do not think that there was less effective refinement, less consideration for others, less polite suppression of self. I speak of the best among my fellow-passengers; for in the steerage, as well as in the saloon, there is a mixture. Those, then, with whom I found myself in sympathy, and of whom I may therefore hope to write with a greater measure of truth, were not only as good in their manners, but endowed with very much the same natural capacities, and about as wise in deduction, as the bankers and barristers of what is called society. One and all were too much interested in disconnected facts, and loved information for its own sake with too rash a devotion; but people in all classes display the same appetite as they gorge themselves daily with the miscellaneous gossip of the newspaper. Newspaper reading, as far as I can make out, is often rather a sort of brown study than an act of culture. I have myself palmed off yesterday's issue on a friend, and seen him re-peruse it for a continuance of minutes with an air at once refreshed and solemn. Workmen, perhaps, pay more attention; but though they may be eager listeners, they have rarely seemed to me either willing or careful thinkers. Culture is not measured by the greatness of the field which is covered by our knowledge, but by the nicety with which we can perceive relations in that field, whether great or small. Workmen, certainly those who were on board with me, I found wanting in this quality or habit of the mind. They did not perceive relations, but leaped to a so-called cause, and thought the problem settled. Thus the cause of everything in England was the form of government, and the cure for all evils was, by consequence, a revolution. It is surprising how many of them said this, and that none should have had a definite thought in his head as he said it. Some hated the Church because they disagreed with it; some hated Lord Beaconsfield because of war and taxes; all hated the masters, possibly with reason. But these feelings were not at the root of the matter; the true reasoning of their souls ran thus — I have not got on; I ought to have got on; if there was a revolution I should get on. How? They had no idea. Why? Because — because — well, look at America!

To be politically blind is no distinction; we are all so, if you come to that. At bottom, as it seems to me, there is but one question in modern home politics, though it appears in many shapes, and that is the question of money; and but one political remedy, that the people should grow wiser and better. My work-men fellow-passengers were as impatient and dull of hearing on the second of these points as any member of Parliament; but they had some glimmerings of the first. They would not hear of improvement on their part, but wished the world made over again in a crack, so that they might remain improvident and idle and debauched, and yet enjoy the comfort and respect that should accompany the opposite virtues; and it was in this expectation, as far as I could see, that many of them were now on their way to America. But on the point of money they saw clearly enough that inland

politics, so far as they were concerned, were reducible
to the question of annual income; a question which
should long ago have been settled by a revolution, they
did not know how, and which they were now about
to settle for themselves, once more they knew not how,
by crossing the Atlantic in a steamship of considerable
tonnage.

And yet it has been amply shown them that the second or income question is in itself nothing, and may as
well be left undecided, if there be no wisdom and virtue to profit by the change. It is not by a man's purse,
but by his character, that he is rich or poor. Barney
will be poor, Alick will be poor, Mackay will be poor;
let them go where they will, and wreck all the govern-
ments under heaven, they will be poor until they die.

Nothing is perhaps more notable in the average
workman than his surprising idleness, and the candour
with which he confesses to the failing. It has to me
been always something of a relief to find the poor, as a
general rule, so little oppressed with work. I can in
consequence enjoy my own more fortunate beginning
with a better grace. The other day I was living with
a farmer in America, an old frontiersman, who had
worked and fought, hunted and farmed, from his childhood up. He excused himself for his defective education on the ground that he had been overworked from
first to last. Even now, he said, anxious as he was,
he had never the time to take up a book. In consequence of this, I observed him closely; he was occupied
for four or, at the extreme outside, for five hours out of
the twenty-four, and then principally in walking; and
the remainder of the day he passed in born idleness,

either eating fruit or standing with his back against a
door. I have known men do hard literary work all
morning, and then undergo quite as much physical fatigue by way of relief as satisfied this powerful frontiersman for the day. He, at least, like all the educated
class, did so much homage to industry as to persuade
himself he was industrious. But the average mechanic
recognises his idleness with effrontery; he has even, as
I am told, organized it.

I give the story as it was told me, and it was told
me for a fact. A man fell from a housetop in the city
of Aberdeen, and was brought into hospital with broken
bones. He was asked what was his trade, and replied
that he was a *tapper*. No one had ever heard of such
a thing before; the officials were filled with curiosity;
they besought an explanation. It appeared that when a
party of slaters were engaged upon a roof, they would
now and then be taken with a fancy for the public-
house. Now a seamstress, for example, might slip
away from her work and no one be the wiser; but if
these fellows adjourned, the tapping of the mallets
would cease, and thus the neighbourhood be advertised
of their defection. Hence the career of the tapper. He
has to do the tapping and keep up an industrious bustle on the housetop during the absence of the slaters.
When he taps for only one or two the thing is child's-
play, but when he has to represent a whole troop, it is
then that he earns his money in the sweat of his brow.
Then must he bound from spot to spot, reduplicate,
triplicate, sexduplicate his single personality, and swell
and hasten his blows, until he produce a perfect illusion
for the ear, and you would swear that a crowd of emu-

lous masons were continuing merrily to roof the house. It must be a strange sight from an upper window.

I heard nothing on board of the tapper; but I was astonished at the stories told by my companions. Skulking, shirking, malingering, were all established tactics, it appeared. They could see no dishonesty where a man who is paid for an hour's work gives half an hour's consistent idling in its place. Thus the tapper would refuse to watch for the police during a burglary, and call himself an honest man. It is not sufficiently recognised that our race detests to work. If I thought that I should have to work every day of my life as hard as I am working now, I should be tempted to give up the struggle. And the workman early begins on his career of toil. He has never had his fill of holidays in the past, and his prospect of holidays in the future is both distant and uncertain. In the circumstances, it would require a high degree of virtue not to snatch alleviations for the moment.

There were many good talkers on the ship; and I believe good talking of a certain sort is a common accomplishment among working men. Where books are comparatively scarce, a greater amount of information will be given and received by word of mouth; and this tends to produce good talkers, and, what is no less needful for conversation, good listeners. They could all tell a story with effect. I am sometimes tempted to think that the less literary class show always better in narration; they have so much more patience with detail, are so much less hurried to reach the points, and preserve so much juster a proportion among the facts. At the same time their talk is dry; they pursue a topic plod-

79

dingly, have not an agile fancy, do not throw sudden lights from unexpected quarters, and when the talk is over they often leave the matter where it was. They mark time instead of marching. They think only to argue, not to reach new conclusions, and use their reason rather as a weapon of offence than as a tool for self-improvement. Hence the talk of some of the cleverest was unprofitable in result, because there was no give and take; they would grant you as little as possible for premise, and begin to dispute under an oath to conquer or to die.

But the talk of a workman is apt to be more interesting than that of a wealthy merchant, because the thoughts, hopes, and fears of which the workman's life is built lie nearer to necessity and nature. They are more immediate to human life. An income calculated by the week is a far more human thing than one calculated by the year, and a small income, simply from its smallness, than a large one. I never wearied listening to the details of a workman's economy, because every item stood for some real pleasure. If he could afford pudding twice a week, you know that twice a week the man ate with genuine gusto and was physically happy; while if you learn that a rich man has seven courses a day, ten to one the half of them remain untasted, and the whole is but misspent money and a weariness to the flesh.

The difference between England and America to a working man was thus most humanly put to me by a fellow-passenger: "In America," said he, "you get pies and puddings." I do not hear enough, in economy books, of pies and pudding. A man lives in and for the delicacies, adornments, and accidental attributes of life, such as pudding to eat and pleasant books and theatres to occupy his leisure. The bare terms of existence would be rejected with contempt by all. If a man feeds on bread and butter, soup and porridge, his appetite grows wolfish after dainties. And the workman dwells in a borderland, and is always within sight of those cheerless regions where life is more difficult to sustain than worth sustaining. Every detail of our existence, where it is worth while to cross the ocean after pie and pudding, is made alive and enthralling by the presence of genuine desire; but it is all one to me whether Crœsus has a hundred or a thousand thousands in the bank. There is more adventure in the life of the working man who descends as a common soldier into the battle of life, than in that of the millionaire who sits apart in an office, like Von Moltke, and only directs the manœuvres by telegraph. Give me to hear about the career of him who is in the thick of the business; to whom one change of market means an empty belly, and another a copious and savoury meal. This is not the philosophical, but the human side of economics; it interests like a story; and the life of all who are thus situated partakes in a small way of the charm of *Robinson Crusoe;* for every step is critical, and human life is presented to you naked and verging to its lowest terms.

NEW YORK

As we drew near to New York I was at first amused,
and then somewhat staggered, by the cautious and the
grisly tales that went the round. You would have
thought we were to land upon a cannibal island. You
must speak to no one in the streets, as they would not
leave you till you were rooked and beaten. You must
enter a hotel with military precautions; for the least you
had to apprehend was to awake next morning without
money or baggage, or necessary raiment, a lone forked
radish in a bed; and if the worst befell, you would instantly and mysteriously disappear from the ranks of
mankind.

I have usually found such stories correspond to the
least modicum of fact. Thus I was warned, I remember, against the roadside inns of the Cévennes, and that
by a learned professor; and when I reached Pradelles
the warning was explained — it was but the far-away
rumour and reduplication of a single terrifying story
already half a century old, and half forgotten in the theatre of the events. So I was tempted to make light of
these reports against America. But we had on board
with us a man whose evidence it would not do to put
aside. He had come near these perils in the body; he

had visited a robber inn. The public has an old and well-grounded favour for this class of incident, and shall be gratified to the best of my power.

My fellow-passenger, whom we shall call M'Naughten, had come from New York to Boston with a comrade, seeking work. They were a pair of rattling blades; and, leaving their baggage at the station, passed the day in beer-saloons, and with congenial spirits, until midnight struck. Then they applied themselves to find a lodging, and walked the streets till two, knocking at houses of entertainment and being refused admittance, or themselves declining the terms. By two the inspiration of their liquor had begun to wear off; they were weary and humble, and after a great circuit found themselves in the same street where they had begun their search, and in front of a French hotel where they had already sought accommodation. Seeing the house still open, they returned to the charge. A man in a white cap sat in an office by the door. He seemed to welcome them more warmly than when they had first presented themselves, and the charge for the night had somewhat unaccountably fallen from a dollar to a quarter. They thought him ill-looking, but paid their quarter apiece, and were shown upstairs to the top of the house. There, in a small room, the man in the white cap wished them pleasant slumbers.

It was furnished with a bed, a chair, and some conveniences. The door did not lock on the inside; and the only sign of adornment was a couple of framed pictures, one close above the head of the bed, and the other opposite the foot, and both curtained, as we may sometimes see valuable water-colours, or the portraits of the dead, or works of art more than usually skittish in the subject. It was perhaps in the hope of finding something of this last description that M'Naughten's comrade pulled aside the curtain of the first. He was startlingly disappointed. There was no picture. The frame surrounded, and the curtain was designed to hide, an oblong aperture in the partition, through which they looked forth into the dark corridor. A person standing without could easily take a purse from under the pillow, or even strangle a sleeper as he lay abed. M'Naughten and his comrade stared at each other like Vasco's seamen, "with a wild surmise;" and then the latter, catching up the lamp, ran to the other frame and roughly raised the curtain. There he stood, petrified; and M'Naughten, who had followed, grasped him by the wrist in terror. They could see into another room, larger in size than that which they occupied, where three men sat crouching and silent in the dark. For a second or so these five persons looked each other in the eyes, then the curtain was dropped, and M'Naughten and his friend made but one bolt of it out of the room and downstairs. The man in the white cap said nothing as they passed him; and they were so pleased to be once more in the open night that they gave up all notion of a bed, and walked the streets of Boston till the morning.

No one seemed much cast down by these stories, but all inquired after the address of a respectable hotel; and I, for my part, put myself under the conduct of Mr. Jones. Before noon of the second Sunday we sighted the low shores outside of New York harbour; the steerage passengers must remain on board to pass through

Castle Garden on the following morning; but we of the second cabin made our escape along with the lords of the saloon; and by six o'clock Jones and I issued into West Street, sitting on some straw in the bottom of an open baggage-wagon. It rained miraculously; and from that moment till on the following night I left New York, there was scarce a lull, and no cessation of the down-pour. The roadways were flooded; a loud strident noise of falling water filled the air; the restaurants smelt heavily of wet people and wet clothing.

It took us but a few minutes, though it cost us a good deal of money, to be rattled along West Street to our destination: "Reunion House, No. 10 West Street, one minute's walk from Castle Garden; convenient to Castle Garden, the Steamboat Landings, California Steamers and Liverpool Ships; Board and Lodging per day 1 dollar, single meals 25 cents, lodging per night 25 cents; private rooms for families; no charge for storage or baggage; satisfaction guaranteed to all persons; Michael Mitchell, Proprietor." Reunion House was, I may go the length of saying, a humble hostelry. You entered through a long bar-room, thence passed into a little dining-room, and thence into a still smaller kitchen. The furniture was of the plainest; but the bar was hung in the American taste, with encouraging and hospitable mottoes.

Jones was well known; we were received warmly; and two minutes afterwards I had refused a drink from the proprietor, and was going on, in my plain European fashion, to refuse a cigar, when Mr. Mitchell sternly interposed, and explained the situation. He was offering to treat me, it appeared; whenever an American bar-keeper proposes anything, it must be borne in mind that he is offering to treat; and if I did not want a drink, I must at least take the cigar. I took it bashfully, feeling I had begun my American career on the wrong foot. I did not enjoy that cigar; but this may have been from a variety of reasons, even the best cigar often failing to please if you smoke three-quarters of it in a drenching rain.

For many years America was to me a sort of promised land; "westward the march of empire holds its way"; the race is for the moment to the young; what has been and what is we imperfectly and obscurely know; what is to be yet lies beyond the flight of our imaginations. Greece, Rome and Judæa are gone by forever, leaving to generations the legacy of their accomplished work; China still endures, an old-inhabited house in the brand-new city of nations; England has already declined, since she has lost the States; and to these States, therefore, yet undeveloped, full of dark possibilities, and grown, like another Eve, from one rib out of the side of their own old land, the minds of young men in England turn naturally at a certain hopeful period of their age. It will be hard for an American to understand the spirit. But let him imagine a young man, who shall have grown up in an old and rigid circle, following bygone fashions and taught to distrust his own fresh instincts, and who now suddenly hears of a family of cousins, all about his own age, who keep house together by themselves and live far from restraint and tradition; let him imagine this, and he will have some imperfect notion of the sentiment with which spirited English youths turn to the thought of the American Republic. It seems to them as if, out west, the war of life was still conducted in the open air, and on free barbaric terms; as if it had not yet been narrowed into parlours, nor begun to be conducted, like some unjust and dreary arbitration, by compromise, costume, forms of procedure, and sad, senseless self-denial. Which of these two he prefers, a man with any youth still left in him will decide rightly for himself. He would rather be houseless than denied a pass-key; rather go without food than partake of a stalled ox in stiff, respectable society; rather be shot out of hand than direct his life according to the dictates of the world.

He knows or thinks nothing of the Maine Laws, the Puritan sourness, the fierce, sordid appetite for dollars, or the dreary existence of country towns. A few wild story-books which delighted his childhood form the imaginative basis of his picture of America. In course of time, there is added to this a great crowd of stimulating details — vast cities that grow up as by enchantment; the birds, that have gone south in autumn, returning with the spring to find thousands camped upon their marshes, and the lamps burning far and near along populous streets; forests that disappear like snow; countries larger than Britain that are cleared and settled, one man running forth with his household gods before another, while the bear and the Indian are yet scarce aware of their approach; oil that gushes from the earth; gold that is washed or quarried in the brooks or glens of the Sierras; and all that bustle, courage, action, and constant kaleidoscopic change that Walt Whitman has seized and set forth in his vigorous, cheerful, and loquacious verses.

Here I was at last in America, and was soon out upon

New York streets, spying for things foreign. The place had to me an air of Liverpool; but such was the rain that not Paradise itself would have looked inviting. We were a party of four, under two umbrellas; Jones and I and two Scots lads, recent immigrants, and not indisposed to welcome a compatriot. They had been six weeks in New York, and neither of them had yet found a single job or earned a single halfpenny. Up to the present they were exactly out of pocket by the amount of the fare.

The lads soon left us. Now I had sworn by all my gods to have such a dinner as would rouse the dead; there was scarce any expense at which I should have hesitated; the devil was in it but Jones and I should dine like heathen emperors. I set to work, asking after a restaurant; and I chose the wealthiest and most gastronomical-looking passers-by to ask from. Yet, although I had told them I was willing to pay anything in reason, one and all sent me off to cheap, fixed-price houses, where I would not have eaten that night for the cost of twenty dinners. I do not know if this were characteristic of New York, or whether it was only Jones and I who looked un-dinerly and discouraged enterprising suggestions. But at length, by our own sagacity, we found a French restaurant, where there was a French waiter, some fair French cooking, some so-called French wine, and French coffee to conclude the whole. I never entered into the feelings of Jack on land so completely as when I tasted that coffee.

I suppose we had one of the " private rooms for families " at Reunion House. It was very small, furnished with a bed, a chair, and some clothes-pegs; and it de-rived all that was necessary for the life of the human animal through two borrowed lights; one looking into the passage, and the second opening, without sash, into another apartment, where three men fitfully snored, or in intervals of wakefulness, drearily mumbled to each other all night long. It will be observed that this was almost exactly the disposition of the room in M'Naughten's story. Jones had the bed; I pitched my camp upon the floor; he did not sleep until near morning, and I, for my part, never closed an eye.

At sunrise I heard a cannon fired; and shortly afterwards the men in the next room gave over snoring for good, and began to rustle over their toilettes. The sound of their voices as they talked was low and moaning, like that of people watching by the sick. Jones, who had at last begun to doze, tumbled and murmured, and every now and then opened unconscious eyes upon me where I lay. I found myself growing eerier and eerier, for I daresay I was a little fevered by my restless night, and hurried to dress and get downstairs.

You had to pass through the rain, which still fell thick and resonant, to reach a lavatory on the other side of the court. There were three basin-stands, and a few crumpled towels and pieces of wet soap, white and slippery like fish; nor should I forget a looking-glass and a pair of questionable combs. Another Scots lad was here, scrubbing his face with a good will. He had been three months in New York and had not yet found a single job nor earned a single halfpenny. Up to the present, he also was exactly out of pocket by the amount of the fare. I began to grow sick at heart for my fellow-emigrants.

Of my nightmare wanderings in New York I spare to tell. I had a thousand and one things to do; only the day to do them in, and a journey across the continent before me in the evening. It rained with patient fury; every now and then I had to get under cover for a while in order, so to speak, to give my mackintosh a rest; for under this continued drenching it began to grow damp on the inside. I went to banks, post-offices, railway-offices, restaurants, publishers, book-sellers, money-changers, and wherever I went a pool would gather about my feet, and those who were careful of their floors would look on with an unfriendly eye. Wherever I went, too, the same traits struck me: the people were all surprisingly rude and surprisingly kind. The money-changer cross-questioned me like a French commissary, asking my age, my business, my average income, and my destination, beating down my attempts at evasion, and receiving my answers in silence; and yet when all was over, he shook hands with me up to the elbows, and sent his lad nearly a quarter of a mile in the rain to get me books at a reduction. Again, in a very large publishing and bookselling establishment, a man, who seemed to be the manager, received me as I had certainly never before been received in any human shop, indicated squarely that he put no faith in my honesty, and refused to look up the names of books or give me the slightest help or information, on the ground, like the steward, that it was none of his business. I lost my temper at last, said I was a stranger in America and not learned in their etiquette; but I would assure him, if he went to any bookseller in England, of more handsome usage. The boast was perhaps exaggerated; but like many a long shot, it struck the gold. The manager passed at once from one extreme to the other; I may say that from that moment he loaded me with kindness; he gave me all sorts of good advice, wrote me down addresses, and came bare-headed into the rain to point me out a restaurant, where I might lunch, nor even then did he seem to think that he had done enough. These are (it is as well to be bold in statement) the manners of America. It is this same opposition that has most struck me in people of almost all classes and from east to west. By the time a man had about strung me up to be the death of him by his insulting behaviour, he himself would be just upon the point of melting into confidence and service-able attentions. Yet I suspect, although I have met with the like in so many parts, that this must be the character of some particular state or group of states; for in America, and this again in all classes, you will find some of the softest-mannered gentlemen in the world.

I was so wet when I got back to Mitchell's toward the evening, that I had simply to divest myself of my shoes, socks and trousers, and leave them behind for the benefit of New York city. No fire could have dried them ere I had to start; and to pack them in their pres-ent condition was to spread ruin among my other pos-sessions. With a heavy heart I said farewell to them as they lay a pulp in the middle of a pool upon the floor of Mitchell's kitchen. I wonder if they are dry by now. Mitchell hired a man to carry my baggage to the station, which was hard by, accompanied me thither himself, and recommended me to the particular attention of the officials. No one could have been kinder. Those who are out of pocket may go safely to Reunion House, where they will get decent meals and find an honest and obliging landlord. I owed him this word of thanks, before I enter fairly on the second and far less agreeable chapter of my emigrant experience.

ACROSS THE PLAINS
WITH OTHER MEMORIES AND ESSAYS

TO
PAUL BOURGET

TRAVELLER and student and curious as you are, you will never have heard the name of Vailima, most likely not even that of Upolu, and Samoa itself may be strange to your ears. To these barbaric seats there came the other day a yellow book with your name on the title, and filled in every page with the exquisite gifts of your art. Let me take and change your own words: *J'ai beau admirer les autres de toutes mes forces, c'est avec vous que je me complais à vivre.*

R. L. S.

VAILIMA,
   UPOLU,
      SAMOA.

LETTER TO THE AUTHOR

My Dear Stevenson:

You have trusted me with the choice and arrangement of these papers, written before you departed to the South Seas, and have asked me to add a preface to the volume. But it is your prose the public wish to read, not mine; and I am sure they will willingly be spared the preface. Acknowledgments are due in your name to the publishers of the several magazines from which the papers are collected, viz. *Fraser's, Longman's,* the *Magazine of Art,* and *Scribner's.* I will only add, lest any reader should find the tone of the concluding pieces less inspiriting than your wont, that they were written under circumstances of especial gloom and sickness. "I agree with you the lights seem a little turned down," so you write to me now; "the truth is I was far through, and came none to soon to the South Seas, where I was to recover peace of body and mind. And however low the lights, the stuff is true. . . ." Well, inasmuch as the South Sea sirens have breathed new life into you, we are bound to be heartily grateful to them, though as they keep you so far removed from us, it is difficult not to bear them a grudge; and if they would reconcile us quite, they have but to do two things more—to teach you new tales that shall charm us like your old, and to spare you, at least once in a while in summer, to climates within reach of us who are task-bound for ten months in the year beside the Thames.

Yours ever,

SIDNEY COLVIN.

February, 1892.

I. ACROSS THE PLAINS

LEAVES FROM THE NOTEBOOK OF AN EMIGRANT BETWEEN
NEW YORK AND SAN FRANCISCO

MONDAY.—It was, if I remember rightly, five o'clock when we were all signalled to be present at the Ferry Depôt of the railroad. An emigrant ship had arrived at New York on the Saturday night, another on the Sunday morning, our own on Sunday afternoon, a fourth early on Monday; and as there is no emigrant train on Sunday, a great part of the passengers from these four ships was concentrated on the train by which I was to travel. There was a babel of bewildered men, women, and children. The wretched little booking office, and the baggage-room, which was not much larger, were crowded thick with emigrants, and were heavy and rank with the atmosphere of dripping clothes. Open carts full of bedding stood by the half-hour in the rain. The officials loaded each other with recriminations. A bearded, mildewed little man, whom I take to have been an emigrant agent, was all over the place, his mouth full of brimstone, blustering and interfering. It was plain that the whole system, if system there was, had utterly broken down under the strain of so many passengers.

My own ticket was given me at once, and an oldish man, who preserved his head in the midst of this turmoil, got my baggage registered, and counselled me to stay quietly where I was till he should give me the word to move. I had taken along with me a small valise, a knapsack, which I carried on my shoulders, and in the bag of my railway rug the whole of *Bancroft's History of the United States,* in six fat volumes. It was as much as I could carry with convenience even for short distances, but it insured me plenty of clothing, and the valise was at that moment, and often after, useful for a stool. I am sure I sat for an hour in the baggage-room, and wretched enough it was; yet, when at last the word was passed to me and I picked up my bundles and got under way, it was only to exchange discomfort for downright misery and danger.

I followed the porters into a long shed reaching down-hill from West Street to the river. It was dark, the wind blew clean through it from end to end; and here I found a great block of passengers and baggage, hundreds of one and tons of the other. I feel I shall have a difficulty to make myself believed; and certainly the scene must have been exceptional, for it was too dangerous for daily repetition. It was a tight jam; there was no fair way through the mingled mass of brute and living obstruction. Into the upper skirts of the crowd porters, infuriated by hurry and overwork, clove their way with shouts. I may say that we stood like sheep, and that the porters charged among us like so many maddened sheep-dogs; and I believe these men were no longer answerable for their acts. It mattered not what they were carrying, they drove straight into the press, and when they could get no farther, blindly discharged their barrowful. With my own hand, for in-

stance, I saved the life of a child as it sat upon its
mother's knee, she sitting on a box; and since I heard
of no accident, I must suppose that there were many
similar interpositions in the course of the evening. It will
give some idea of the state of mind to which we were reduced if I tell you that neither the porter nor the mother
of the child paid the least attention to my act. It was
not till some time after that I understood what I had
done myself, for to ward off heavy boxes seemed at the
moment a natural incident of human life. Cold, wet,
clamour, dead opposition to progress, such as one encounters in an evil dream, had utterly daunted the spirits. We had accepted this purgatory as a child accepts
the conditions of the world. For my part, I shivered a
little, and my back ached wearily; but I believe I had
neither a hope nor a fear, and all the activities of my
nature had become tributary to one massive sensation
of discomfort.

At length, and after how long an interval I hesitate to
guess, the crowd began to move, heavily straining
through itself. About the same time some lamps were
lighted, and threw a sudden flare over the shed. We
were being filtered out into the river boat for Jersey City.
You may imagine how slowly this filtering proceeded,
through the dense, choking crush, every one overladen
with packages or children, and yet under the necessity
of fishing out his ticket by the way; but it ended at
length for me, and I found myself on deck under a flimsy
awning and with a trifle of elbow-room to stretch and
breathe in. This was on the starboard; for the bulk of
the emigrants stuck hopelessly on the port side, by
which we had entered. In vain the seamen shouted to

them to move on, and threatened them with shipwreck. These poor people were under a spell of stupor, and did not stir a foot. It rained as heavily as ever, but the wind now came in sudden claps and capfuls, not without danger to a boat so badly ballasted as ours; and we crept over the river in the darkness, trailing one paddle in the water like a wounded duck, and passed ever and again by huge, illuminated steamers running many knots, and heralding their approach by strains of music. The contrast between these pleasure embarkations and our own grim vessel, with her list to port and her freight of wet and silent emigrants, was of that glaring description which we count too obvious for the purposes of art.

The landing at Jersey City was done in a stampede. I had a fixed sense of calamity, and to judge by conduct, the same persuasion was common to us all. A panic selfishness, like that produced by fear, presided over the disorder of our landing. People pushed, and elbowed, and ran, the families following how they could. Children fell, and were picked up to be rewarded by a blow. One child, who had lost her parents, screamed steadily and with increasing shrillness, as though verging towards a fit; an official kept her by him, but no one else seemed so much as to remark her distress; and I am ashamed to say that I ran among the rest. I was so weary that I had twice to make a halt and set down my bundles in the hundred yards or so between the pier and the railway station, so that I was quite wet by the time that I got under cover. There was no waiting-room, no refreshment room; the cars were locked; and for at least another hour, or so it seemed, we had to camp upon the draughty, gaslit platform. I sat on my valise, too crushed to observe my neighbours; but as they were all cold, and wet, and weary, and driven stupidly crazy by the mismanagement to which we had been subjected, I believe they can have been no happier than myself. I bought half a dozen oranges from a boy, for oranges and nuts were the only refection to be had. As only two of them had even a pretence of juice, I threw the other four under the cars, and beheld, as in a dream, grown people and children groping on the track after my leavings.

At last we were admitted into the cars, utterly dejected, and far from dry. For my own part, I got out a clothes-brush, and brushed my trousers as hard as I could till I had dried them and warmed my blood into the bargain; but no one else, except my next neighbour to whom I lent the brush, appeared to take the least precaution. As they were, they composed themselves to sleep. I had seen the lights of Philadelphia, and been twice ordered to change carriages and twice countermanded, before I allowed myself to follow their example.

Tuesday.— When I awoke, it was already day; the train was standing idle; I was in the last carriage, and, seeing some others strolling to and fro about the lines, I opened the door and stepped forth, as from a caravan by the wayside. We were near no station, nor even, as far as I could see, within reach of any signal. A green, open, undulating country stretched away upon all sides. Locust trees and a single field of Indian corn gave it a foreign grace and interest; but the contours of the land were soft and English. It was not quite England, neither was it quite France; yet like enough either to seem natural in my eyes. And it was in the sky, and not upon the earth, that I was surprised to find a change. Explain it how you may, and for my part I cannot explain it at all, the sun rises with a different spendour in America and Europe. There is more clear gold and scarlet in our old country mornings; more purple, brown, and smoky orange in those of the new. It may be from habit, but to me the coming of day is less fresh and inspiriting in the latter; it has a duskier glory, and more nearly resembles sunset; it seems to fit some subsequential, evening epoch of the world, as though America were in fact, and not merely in fancy, farther from the orient of Aurora and the springs of day. I thought so then, by the railroad side in Pennsylvania, and I have thought so a dozen times since in far distant parts of the continent. If it be an illusion it is one very deeply rooted, and in which my eyesight is accomplice.

Soon after a train whisked by, announcing and accompanying its passage by the swift beating of a sort of chapel bell upon the engine; and as it was for this we had been waiting, we were summoned by the cry of "All aboard!" and went on again upon our way. The whole line, it appeared, was topsy-turvy; an accident at midnight having thrown all the traffic hours into arrear. We paid for this in the flesh, for we had no meals all that day. Fruit we could buy upon the cars; and now and then we had a few minutes at some station with a meagre show of rolls and sandwiches for sale; but we were so many and so ravenous that, though I tried at every opportunity, the coffee was always exhausted before I could elbow my way to the counter.

Our American sunrise had ushered in a noble summer's day. There was not a cloud; the sunshine was baking; yet in the woody river valleys among which we wound our way, the atmosphere preserved a sparkling freshness till late in the afternoon. It had an inland sweetness and variety to one newly from the sea; it smelt of woods, rivers, and the delved earth. These, though in so far a country, were airs from home. I stood on the platform by the hour; and as I saw, one after another, pleasant villages, carts upon the highway and fishers by the stream, and heard cockcrows and cheery voices in the distance, and beheld the sun, no longer shining blankly on the plains of ocean, but striking among shapely hills and his light dispersed and coloured by a thousand accidents of form and surface, I began to exult with myself upon this rise in life like a man who had come into a rich estate. And when I had asked the name of a river from the brakesman, and heard that it was called the Susquehanna, the beauty of the name seemed to be part and parcel of the beauty of the land. As when Adam with divine fitness named the creatures, so this word Susquehanna was at once accepted by the fancy. That was the name, as no other could be, for that shining river and desirable valley.

None can care for literature in itself who do not take a special pleasure in the sound of names; and there is no part of the world where nomenclature is so rich, poetical, humorous, and picturesque as the United States of America. All times, races, and languages have brought their contribution. Pekin is in the same State with Euclid, with Bellefontaine, and with Sandusky. Chelsea, with its London associations of red brick, Sloane

Square, and the King's Road, is own suburb to stately
and primeval Memphis; there they have their seat,
translated names of cities, where the Mississippi runs
by Tennessee and Arkansas;[1] and both, while I was
crossing the continent, lay, watched by armed men, in
the horror and isolation of a plague. Old, red Manhat-
tan lies, like an Indian arrowhead under a steam factory, below anglified New York. The names of the
States and Territories themselves form a chorus of sweet
and most romantic vocables: Delaware, Ohio, Indiana,
Florida, Dakota, Iowa, Wyoming, Minnesota, and the
Carolinas; there are few poems with a nobler music for
the ear: a songful, tuneful land; and if the new Homer
shall arise from the Western continent, his verse will
be enriched, his pages sing spontaneously, with the
names of states and cities that would strike the fancy
in a business circular.

Late in the evening we were landed in a waiting-
room at Pittsburg. I had now under my charge a
young and sprightly Dutch widow with her children;
these I was to watch over providentially for a certain
distance farther on the way; but as I found she was
furnished with a basket of eatables, I left her in the
waiting-room to seek a dinner for myself.

I mention this meal, not only because it was the first
of which I had partaken for about thirty hours, but because it was the means of my first introduction to a
coloured gentleman. He did me the honour to wait
upon me after a fashion, while I was eating; and with
every word, look, and gesture marched me farther into
the country of surprise. He was indeed strikingly un-

1 Please pronounce Arkansaw, with the accent on the first.

like the negroes of Mrs. Beecher Stowe, or the Christy
Minstrels of my youth.   Imagine a gentleman, certainly
somewhat dark, but of a pleasant warm hue, speaking
English with a slight and rather odd foreign accent,
every inch a man of the world, and armed with manners so patronisingly superior that I am at a loss to
name their parallel in England.   A butler perhaps rides
as high over the unbutlered, but then he sets you right
with a reserve and a sort of sighing patience which one
is often moved to admire.   And again, the abstract
butler never stoops to familiarity.   But the coloured
gentleman will pass you a wink at a time; he is familiar
like an upper form boy to a fag; he unbends to you like
Prince Hal with Poins and Falstaff.   He makes himself
at home and welcome.   Indeed, I may say, this waiter
behaved himself to me throughout that supper much as,
with us, a young, free, and not very self-respecting
master might behave to a good-looking chambermaid.
I had come prepared to pity the poor negro, to put him
at his ease, to prove in a thousand condescensions that
I was no sharer in the prejudice of race; but I assure
you I put my patronage away for another occasion, and
had the grace to be pleased with that result.

Seeing he was a very honest fellow, I consulted him
upon a point of etiquette: if one should offer to tip the
American waiter?   Certainly not, he told me.   Never.
It would not do.   They considered themselves too
highly to accept.   They would even resent the offer.   As
for him and me, we had enjoyed a very pleasant conversation; he, in particular, had found much pleasure in
my society; I was a stranger; this was exactly one of
those rare conjunctures. . . .   Without being very clear

seeing, I can still perceive the sun at noonday; and the coloured gentleman deftly pocketed a quarter.

Wednesday. — A little after midnight I convoyed my widow and orphans on board the train; and morning found us far into Ohio. This had early been a favourite home of my imagination; I have played at being in Ohio by the week, and enjoyed some capital sport there with a dummy gun, my person being still unbreeched. My preference was founded on a work which appeared in *Cassell's Family Paper,* and was read aloud to me by my nurse. It narrated the doings of one Custaloga, an Indian brave, who, in the last chapter, very obligingly washed the paint off his face and became Sir Reginald Somebody-or-other; a trick I never forgave him. The idea of a man being an Indian brave, and then giving that up to be a baronet, was one which my mind rejected. It offended verisimilitude, like the pretended anxiety of Robinson Crusoe and others to escape from uninhabited islands.

But Ohio was not at all as I had pictured it. We were now on those great plains which stretch unbroken to the Rocky Mountains. The country was flat like Holland, but far from being dull. All through Ohio, Indiana, Illinois, and Iowa, or for as much as I saw of them from the train and in my waking moments, it was rich and various, and breathed an elegance peculiar to itself. The tall corn pleased the eye; the trees were graceful in themselves, and framed the plain into long, aërial vistas; and the clean, bright, gardened townships spoke of country fare and pleasant summer evenings on the stoop. It was a sort of flat paradise; but, I am afraid, not unfrequented by the devil. That morning dawned with such a freezing chill as I have rarely felt; a chill that was not perhaps so measurable by instrument, as it struck home upon the heart and seemed to travel with the blood. Day came in with a shudder. White mists lay thinly over the surface of the plain, as we see them more often on a lake; and though the sun had soon dispersed and drunk them up, leaving an atmosphere of fever heat and crystal pureness from horizon to horizon, the mists had still been there, and we knew that this paradise was haunted by killing damps and foul malaria. The fences along the line bore but two descriptions of advertisement; one to recommend tobaccos, and the other to vaunt remedies against the ague. At the point of day, and while we were all in the grasp of that first chill, a native of the state, who had got in at some way station, pronounced it, with a doctoral air, "a fever and ague morning."

The Dutch widow was a person of some character. She had conceived at first sight a great aversion for the present writer, which she was at no pains to conceal. But being a woman of a practical spirit, she made no difficulty about accepting my attentions, and encouraged me to buy her children fruits and candies, to carry all her parcels, and even to sleep upon the floor that she might profit by my empty seat. Nay, she was such a rattle by nature, and so powerfully moved to autobiographical talk, that she was forced, for want of a better, to take me into confidence and tell me the story of her life. I heard about her late husband, who seemed to have made his chief impression by taking her out pleasuring on Sundays. I could tell you her prospects, her hopes, the amount of her fortune, the cost of her house-

keeping by the week, and a variety of particular matters
that are not usually disclosed except to friends. At one
station, she shook up her children to look at a man on
the platform and say if he were not like Mr. Z.; while
to me she explained how she had been keeping company with this Mr. Z., how far matters had proceeded,
and how it was because of his desistance that she was
now travelling to the west. Then, when I was thus put
in possession of the facts, she asked my judgment on
that type of manly beauty. I admired it to her heart's
content. She was not, I think, remarkably veracious in
talk, but broidered as fancy prompted, and built castles
in the air out of her past; yet she had that sort of candour, to keep me, in spite of all these confidences, steadily aware of her aversion. Her parting words were
ingeniously honest. "I am sure," said she, "we all
ought to be very much obliged to you." I cannot pretend that she put me at my ease; but I had a certain
respect for such a genuine dislike. A poor nature would
have slipped, in the course of these familiarities, into a
sort of worthless toleration for me.

We reached Chicago in the evening. I was turned
out of the cars, bundled into an omnibus, and driven off
through the streets to the station of a different railroad.
Chicago seemed a great and gloomy city. I remember
having subscribed, let us say sixpence, towards its res-
toration at the period of the fire; and now when I beheld street after street of ponderous houses and crowds
of comfortable burghers, I thought it would be a graceful act for the corporation to refund that sixpence, or, at
the least, to entertain me to a cheerful dinner. But
there was no word of restitution. I was that city's ben-

efactor, yet I was received in a third-class waiting-room, and the best dinner I could get was a dish of ham and eggs at my own expense.

I can safely say, I have never been so dog-tired as that night in Chicago. When it was time to start, I descended the platform like a man in a dream. It was a long train, lighted from end to end; and car after car, as I came up with it, was not only filled but overflowing. My valise, my knapsack, my rug, with those six ponderous tomes of Bancroft, weighed me double; I was hot, feverish, painfully athirst; and there was a great darkness over me, an internal darkness, not to be dispelled by gas. When at last I found an empty bench, I sank into it like a bundle of rags, the world seemed to swim away into the distance, and my consciousness dwindled within me to a mere pin's head, like a taper on a foggy night.

When I came a little more to myself, I found that there had sat down beside me a very cheerful, rosy little German gentleman, somewhat gone in drink, who was talking away to me, nineteen to the dozen, as they say. I did my best to keep up the conversation; for it seemed to me dimly as if something depended upon that. I heard him relate, among many other things, that there were pickpockets on the train, who had already robbed a man of forty dollars and a return ticket; but though I caught the words, I do not think I properly understood the sense until next morning; and I believe I replied at the time that I was very glad to hear it. What else he talked about I have no guess; I remember a gabbling sound of words, his profuse gesticulation, and his smile, which was highly explanatory; but no more. And I suppose I must have shown my confusion very plainly; for, first, I saw him knit his brows at me like one who has conceived a doubt; next, he tried me in German, supposing perhaps that I was unfamiliar with the English tongue; and finally, in despair, he rose and left me. I felt chagrined; but my fatigue was too crushing for delay, and, stretching myself as far as that was possible upon the bench, I was received at once into a dreamless stupor.

The little German gentleman was only going a little way into the suburbs after a *diner fin,* and was bent on entertainment while the journey lasted. Having failed with me, he pitched next upon another emigrant, who had come through from Canada, and was not one jot less weary than myself. Nay, even in a natural state, as I found next morning when we scraped acquaintance, he was a heavy, uncommunicative man. After trying him on different topics, it appears that the little German gentleman flounced into a temper, swore an oath or two, and departed from that car in quest of livelier society. Poor little gentleman! I suppose he thought an emigrant should be a rollicking, free-hearted blade, with a flask of foreign brandy and a long, comical story to beguile the moments of digestion.

Thursday. — I suppose there must be a cycle in the fatigue of travelling, for when I awoke next morning, I was entirely renewed in spirits and ate a hearty breakfast of porridge, with sweet milk, and coffee and hot cakes, at Burlington upon the Mississippi. Another long day's ride followed, with but one feature worthy of remark. At a place called Creston, a drunken man got in. He was aggressively friendly, but, according to

English notions, not at all unpresentable upon a train. For one stage he eluded the notice of the officials; but just as we were beginning to move out of the next station, Cromwell by name, by came the conductor. There was a word or two of talk; and then the official had the man by the shoulders, twitched him from his seat, marched him through the car, and sent him flying on to the track. It was done in three motions, as exact as a piece of drill. The train was still moving slowly, although beginning to mend her pace, and the drunkard got his feet without a fall. He carried a red bundle, though not so red as his cheeks; and he shook this menacingly in the air with one hand, while the other stole behind him to the region of the kidneys. It was the first indication that I had come among revolvers, and I observed it with some emotion. The conductor stood on the steps with one hand on his hip, looking back at him; and perhaps this attitude imposed upon the creature, for he turned without further ado, and went off staggering along the track towards Cromwell, followed by a peal of laughter from the cars. They were speaking English all about me, but I knew I was in a foreign land.

Twenty minutes before nine that night, we were deposited at the Pacific Transfer Station near Council Bluffs, on the eastern bank of the Missouri river. Here we were to stay the night at a kind of caravanserai, set apart for emigrants. But I gave way to a thirst for luxury, separated myself from my companions, and marched with my effects into the Union Pacific Hotel. A white clerk and a coloured gentleman whom, in my plain European way, I should call the boots, were installed behind a counter like bank tellers. They took my name, assigned me a number, and proceeded to deal with my packages. And here came the tug of war. I wished to give up my packages into safe keeping; but I did not wish to go to bed. And this, it appeared, was impossible in an American hotel.

It was, of course, some inane misunderstanding, and sprang from my unfamiliarity with the language. For although two nations use the same words and read the same books, intercourse is not conducted by the dictionary. The business of life is not carried on by words, but in set phrases, each with a special and almost a slang signification. Some international obscurity prevailed between me and the coloured gentleman at Council Bluffs; so that what I was asking, which seemed very natural to me, appeared to him a monstrous exigency. He refused, and that with the plainness of the West. This American manner of conducting matters of business is, at first, highly unpalatable to the European. When we approach a man in the way of his calling, and for those services by which he earns his bread, we consider him for the time being our hired servant. But in the American opinion, two gentlemen meet and have a friendly talk with a view to exchanging favours if they shall agree to please. I know not which is the more convenient, nor even which is the more truly courteous. The English stiffness unfortunately tends to be continued after the particular transaction is at an end, and thus favours class separations. But on the other hand, these equalitarian plainnesses leave an open field for the insolence of Jack-in-office.

I was nettled by the coloured gentleman's refusal,

114

and unbuttoned my wrath under the similitude of iron-ical submission. I knew nothing, I said, of the ways of American hotels; but I had no desire to give trouble. If there was nothing for it but to get to bed immedi-ately, let him say the word, and though it was not my habit, I should cheerfully obey.

He burst into a shout of laughter. "Ah!" said he, "you do not know about America. They are fine people in America. Oh! you will like them very well. But you mustn't get mad. I know what you want. You come along with me."

And issuing from behind the counter, and taking me by the arm like an old acquaintance, he led me to the bar of the hotel.

"There," said he, pushing me from him by the shoulder, "go and have a drink!"

THE EMIGRANT TRAIN

ALL this while I had been travelling by mixed trains, where I might meet with Dutch widows and little Ger-man gentry fresh from table. I had been but a latent emigrant; now I was to be branded once more, and put apart with my fellows. It was about two in the afternoon of Friday that I found myself in front of the Emigrant House, with more than a hundred others, to be sorted and boxed for the journey. A white-haired official, with a stick under one arm, and a list in the other hand, stood apart in front of us, and called name after name in the tone of a command. At each name you would see a family gather up its brats and bundles and run for the hindmost of the three cars that stood awaiting us, and I soon concluded that this was to be set apart for the women and children. The second or central car, it turned out, was devoted to men travelling alone, and the third to the Chinese. The official was easily moved to anger at the least delay; but the emigrants were both quick at answering their names, and speedy in getting themselves and their effects on board.

The families once housed, we men carried the second car without ceremony by simultaneous assault. I suppose the reader has some notion of an American railroad-car, that long, narrow wooden box, like a flat-roofed Noah's ark, with a stove and a convenience, one at either end, a passage down the middle, and transverse benches upon either hand. Those destined for emigrants on the Union Pacific are only remarkable for their extreme plainness, nothing but wood entering in any part into their constitution, and for the usual inefficacy of the lamps, which often went out and shed but a dying glimmer even while they burned. The benches are too short for anything but a young child. Where there is scarce elbow-room for two to sit, there will not be be space enough for one to lie. Hence the company, or rather, as it appears from certain bills about the Transfer Station, the company's servants, have conceived a plan for the better accommodation of travellers. They prevail on every two to chum together. To each of the chums they sell a board and three square cushions stuffed with straw, and covered with thin cotton. The benches can be made to face each other in pairs, for the backs are reversible. On the approach of night the boards are laid from bench to bench, making a couch wide enough for two, and long enough for a man of the middle height; and the chums lie down side by side upon the cushions with the head to the conductor's van and the feet to the engine. When the train is full, of course this plan is impossible, for there must not be more than one to every bench, neither can it be carried out unless the chums agree. It was to bring about this last condition that our white-haired official now bestirred himself. He made a most active master of ceremonies, introducing likely couples, and even guaranteeing the amiability and honesty of each. The greater the number of happy couples the better for his pocket, for it was he who sold the raw material of the beds. His price for one board and three straw cushions began with two dollars and a half; but before the train left, and, I am sorry to say, long after I had purchased mine, it had fallen to one dollar and a half.

The match-maker had a difficulty with me; perhaps, like some ladies, I showed myself too eager for union at any price; but certainly the first who was picked out to be my bedfellow, declined the honour without thanks. He was an old, heavy, slow-spoken man, I think from Yankeeland, looked me all over with great timidity, and then began to excuse himself in broken phrases. He didn't know the young man, he said. The young man might be very honest, but how was he to know that? There was another young man whom he had met already in the train; he guessed *he* was honest, and would prefer to chum with *him* upon the whole. All this without any sort of excuse, as though I had been inanimate or absent. I began to tremble lest everyone should refuse my company, and I be left rejected. But the next in turn was a tall, strapping, long-limbed, small-headed, curly-haired Pennsylvania Dutchman, with a soldierly smartness in his manner. To be exact, he had acquired it in the navy. But that was all one; he had at least been trained to desperate resolves, so he accepted the match, and the white-haired swindler pronounced the connubial benediction, and pocketed his fees.

The rest of the afternoon was spent in making up the train. I am afraid to say how many baggage-waggons followed the engine, certainly a score; then came the Chinese, then we, then the families, and the rear was brought up by the conductor in what, if I have it rightly, is called his caboose. The class to which I belonged was of course far the largest, and we ran over, so to speak, to both sides; so that there were some Caucasians among the Chinamen, and some bachelors among the families. But our own car was pure from admixture, save for one little boy of eight or nine, who had the whooping-cough. At last, about six, the long train crawled out of the Transfer Station and across the wide Missouri river to Omaha, westward bound.

It was a troubled uncomfortable evening in the cars. There was thunder in the air, which helped to keep us restless. A man played many airs upon the cornet, and none of them were much attended to, until he came to "Home, sweet home." It was truly strange to note how the talk ceased at that, and the faces began to lengthen. I have no idea whether musically this air is to be considered good or bad; but it belongs to that class of art which may be best described as a brutal assault upon the feelings. Pathos must be relieved by dignity of treatment. If you wallow naked in the pathetic, like the author of "Home, sweet home," you make your hearers weep in an unmanly fashion; and even while yet they are moved, they despise themselves and hate the occasion of their weakness. It did not come to tears that night, for the experiment was interrupted. An elderly, hard-looking man, with a goatee beard and about as much appearance of sentiment as you would expect from a retired slaver, turned with a start and bade the performer stop that "damned thing." "I've heard about enough of that," he added; "give us something about the good country we're going to." A murmur of adhesion ran round the car; the performer took the instrument from his lips, laughed and nodded, and then struck into a dancing measure; and, like a new Timotheus, stilled immediately the emotion he had raised.

The day faded; the lamps were lit; a party of wild young men, who got off next evening at North Platte, stood together on the stern platform, singing "The Sweet By-and-bye" with very tuneful voices; the chums began to put up their beds; and it seemed as if the business of the day were at an end. But it was not so; for, the train stopping at some station, the cars were instantly thronged with the natives, wives and fathers, young men and maidens, some of them in little more than nightgear, some with stable lanterns, and all offering beds for sale. Their charge began with twenty-five cents a cushion, but fell, before the train went on again, to fifteen, with the bed-board gratis, or less than one-fifth of what I had paid for mine at the Transfer. This is my contribution to the economy of future emigrants.

A great personage on an American train is the newsboy. He sells books (such books!), papers, fruit, lollipops, and cigars; and on emigrant journeys, soap, towels, tin washing dishes, tin coffee pitchers, coffee, tea, sugar, and tinned eatables, mostly hash or beans and bacon. Early next morning the newsboy went around the cars, and chumming on a more extended principle became the order of the hour. It requires but a copartnery of two to manage beds; but washing and eating can be carried on most economically by a syndicate of three. I myself entered a little after sunrise into articles of agreement, and became one of the firm of Pennsylvania, Shakespeare, and Dubuque. Shakespeare was my own nickname on the cars; Pennsylvania that of my bedfellow; and Dubuque, the name of a place in the State of Iowa, that of an amiable young fellow going west to cure an asthma, and retarding his recovery by incessantly chewing or smoking, and sometimes chewing and smoking together. I have never seen tobacco so sillily abused. Shakespeare bought a tin washing-dish, Dubuque a towel, and Pennsylvania a brick of soap. The partners used these instruments, one after another, according to the order of their first awaking; and when the firm had finished there was no want of borrowers. Each filled the tin dish at the water filter opposite the stove, and retired with the whole stock in trade to the platform of the car. There he knelt down, supporting himself by a shoulder against the woodwork or one elbow crooked about the railing, and made a shift to wash his face and neck and hands; a cold, an insufficient, and, if the train is moving rapidly, a somewhat dangerous toilet.

On a similar division of expense, the firm of Pennsylvania, Shakespeare, and Dubuque supplied themselves with coffee, sugar, and necessary vessels; and their operations are a type of what went on through all the cars. Before the sun was up the stove would be brightly burning; at the first station the natives would come on board with milk and eggs and coffee cakes; and soon from end to end the car would be filled with little parties breakfasting upon the bed-boards. It was the pleasantest hour of the day.

There were meals to be had, however, by the wayside: a breakfast in the morning, a dinner somewhere between eleven and two, and supper from five to eight or nine at night. We had rarely less than twenty minutes for each; and if we had not spent many another twenty minutes waiting for some express upon a side track among miles of desert, we might have taken an hour to each repast and arrived at San Francisco up to time. For haste is not the foible of an emigrant train. It gets through on sufferance, running the gauntlet among its more considerable brethren; should there be a block, it is unhesitatingly sacrificed; and they cannot, in consequence, predict the length of the passage within a day or so. Civility is the main comfort that you miss. Equality, though conceived very largely in America, does not extend so low down as to an emigrant. Thus in all other trains, a warning cry of " All aboard! " recalls the passengers to take their seats; but as soon as I was alone with emigrants, and from the Transfer all the way to San Francisco, I found this ceremony was pretermitted; the train stole from the station without note of warning, and you had to keep an eye upon it even while you ate. The annoyance is considerable, and the disrespect both wanton and petty.

Many conductors, again, will hold no communication with an emigrant. I asked a conductor one day at what time the train would stop for dinner; as he made no answer I repeated the question, with a like result; a third time I returned to the charge, and then Jack-in-office looked me coolly in the face for several seconds and turned ostentatiously away. I believe he was half ashamed of his brutality; for when another person made the same inquiry, although he still refused the information, he condescended to answer, and even to justify his reticence in a voice loud enough for me to hear. It was, he said, his principle not to tell people where they were to dine; for one answer led to many other questions, as what o'clock it was? or, how soon should we be there? and he could not afford to be eternally worried.

As you are thus cut off from the superior authorities, a great deal of your comfort depends on the character of the newsboy. He has it in his power indefinitely to better and brighten the emigrant's lot. The newsboy with whom we started from the Transfer was a dark, bullying, contemptuous, insolent scoundrel, who treated us like dogs. Indeed, in his case, matters came nearly to a fight. It happened thus: he was going his rounds through the cars with some commodities for sale, and coming to a party who were at *Seven-up* or *Cascino* (our two games), upon a bed-board, slung down a cigar-box in the middle of the cards, knocking one man's hand to the floor. It was the last straw. In a moment the whole party were upon their feet, the cigars were upset, and he was ordered to "get out of that directly, or he would get more than he reckoned for." The fellow grumbled and muttered, but ended by making off, and was less openly insulting in the future. On the other hand, the lad who rode with us in this capacity from Ogden to Sacramento made himself the friend of all, and helped us with information, attention, assistance, and a kind countenance. He told us where and when we should have our meals, and how long the train would stop; kept seats at table for those who were delayed, and watched that we should neither be left behind nor yet unnecessarily hurried. You, who live at home at ease, can hardly realise the greatness of this service, even had it stood alone. When I think of that lad coming and going, train after train, with his bright face and civil words, I see how easily a good man may become the benefactor of his kind. Perhaps he is discontented with himself, perhaps troubled with ambitions; why, if he but knew it, he is a hero of the old Greek stamp; and while he thinks he is only earning a profit of a few cents, and that perhaps exorbitant, he is doing a man's work, and bettering the world.

I must tell here an experience of mine with another newsboy. I tell it because it gives so good an example of that uncivil kindness of the American, which is perhaps their most bewildering character to one newly landed. It was immediately after I had left the emigrant train; and I am told I looked like a man at death's door, so much had this long journey shaken me. I sat at the end of a car, and the catch being broken, and myself feverish and sick, I had to hold the door open with my foot for the sake of air. In this attitude my leg debarred the newsboy from his box of merchandise. I made haste to let him pass when I observed that he was coming; but I was busy with a book, and so once or twice he came upon me unawares. On these occasions he most rudely struck my foot aside; and though I myself apologised, as if to show him the way, he answered me never a word. I chafed furiously, and I fear the next time it would have come to words. But suddenly I felt a touch upon my shoulder, and a large juicy pear was put into my hand. It was the newsboy, who had observed that I was looking ill and so made me this present out of a tender heart. For the rest of the journey I was petted like a sick child; he lent me newspapers, thus depriving himself of his legitimate profit on their sale, and came repeatedly to sit by me and cheer me up.

THE PLAINS OF NEBRASKA

It had thundered on the Friday night, but the sun rose on Saturday without a cloud. We were at sea — there is no other adequate expression — on the plains of Nebraska. I made my observatory on the top of a fruit-waggon, and sat by the hour upon that perch to spy about me, and to spy in vain for something new. It was a world almost without a feature; an empty sky, an empty earth; front and back, the line of railway stretched from horizon to horizon, like a cue across a billiard-board; on either hand, the green plain ran till it touched the skirts of heaven. Along the track innumerable wild sunflowers, no bigger than a crown-piece, bloomed in a continuous flower-bed; grazing beasts were seen upon the prairie at all degrees of distance and diminution; and, now and again we might perceive a few dots beside the railroad which grew more and more distinct as we drew nearer till they turned into wooden cabins, and then dwindled and dwindled in our wake until they melted into their surroundings, and we were once more alone upon the billiard-board. The train toiled over this infinity like a snail; and being the one thing moving, it was wonderful what huge proportions it began to assume in our regard. It seemed miles in length, and either end of it within but a step of the horizon. Even my own body or my own head seemed a great thing in that emptiness. I note the feeling the more readily as it is the contrary of what I have read of in the experience of others. Day and night, above the roar of the train, our ears were kept busy with the incessant chirp of grasshoppers — a noise like the winding up of countless clocks and watches, which began after a while to seem proper to that land.

To one hurrying through by steam there was a certain exhilaration in this spacious vacancy, this greatness of the air, this discovery of the whole arch of heaven, this straight, unbroken, prison-line of the horizon. Yet one could not but reflect upon the weariness of those who passed by there in old days, at the foot's pace of oxen, painfully urging their teams, and with no landmark but that unattainable evening sun for which they steered, and which daily fled them by an equal stride. They had nothing, it would seem, to overtake; nothing by which to reckon their advance; no sight for repose or for encouragement; but stage after stage, only the dead green waste under foot, and the mocking, fugitive horizon. But the eye, as I have been told, found differences even here; and at the worst the emigrant came, by perseverance, to the end of his toil. It is the settlers, after all, at whom we have a right to marvel. Our consciousness, by which we live, is itself but the creature of variety. Upon what food does it subsist in such a land? What livelihood can repay a human creature for a life spent in this huge sameness? He is cut off from books, from news, from company, from all that can relieve existence but the prosecution of his affairs. A sky full of stars is the most varied spectacle that he can hope. He may walk five miles and see nothing; ten, and it is as though he had not moved; twenty, and still he is in the midst of the same great level, and has approached no nearer to the one object within view, the flat horizon which keeps pace with his advance. We are full at home of the question of agreeable wall-papers, and wise people are of opinion that the temper may be quieted by sedative surroundings. But what is to be said of the Nebraskan settler? His is a wall-paper with a vengeance — one quarter of the universe laid bare in all its gauntness. His eye must embrace at every glance the whole seeming concave of the visible world; it quails before so vast an outlook, it is tortured by distance; yet there is no rest or shelter, till the man runs into his cabin, and can repose his sight upon things near at hand. Hence, I am told, a sickness of the vision peculiar to these empty plains.

Yet perhaps with sunflowers and cicadæ, summer and winter, cattle, wife and family, the settler may create a full and various existence. One person at least I saw upon the plains who seemed in every way superior to her lot. This was a woman who boarded us at a way station, selling milk. She was largely formed; her features were more than comely; she had that great rarity —a fine complexion which became her; and her eyes were kind, dark, and steady. She sold milk with patriarchal grace. There was not a line in her countenance, not a note in her soft and sleepy voice, but spoke of an entire contentment with her life. It would have been fatuous arrogance to pity such a woman. Yet the place where she lived was to me almost ghastly. Less than a dozen wooden houses, all of a shape and all nearly of a size, stood planted along the railway lines. Each stood apart in its own lot. Each opened direct off the billiard-board, as if it were a billiard-board indeed, and these only models that had been set down upon it ready made. Her own, into which I looked, was clean but very empty, and showed nothing homelike but the burning fire. This extreme newness, above all in so naked and flat a country, gives a strong impression of artificiality. With none of the litter and discolouration of human life; with the paths unworn, and the houses still sweating from the axe, such a settlement as this seems purely scenic. The mind is loth to accept it for a piece of reality; and it seems incredible that life can go on with so few properties, or the great child, man, find entertainment in so bare a playroom.

And truly it is as yet an incomplete society in some points; or at least it contained, as I passed through, one person incompletely civilised. At North Platte, where we supped that evening, one man asked another to pass the milk-jug. This other was well-dressed and of what we should call a respectable appearance; a darkish man, high spoken, eating as though he had some usage of society; but he turned upon the first speaker with extraordinary vehemence of tone ——

" There's a waiter here! " he cried.

"I only asked you to pass the milk," explained the first. Here is the retort verbatim ——

" Pass! Hell! I'm not paid for that business; the waiter's paid for it. You should use civility at table, and, by God, I'll show you how! "

The other man very wisely made no answer, and the bully went on with his supper as though nothing had occurred. It pleases me to think that some day soon he will meet with one of his own kidney; and that perhaps both may fall.

THE DESERT OF WYOMING

To cross such a plain is to grow homesick for the mountains. I longed for the Black Hills of Wyoming, which I knew we were soon to enter, like an ice-bound whaler for the spring. Alas! and it was a worse country than the other. All Sunday and Monday we travelled through these sad mountains, or over the main ridge of the Rockies, which is a fair match to them for misery of aspect. Hour after hour it was the same unhomely and unkindly world about our onward path; tumbled boulders, cliffs that drearily imitate the shape of monuments and fortifications — how drearily, how tamely, none can tell who has not seen them; not a tree, not a patch of sward, not one shapely or commanding mountain form; sage-brush, eternal sagebrush; over all, the same weariful and gloomy colouring, grays warming into brown, grays darkening towards black; and for sole sign of life, here and there a few fleeing antelopes; here and there, but at incredible intervals, a creek running in a cañon. The plains have a grandeur of their own; but here there is nothing but a contorted smallness. Except for the air, which was light and stimulating, there was not one good circumstance in that God-forsaken land.

I had been suffering in my health a good deal all the way; and at last, whether I was exhausted by my complaint or poisoned in some wayside eating-house, the evening we left Laramie, I fell sick outright. That was a night which I shall not readily forget. The lamps did not go out; each made a faint shining in its own neighbourhood, and the shadows were confounded together in the long, hollow box of the car. The sleepers lay in uneasy attitudes; here two chums alongside, flat upon their backs like dead folk; there a man sprawling on the floor, with his face upon his arm; there another half seated with his head and shoulders on the bench. The most passive were continually and roughly shaken by the movement of the train; others stirred, turned, or stretched out their arms like children; it was surprising how many groaned and murmured in their sleep; and as I passed to and fro, stepping across the prostrate, and caught now a snore, now a gasp, now a half-formed word, it gave me a measure of the worthlessness of rest in that unresting vehicle. Although it was chill, I was obliged to open my window, for the degradation of the air soon became intolerable to one who was awake and using the full supply of life. Outside, in a glimmering night, I saw the black, amorphous hills shoot by unweariedly into our wake. They that long for morning have never longed for it more earnestly than I.

And yet when day came, it was to shine upon the same broken and unsightly quarter of the world. Mile upon mile, and not a tree, a bird, or a river. Only down the long, sterile cañons, the train shot hooting and awoke the resting echo. That train was the one piece of life in all the deadly land; it was the one actor, the one spectacle fit to be observed in this paralysis of man and nature. And when I think how the railroad has been pushed through this unwatered wilderness and haunt of savage tribes, and now will bear an emigrant for some £12 from the Atlantic to the Golden Gates; how at each stage of the construction, roaring, impromptu cities, full of gold and lust and death, sprang up and then died away again, and are now but wayside stations in the desert; how in these uncouth places pigtailed Chinese pirates worked side by side with border ruffians and broken men from Europe, talking together in a mixed dialect, mostly oaths, gambling, drinking, quarrelling and murdering like wolves; how the plumed hereditary lord of all America heard, in this last fastness, the scream of the "bad medicine waggon" charioting his foes; and then when I go on to remember that all this epical turmoil was conducted by gentlemen in frock coats, and with a view to nothing more extraordinary than a fortune and a subsequent visit to Paris, it seems to me, I own, as if this railway were the one typical achievement of the age in which we live, as if it brought together into one plot all the ends of the world and all the degrees of social rank, and offered to some great writer the busiest, the most extended, and the most varied subject for an enduring literary work. If it be romance, if it be contrast, if it be heroism that we require, what was Troy town to this? But, alas! it is not these things that are necessary — it is only Homer.

Here also we are grateful to the train, as to some god who conducts us swiftly through these shades and by so many hidden perils. Thirst, hunger, the sleight and ferocity of Indians are all no more feared, so lightly do we skim these horrible lands; as the gull, who wings safely through the hurricane and past the shark. Yet we should not be forgetful of these hardships of the past; and to keep the balance true, since I have complained of the trifling discomforts of my journey, perhaps more than was enough, let me add an original document. It was not written by Homer, but by a boy of eleven, long since dead, and is dated only twenty years ago. I shall punctuate, to make things clearer, but not change the spelling.

"My dear sister Mary,—I am afraid you will go nearly crazy when you read my letter. If Jerry" (the writer's eldest brother) "has not written to you before now, you will be surprised to heare that we are in California, and that poor Thomas" (another brother, of fifteen) "is dead. We started from —————— in July, with plenty of provisions and too yoke oxen. We went along very well till we got within six or seven hundred miles of California, when the Indians attacked us. We found places where they had killed the emigrants. We had one passenger with us, too guns, and one revolver; so we ran all the lead We had into bullets (and) hung the guns up in the wagon so that we could get at them in a minit. It was about two o'clock in the afternoon; droave the cattel

*a little way; when a prairie chicken alited a little way
from the wagon.*

*" Jerry took out one of the guns to shoot it, and told
Tom to drive the oxen. Tom and I drove the oxen, and
Jerry and the passenger went on. Then, after a little,
I left Tom and caught up with Jerry and the other man.
Jerry stopped for Tom to come up; me and the man went
on and sit down by a little stream. In a few minutes,
we heard some noise; then three shots (they all struck
poor Tom, I suppose); then they gave the war hoop, and
as many as twenty of the red skins came down upon us.
The three that shot Tom was hid by the side of the road
in the bushes.*

*" I thought the Tom and Jerry were shot; so I told the
other man that Tom and Jerry were dead, and that we
had better try to escape, if possible. I had no shoes on;
having a sore foot, I thought I would not put them on.
The man and me run down the road, but We was soon
stopt by an Indian on a pony. We then turend the other
way, and run up the side of the Mountain, and hid behind some cedar trees, and stayed there till dark. The
Indians hunted all over after us, and verry close to us,
so close that we could here there tomyhawks Jingle. At
dark the man and me started on, I stubing my toes against
sticks and stones. We traveld on all night; and next
morning, Just as it was getting gray, we saw something
in the shape of a man. It layed Down in the grass. We
went up to it, and it was Jerry. He thought we ware
Indians. You can imagine how glad he was to see me.
He thought we was all dead but him, and we thought him
and Tom was dead. He had the gun that he took out of*

*the wagon to shoot the prairie Chicken; all he had was
the load that was in it.*

"*We traveld on till about eight o'clock, We caught
up with one wagon with too men with it. We had traveld with them before one day; we stopt and they Drove
on; we knew that they was ahead of us, unless they had
been killed to. My feet was so sore when we caught up
with them that I had to ride; I could not step. We traveld on for too days, when the men that owned the cattle
said they would (could) not drive them another inch. We
unyoked the oxen; we had about seventy pounds of flour;
we took it out and divided it into four packs. Each of
the men took about 18 pounds apiece and a blanket. I
carried a little bacon, dried meat, and little quilt; I had
in all about twelve pounds. We had one pint of flour a day
for our alloyance. Sometimes we made soup of it; sometimes we (made) pancakes; and sometimes mixed it up with
cold water and eat it that way. We traveld twelve or fourteen days. The time came at last when we should have to
reach some place or starve. We saw fresh horse and cattle
tracks. The morning come, we scraped all the flour out of
the sack, mixed it up, and baked it into bread, and made
some soup, and eat everything we had. We traveld on all
day without anything to eat, and that evening we Caught up
with a sheep train of eight wagons. We traveld with them
till we arrived at the settlements; and know I am safe in
California, and got to good home, and going to school.*

"*Jerry is working in* ———. *It is a good country.
You can get from 50 to 60 and 75 Dollars for cooking.
Tell me all about the affairs in the States, and how all the
folks get along.*"

And so ends this artless narrative. The little man was at school again, God bless him, while his brother lay scalped upon the deserts.

FELLOW PASSENGERS

At Ogden we changed cars from the Union Pacific to the Central Pacific line of railroad. The change was doubly welcome; for, first, we had better cars on the new line; and, second, those in which we had been cooped for more than ninety hours had begun to stink abominably. Several yards away, as we returned, let us say from dinner, our nostrils were assailed by rancid air. I have stood on a platform while the whole train was shunting; and as the dwelling-cars drew near, there would come a whiff of pure menagerie, only a little sourer, as from men instead of monkeys. I think we are human only in virtue of open windows. Without fresh air, you only require a bad heart, and a remarkable command of the Queen's English, to become such another as Dean Swift; a kind of leering, human goat, leaping and wagging your scut on mountains of offence. I do my best to keep my head the other way, and look for the human rather than the bestial in this Yahoo-like business of the emigrant train. But one thing I must say, the car of the Chinese was notably the least offensive.

The cars on the Central Pacific were nearly twice as high, and so proportionally airier; they were freshly varnished, which gave us all a sense of cleanliness as though we had bathed; the seats drew out and joined in the centre, so that there was no more need for bed boards; and there was an upper tier of berths which could be closed by day and opened at night.

I had by this time some opportunity of seeing the people whom I was among. They were in rather marked contrast to the emigrants I had met on board ship while crossing the Atlantic. They were mostly lumpish fellows, silent and noisy, a common combination; somewhat sad, I should say, with an extraordinary poor taste in humour, and little interest in their fellow-creatures beyond that of a cheap and merely external curiosity. If they heard a man's name and business, they seemed to think they had the heart of that mystery; but they were as eager to know that much as they were indifferent to the rest. Some of them were on nettles till they learned your name was Dickson and you a journeyman baker; but beyond that, whether you were Catholic or Mormon, dull or clever, fierce or friendly, was all one to them. Others who were not so stupid, gossiped a little, and, I am bound to say, unkindly. A favourite witticism was for some lout to raise the alarm of "All aboard!" while the rest of us were dining, thus contributing his mite to the general discomfort. Such a one was always much applauded for his high spirits. When I was ill coming through Wyoming, I was astonished — fresh from the eager humanity on board ship — to meet with little but laughter. One of the young men even amused himself by incommoding me, as was then very easy; and that not from ill-nature, but mere clodlike incapacity to think, for he expected me to join the laugh. I did so, but it was phantom merriment. Later on, a man from Kansas had three violent epileptic fits, and though, of course, there were not wanting some to help him, it was rather superstitious terror than sympathy that his case evoked among his fellow-passengers. "Oh, I hope he's not going to die!" cried a woman; "it would be terrible to have a dead body!" And there was a very general movement to leave the man behind at the next station. This, by good fortune, the conductor negatived.

There was a good deal of story-telling in some quarters; in others, little but silence. In this society, more than any other that ever I was in, it was the narrator alone who seemed to enjoy the narrative. It was rarely that any one listened for the listening. If he lent an ear to another man's story, it was because he was in immediate want of a hearer for one of his own. Food and the progress of the train were the subjects most generally treated; many joined to discuss these who otherwise would hold their tongues. One small knot had no better occupation than to worm out of me my name; and the more they tried, the more obstinately fixed I grew to baffle them. They assailed me with artful questions and insidious offers of correspondence in the future; but I was perpetually on my guard, and parried their assaults with inward laughter. I am sure Dubuque would have given me ten dollars for the secret. He owed me far more, had he understood life, for thus preserving him a lively interest throughout the journey. I met one of my fellow-passengers months after, driving a street tramway car in San Francisco; and, as the joke was now out of season, told him my name without subterfuge. You never saw a man more chopfallen. But had my name been Demogorgon, after so prolonged a mystery he had still been disappointed.

There were no emigrants direct from Europe — save one German family and a knot of Cornish miners who kept grimly by themselves, one reading the New Testament all day long through steel spectacles, the rest discussing privately the secrets of their old-world, mysterious race. Lady Hester Stanhope believed she could make something great of the Cornish; for my part, I can make nothing of them at all. A division of races, older and more original than that of Babel, keeps this close, esoteric family apart from neighbouring Englishmen. Not even a Red Indian seems more foreign in my eyes. This is one of the lessons of travel — that some of the strangest races dwell next door to you at home.

The rest were all American born, but they came from almost every quarter of that Continent. All the States of the North had sent out a fugitive to cross the plains with me. From Virginia, from Pennsylvania, from New York, from far western Iowa and Kansas, from Maine that borders on the Canadas, and from the Canadas themselves — some one or two were fleeing in quest of a better land and better wages. The talk in the train, like the talk I heard on the steamer, ran upon hard times, short commons, and hope that moves ever westward. I thought of my shipful from Great Britain with a feeling of despair. They had come 3000 miles, and yet not far enough. Hard times bowed them out of the Clyde, and stood to welcome them at Sandy Hook. Where were they to go? Pennsylvania, Maine, Iowa, Kansas? These were not places for immigration, but for emigration, it appeared; not one of them, but I knew a man who had lifted up his heel and left it for an ungrateful country. And it was still westward that they ran. Hunger, you would have thought, came out of the east like the sun, and the evening was made of edible gold. And, meantime, in the car in front of me, were there not half a hundred emigrants from the opposite quarter? Hungry Europe and hungry China, each pouring from their gates in search of provender, had here come face to face. The two waves had met; east and west had alike failed; the whole round world had been prospected and condemned; there was no El Dorado anywhere; and till one could emigrate to the moon, it seemed as well to stay patiently at home. Nor was there wanting another sign, at once more picturesque and more disheartening; for, as we continued to steam westward toward the land of gold, we were continually passing other emigrant trains upon the journey east; and these were as crowded as our own. Had all these return voyagers made a fortune in the mines? Were they all bound for Paris, and to be in Rome by Easter? It would seem not, for, whenever we met them, the passengers ran on the platform and cried to us through the windows, in a kind of wailing chorus, to "Come back." On the plains of Nebraska, in the mountains of Wyoming, it was still the same cry, and dismal to my heart, "Come back!" That was what we heard by the way "about the good country we were going to." And at that very hour the Sand-lot of San Francisco was crowded with the unemployed, and the echo from the other side of Market Street was repeating the rant of demagogues.

If, in truth, it were only for the sake of wages that men emigrate, how many thousands would regret the

bargain! But wages, indeed, are only one consideration out of many; for we are a race of gipsies, and
love change and travel for themselves.

DESPISED RACES

Of all stupid ill-feelings, the sentiment of my fellow-
Caucasians towards our companions in the Chinese car
was the most stupid and the worst. They seemed
never to have looked at them, listened to them, or
thought of them, but hated them *a priori*. The Mongols
were their enemies in that cruel and treacherous battle-
field of money. They could work better and cheaper
in half a hundred industries, and hence there was no
calumny too idle for the Caucasians to repeat, and even
to believe. They declared them hideous vermin, and
affected a kind of choking in the throat when they beheld them. Now, as a matter of fact, the young Chinese man is so like a large class of European women,
that on raising my head and suddenly catching sight of
one at a considerable distance, I have for an instant
been deceived by the resemblance. I do not say it is
the most attractive class of our women, but for all that
many a man's wife is less pleasantly favoured. Again,
my emigrants declared that the Chinese were dirty.
I cannot say they were clean, for that was impossible
upon the journey; but in their efforts after cleanliness
they put the rest of us to shame. We all pigged and
stewed in one infamy, wet our hands and faces for half
a minute daily on the platform, and were unashamed.
But the Chinese never lost an opportunity, and you
would see them washing their feet — an act not dreamed

of among ourselves—and going as far as decency permitted to wash their whole bodies. I may remark by the way that the dirtier people are in their persons the more delicate is their sense of modesty. A clean man strips in a crowded boathouse; but he who is unwashed slinks in and out of bed without uncovering an inch of skin. Lastly, these very foul and malodorous Caucasians entertained the surprising illusion that it was the Chinese waggon, and that alone, which stank. I have said already that it was the exception, and notably the freshest of the three.

These judgments are typical of the feeling in all Western America. The Chinese are considered stupid, because they are imperfectly acquainted with English. They are held to be base, because their dexterity and frugality enable them to underbid the lazy, luxurious Caucasian. They are said to be thieves; I am sure they have no monopoly of that. They are called cruel; the Anglo-Saxon and the cheerful Irishman may each reflect before he bears the accusation. I am told, again, that they are of the race of river pirates, and belong to the most despised and dangerous class in the Celestial Empire. But if this be so, what remarkable pirates have we here! and what must be the virtues, the industry, the education, and the intelligence of their superiors at home!

Awhile ago it was the Irish, now it is the Chinese that must go. Such is the cry. It seems, after all, that no country is bound to submit to immigration any more than to invasion: each is war to the knife, and resistance to either but legitimate defence. Yet we may regret the free tradition of the republic, which loved to depict herself with open arms, welcoming all unfortunates. And certainly, as a man who believes that he loves freedom, I may be excused some bitterness when I find her sacred name misused in the contention. It was but the other day that I heard a vulgar fellow in the Sand-lot, the popular tribune of San Francisco, roaring for arms and butchery. "At the call of Abreham Lincoln," said the orator, "ye rose in the name of freedom to set free the negroes; can ye not rise and liberate yourselves from a few dhirty Mongolians?"

For my own part, I could not look but with wonder and respect on the Chinese. Their forefathers watched the stars before mine had begun to keep pigs. Gunpowder and printing, which the other day we imitated, and a school of manners which we never had the delicacy so much as to desire to imitate, were theirs in a long-past antiquity. They walk the earth with us, but it seems they must be of different clay. They hear the clock strike the same hour, yet surely of a different epoch. They travel by steam conveyance, yet with such a baggage of old Asiatic thoughts and superstitions as might check the locomotive in its course. Whatever is thought within the circuit of the Great Wall; what the wry-eyed, spectacled schoolmaster teaches in the hamlets round Pekin; religions so old that our language looks a halfling boy alongside; philosophy so wise that our best philosophers find things therein to wonder at; all this travelled alongside of me for thousands of miles over plain and mountain. Heaven knows if we had one common thought or fancy all that way, or whether our eyes, which yet were formed upon the same design, beheld the same world out of the railway windows.

And when either of us turned his thoughts to home and childhood, what a strange dissimilarity must there not have been in these pictures of the mind — when I beheld that old, gray, castled city, high throned above the firth, with the flag of Britain flying, and the red-coat sentry pacing over all; and the man in the next car to me would conjure up some junks and a pagoda and a fort of porcelain, and call it, with the same affection, home.

Another race shared among my fellow-passengers in the disfavour of the Chinese; and that, it is hardly necessary to say, was the noble red man of old story — he over whose own hereditary continent we had been steaming all these days. I saw no wild or independent Indian; indeed, I hear that such avoid the neighbourhood of the train; but now and again at way stations, a husband and wife and a few children, disgracefully dressed out with the sweepings of civilisation, came forth and stared upon the emigrants. The silent stoicism of their conduct, and the pathetic degradation of their appearance, would have touched any thinking creature, but my fellow-passengers danced and jested round them with a truly Cockney baseness. I was ashamed for the thing we call civilisation. We should carry upon our consciences so much, at least, of our forefathers' misconduct as we continue to profit by ourselves.

If oppression drives a wise man mad, what should be raging in the hearts of these poor tribes, who have been driven back and back, step after step, their promised reservations torn from them one after another as the States extended westward, until at length they are shut up into these hideous mountain deserts of the centre —

and even there find themselves invaded, insulted, and hunted out by ruffianly diggers? The eviction of the Cherokees (to name but an instance), the extortion of Indian agents, the outrages of the wicked, the ill-faith of all, nay, down to the ridicule of such poor beings as were here with me upon the train, make up a chapter of injustice and indignity such as a man must be in some ways base if his heart will suffer him to pardon or forget. These old, well-founded, historical hatreds have a savour of nobility for the independent. That the Jew should not love the Christian, nor the Irishman love the English, nor the Indian brave tolerate the thought of the American, is not disgraceful to the nature of man; rather, indeed, honourable, since it depends on wrongs ancient like the race, and not personal to him who cherishes the indignation.

TO THE GOLDEN GATES

A LITTLE corner of Utah is soon traversed, and leaves no particular impressions on the mind. By an early hour on Wednesday morning we stopped to breakfast at Toano, a little station on a bleak, high-lying plateau in Nevada. The man who kept the station eating-house was a Scot, and learning that I was the same, he grew very friendly, and gave me some advice on the country I was now entering. "You see," said he, "I tell you this, because I come from your country." Hail, brither Scots!

His most important hint was on the moneys of this part of the world. There is something in the simplicity of a decimal coinage which is revolting to the human mind; thus the French, in small affairs, reckon strictly

by halfpence; and you have to solve, by a spasm of
mental arithmetic, such posers as thirty-two, forty-five,
or even a hundred halfpence. In the Pacific States they
have made a bolder push for complexity, and settle their
affairs by a coin that no longer exists—the *bit,* or old
Mexican real. The supposed value of the bit is twelve
and a half cents, eight to the dollar. When it comes
to two bits, the quarter-dollar stands for the required
amount. But how about an odd bit? The nearest coin
to it is a dime, which is short by a fifth. That, then, is
called a *short bit.* If you have one, you lay it trium-
phantly down, and save two and a half cents. But if you
have not, and lay down a quarter, the bar-keeper or
shopman calmly tenders you a dime by way of change;
and thus you have paid what is called a *long bit,* and
lost two and a half cents, or even, by comparison with
a short bit, five cents. In country places all over the
Pacific coast, nothing lower than a bit is ever asked or
taken, which vastly increases the cost of life; as even for
a glass of beer you must pay fivepence or sevenpence-
halfpenny, as the case may be. You would say that
this system of mutual robbery was as broad as it was
long; but I have discovered a plan to make it broader,
with which I here endow the public. It is brief and
simple—radiantly simple. There is one place where
five cents are recognised, and that is the post-office. A
quarter is only worth two bits, a short and a long.
Whenever you have a quarter, go to the post-office and
buy five cents' worth of postage-stamps; you will receive
in change two dimes, that is, two short bits. The pur-
chasing power of your money is undiminished. You
can go and have your two glasses of beer all the same;

and you have made yourself a present of five cents' worth of postage-stamps into the bargain. Benjamin Franklin would have patted me on the head for this discovery.

From Toano we travelled all day through deserts of alkali and sand, horrible to man, and bare sage-brush country that seemed little kindlier, and came by supper-time to Elko. As we were standing, after our manner, outside the station, I saw two men whip suddenly from underneath the cars, and take to their heels across country. They were tramps, it appeared, who had been riding on the beams since eleven of the night before; and several of my fellow-passengers had already seen and conversed with them while we broke our fast at Toano. These land stowaways play a great part over here in America, and I should have liked dearly to become acquainted with them.

At Elko an odd circumstance befell me. I was coming out from supper, when I was stopped by a small, stout, ruddy man, followed by two others taller and ruddier than himself.

"Ex-cuse me, sir," he said, "but do you happen to be going on?"

I said I was, whereupon he said he hoped to persuade me to desist from that intention. He had a situation to offer me, and if we could come to terms, why, good and well. "You see," he continued, "I'm running a theatre here, and we're a little short in the orchestra. You're a musician, I guess?"

I assured him that, beyond a rudimentary acquaintance with "Auld Lang Syne" and "The Wearing of the Green," I had no pretension whatever to that style. He seemed much put out of countenance; and one of

145

his taller companions asked him, on the nail, for five dollars.

"You see, sir," added the latter to me, "he bet you were a musician; I bet you weren't. No offence, I hope?"

"None whatever," I said, and the two withdrew to the bar, where I presume the debt was liquidated.

This little adventure woke bright hopes in my fellow-travellers, who thought they had now come to a country where situations went a-begging. But I am not so sure that the offer was in good faith. Indeed, I am more than half persuaded it was but a feeler to decide the bet.

Of all the next day I will tell you nothing, for the best of all reasons, that I remember no more than that we continued through desolate and desert scenes, fiery hot and deadly weary. But some time after I had fallen asleep that night, I was awakened by one of my companions. It was in vain that I resisted. A fire of enthusiasm and whisky burned in his eyes; and he declared we were in a new country, and I must come forth upon the platform and see with my own eyes. The train was then, in its patient way, standing halted in a by-track. It was a clear, moonlit night; but the valley was too narrow to admit the moonshine direct, and only a diffused glimmer whitened the tall rocks and relieved the blackness of the pines. A hoarse clamour filled the air; it was the continuous plunge of a cascade somewhere near at hand among the mountains. The air struck chill, but tasted good and vigorous in the nostrils — a fine, dry, old mountain atmosphere. I was dead sleepy, but I returned to roost with a grateful mountain feeling at my heart.

When I awoke next morning, I was puzzled for a while to know if it were day or night, for the illumination was unusual. I sat up at last, and found we were grading slowly downward through a long snowshed; and suddenly we shot into an open; and before we were swallowed into the next length of wooden tunnel, I had one glimpse of a huge pine-forested ravine upon my left, a foaming river, and a sky already coloured with the fires of dawn. I am usually very calm over the displays of nature; but you will scarce believe how my heart leaped at this. It was like meeting one's wife. I had come home again — home from unsightly deserts to the green and habitable corners of the earth. Every spire of pine along the hill-top, every trouty pool along that mountain river, was more dear to me than a blood relation. Few people have praised God more happily than I did. And thenceforward, down by Blue Cañon, Alta, Dutch Flat, and all the old mining camps, through a sea of mountain forests, dropping thousands of feet toward the far sea-level as we went, not I only, but all the passengers on board, threw off their sense of dirt and heat and weariness, and bawled like schoolboys, and thronged with shining eyes upon the platform and became new creatures within and without. The sun no longer oppressed us with heat, it only shone laughingly along the mountain-side, until we were fain to laugh ourselves for glee. At every turn we could see farther into the land and our own happy futures. At every town the cocks were tossing their clear notes into the golden air, and crowing for the new day and the new country. For this was indeed our destination; this was "the good country" we had been going to so long.

By afternoon we were at Sacramento, the city of gardens in a plain of corn; and the next day before the dawn we were lying to upon the Oakland side of San Francisco Bay. The day was breaking as we crossed the ferry; the fog was rising over the citied hills of San Francisco; the bay was perfect — not a ripple, scarce a stain, upon its blue expanse; everything was waiting, breathless, for the sun. A spot of cloudy gold lit first upon the head of Tamalpais, and then widened downward on its shapely shoulder; the air seemed to awaken, and began to sparkle; and suddenly

"The tall hills Titan discovered,"

and the city of San Francisco, and the bay of gold and corn, were lit from end to end with summer daylight.

[1879.]

148

II. THE OLD PACIFIC CAPITAL

THE WOODS AND THE PACIFIC

THE Bay of Monterey has been compared by no less a person than General Sherman to a bent fishing-hook; and the comparison, if less important than the march through Georgia, still shows the eye of a soldier for topography. Santa Cruz sits exposed at the shank; the mouth of the Salinas river is at the middle of the bend; and Monterey itself is cosily ensconced beside the barb. Thus the ancient capital of California faces across the bay, while the Pacific Ocean, though hidden by low hills and forests, bombards her left flank and rear with never-dying surf. In front of the town, the long line of sea-beach trends north and north-west, and then westward to enclose the bay. The waves which lap so quietly about the jetties of Monterey grow louder and larger in the distance; you can see the breakers leaping high and white by day; at night, the outline of the shore is traced in transparent silver by the moonlight and the flying foam; and from all round, even in quiet weather, the low, distant, thrilling roar of the Pacific hangs over the coast and the adjacent country like smoke above a battle.

These long beaches are enticing to the idle man. It would be hard to find a walk more solitary and at the same time more exciting to the mind. Crowds of ducks and sea-gulls hover over the sea. Sandpipers trot in and out by troops after the retiring waves, trilling together in a chorus of infinitesimal song. Strange sea-tangles, new to the European eye, the bones of whales, or sometimes a whole whale's carcase, white with carrion-gulls and poisoning the wind, lie scattered here and there along the sands. The waves come in slowly, vast and green, curve their translucent necks, and burst with a surprising uproar, that runs, waxing and waning, up and down the long key-board of the beach. The foam of these great ruins mounts in an instant to the ridge of the sand glacis, swiftly fleets back again, and is met and buried by the next breaker. The interest is perpetually fresh. On no other coast that I know shall you enjoy, in calm, sunny weather, such a spectacle of Ocean's greatness, such beauty of changing colour, or such degrees of thunder in the sound. The very air is more than usually salt by this Homeric deep.

Inshore, a tract of sand-hills borders on the beach. Here and there a lagoon, more or less brackish, attracts the birds and hunters. A rough, spotty undergrowth partially conceals the sand. The crouching, hardy, live-oaks flourish singly or in thickets — the kind of wood for murderers to crawl among — and here and there the skirts of the forest extend downward from the hills with a floor of turf and long aisles of pine-trees hung with Spaniard's Beard. Through this quaint desert the railway cars drew near to Monterey from the junction at Salinas City — though that and so many other things are now for ever altered — and it was from here that you had the first view of the old township lying in the sands, its white windmills bickering in the chill, perpetual wind, and the first fogs of the evening drawing drearily around it from the sea.

The one common note of all this country is the haunting presence of the ocean. A great faint sound of breakers follows you high up into the inland cañons; the roar of water dwells in the clean, empty rooms of Monterey as in a shell upon the chimney; go where you will, you have but to pause and listen to hear the voice of the Pacific. You pass out of the town to the southwest, and mount the hill among pine woods. Glade, thicket, and grove surround you. You follow winding sandy tracks that lead nowhither. You see a deer; a multitude of quail arises. But the sound of the sea still follows you as you advance, like that of wind among the trees, only harsher and stranger to the ear; and when at length you gain the summit, out breaks on every hand and with freshened vigour, that same unending, distant, whispering rumble of the ocean; for now you are on the top of Monterey peninsula, and the noise no longer only mounts to you from behind along the beach towards Santa Cruz, but from your right also, round by Chinatown and Pinos lighthouse, and from down before you to the mouth of the Carmello river. The whole woodland is begirt with thundering surges. The silence that immediately surrounds you where you stand is not so much broken as it is haunted by this distant, circling rumour. It sets your senses upon edge; you strain your attention; you are clearly and unusually conscious of small sounds near at hand; you walk listening like an Indian hunter; and that voice of the Pacific is a sort of disquieting company to you in your walk.

When once I was in these woods I found it difficult
to turn homeward. All woods lure a rambler onward;
but in those of Monterey it was the surf that particularly
invited me to prolong my walks. I would push straight
for the shore where I thought it to be nearest. Indeed,
there was scarce a direction that would not, sooner or
later, have brought me forth on the Pacific. The emptiness of the woods gave me a sense of freedom and discovery in these excursions. I never in all my visits met
but one man. He was a Mexican, very dark of hue,
but smiling and fat, and he carried an axe, though his
true business at that moment was to seek for straying
cattle. I asked him what o'clock it was, but he seemed
neither to know nor care; and when he in his turn asked
me for news of his cattle, I showed myself equally indifferent. We stood and smiled upon each other for a
few seconds, and then turned without a word and took
our several ways across the forest.

One day — I shall never forget it — I had taken a trail
that was new to me. After a while the woods began
to open, the sea to sound nearer hand. I came upon a
road, and, to my surprise, a stile. A step or two farther,
and, without leaving the woods, I found myself among
trim houses. I walked through street after street, parallel and at right angles, paved with sward and dotted
with trees, but still undeniable streets, and each with its
name posted at the corner, as in a real town. Facing
down the main thoroughfare — " Central Avenue," as
it was ticketed — I saw an open-air temple, with benches
and sounding-board, as though for an orchestra. The
houses were all tightly shuttered; there was no smoke,
no sound but of the waves, no moving thing. I have never

been in any place that seemed so dreamlike. Pompeii is all in a bustle with visitors, and its antiquity and strangeness deceive the imagination; but this town had plainly not been built above a year or two, and perhaps had been deserted overnight. Indeed, it was not so much like a deserted town as like a scene upon the stage by daylight, and with no one on the boards. The barking of a dog led me at last to the only house still occupied, where a Scotch pastor and his wife pass the winter alone in this empty theatre. The place was " The Pacific Camp Grounds, the Christian Seaside Resort." Thither, in the warm season, crowds come to enjoy a life of teetotalism, religion, and flirtation, which I am willing to think blameless and agreeable. The neighbourhood at least is well selected. The Pacific booms in front. Westward is Point Pinos, with the lighthouse in a wilderness of sand, where you will find the lightkeeper playing the piano, making models and bows and arrows, studying dawn and sunrise in amateur oilpainting, and with a dozen other elegant pursuits and interests to surprise his brave, old-country rivals. To the east, and still nearer, you will come upon a space of open down, a hamlet, a haven among rocks, a world of surge and screaming sea-gulls. Such scenes are very similar in different climates; they appear homely to the eyes of all; to me this was like a dozen spots in Scotland. And yet the boats that ride in the haven are of strange outlandish design; and, if you walk into the hamlet, you will behold costumes and faces and hear a tongue that are unfamiliar to the memory. The jossstick burns, the opium pipe is smoked, the floors are strewn with slips of coloured paper — prayers, you would say, that had somehow missed their destination — and a man guiding his upright pencil from right to left across the sheet, writes home the news of Monterey to the Celestial Empire.

The woods and the Pacific rule between them the climate of this seaboard region. On the streets of Monterey, when the air does not smell salt from the one, it will be blowing perfumed from the resinous tree-tops of the other. For days together a hot, dry air will overhang the town, close as from an oven, yet healthful and aromatic in the nostrils. The cause is not far to seek, for the woods are afire, and the hot wind is blowing from the hills. These fires are one of the great dangers of California. I have seen from Monterey as many as three at the same time, by day a cloud of smoke, by night a red coal of conflagration in the distance. A little thing will start them, and, if the wind be favourable, they gallop over miles of country faster than a horse. The inhabitants must turn out and work like demons, for it is not only the pleasant groves that are destroyed; the climate and the soil are equally at stake, and these fires prevent the rains of the next winter and dry up perennial fountains. California has been a land of promise in its time, like Palestine; but if the woods continue so swiftly to perish, it may become, like Palestine, a land of desolation.

To visit the woods while they are languidly burning is a strange piece of experience. The fire passes through the underbrush at a run. Every here and there a tree flares up instantaneously from root to summit, scattering tufts of flame, and is quenched, it seems, as quickly. But this last is only in semblance. For after this first squib-like conflagration of the dry moss and twigs, there remains behind a deep-rooted and consuming fire in the very entrails of the tree. The resin of the pitch-pine is principally condensed at the base of the bole and in the spreading roots. Thus, after the light, showy, skirmishing flames, which are only as the match to the explosion, have already scampered down the wind into the distance, the true harm is but beginning for this giant of the woods. You may approach the tree from one side, and see it, scorched indeed from top to bottom, but apparently survivor of the peril. Make the circuit, and there, on the other side of the column, is a clear mass of living coal, spreading like an ulcer; while underground, to their most extended fibre, the roots are being eaten out by fire, and the smoke is rising through the fissures to the surface. A little while, and, without a nod of warning, the huge pine-tree snaps off short across the ground and falls prostrate with a crash. Meanwhile the fire continues its silent business; the roots are reduced to a fine ash; and long afterwards, if you pass by, you will find the earth pierced with radiating galleries, and preserving the design of all these subterranean spurs, as though it were the mould for a new tree instead of the print of an old one. These pitchpines of Monterey are, with the single exception of the Monterey cypress, the most fantastic of forest trees. No words can give an idea of the contortion of their growth; they might figure without change in a circle of the nether hell as Dante pictured it; and at the rate at which trees grow, and at which forest fires spring up and gallop through the hills of California, we may look forward to a time when there will not be one of them left standing in that land of their nativity. At least they have not so much to fear from the axe, but perish by what may be called a natural although a violent death; while it is man in his short-sighted greed that robs the country of the nobler red-wood. Yet a little while and perhaps all the hills of sea-board California may be as bald as Tamalpais.

I have an interest of my own in these forest fires, for I came so near to lynching on one occasion, that a braver man might have retained a thrill from the experience. I wished to be certain whether it was the moss, that quaint funereal ornament of Californian forests, which blazed up so rapidly when the flame first touched the tree. I suppose I must have been under the influence of Satan, for instead of plucking off a piece for my experiment, what should I do but walk up to a great pine-tree in a portion of the wood which had escaped so much as scorching, strike a match, and apply the flame gingerly to one of the tassels. The tree went off simply like a rocket; in three seconds it was a roaring pillar of fire. Close by I could hear the shouts of those who were at work combating the original conflagration. I could see the waggon that had brought them tied to a live oak in a piece of open; I could even catch the flash of an axe as it swung up through the underwood into the sunlight. Had any one observed the result of my experiment my neck was literally not worth a pinch of snuff; after a few minutes of passionate expostulation I should have been run up to a convenient bough.

To die for faction is a common evil;
But to be hanged for nonsense is the devil.

I have run repeatedly, but never as I ran that day. At night I went out of town, and there was my own particular fire, quite distinct from the other, and burning as I thought with even greater vigour.

But it is the Pacific that exercises the most direct and obvious power upon the climate. At sunset, for months together, vast, wet, melancholy fogs arise and come shoreward from the ocean. From the hill-top above Monterey the scene is often noble, although it is always sad. The upper air is still bright with sunlight; a glow still rests upon the Gabelano Peak; but the fogs are in possession of the lower levels; they crawl in scarves among the sandhills; they float, a little higher, in clouds of a gigantic size and often of a wild configuration; to the south, where they have struck the seaward shoulder of the mountains of Santa Lucia, they double back and spire up skyward like smoke. Where their shadow touches, colour dies out of the world. The air grows chill and deadly as they advance. The trade-wind freshens, the trees begin to sigh, and all the windmills in Monterey are whirling and creaking and filling their cisterns with the brackish water of the sands. It takes but a little while till the invasion is complete. The sea, in its lighter order, has submerged the earth. Monterey is curtained in for the night in thick, wet, salt, and frigid clouds, so to remain till day returns; and before the sun's rays they slowly disperse and retreat in broken squadrons to the bosom of the sea. And yet often when the fog is thickest and most chill, a few steps out of the town and up the slope, the night will be dry and warm and full of inland perfume.

MEXICANS, AMERICANS, AND INDIANS

THE history of Monterey has yet to be written. Founded by Catholic missionaries, a place of wise beneficence to Indians, a place of arms, a Mexican capital continually wrested by one faction from another, an American capital when the first House of Representatives held its deliberations, and then falling lower and lower from the capital of the State to the capital of a county, and from that again, by the loss of its charter and town lands, to a mere bankrupt village, its rise and decline is typical of that of all Mexican institutions and even Mexican families in California.

Nothing is stranger in that strange State than the rapidity with which the soil has changed hands. The Mexicans, you may say, are all poor and landless, like their former capital; and yet both it and they hold themselves apart and preserve their ancient customs and something of their ancient air.

The town, when I was there, was a place of two or three streets, economically paved with sea-sand, and two or three lanes, which were watercourses in the rainy season, and were, at all times, rent up by fissures four or five feet deep. There were no street lights. Short sections of wooden sidewalk only added to the dangers of the night, for they were often high above the level of the roadway, and no one could tell where they would be likely to begin or end. The houses were, for the most part, built of unbaked adobe brick, many of them old for so new a country, some of very elegant proportions, with low, spacious, shapely rooms, and walls so thick that the heat of summer never dried them to the heart. At the approach of the rainy season a deathly chill and a graveyard smell began to hang about the lower floors; and diseases of the chest are common and fatal among house-keeping people of either sex.

There was no activity but in and around the saloons, where people sat almost all day long playing cards. The smallest excursion was made on horseback. You would scarcely ever see the main street without a horse or two tied to posts, and making a fine figure with their Mexican housings. It struck me oddly to come across some of the *Cornhill* illustrations to Mr. Blackmore's *Erema,* and see all the characters astride on English saddles. As a matter of fact, an Englis saddle is a rarity even in San Francisco, and, you may say, a thing unknown in all the rest of California. In a place so exclusively Mexican as Monterey, you saw not only Mexican saddles but true Vaquero riding — men always at the hand-gallop up hill and down dale, and round the sharpest corner, urging their horses with cries and gesticulations and cruel rotatory spurs, checking them dead with a touch, or wheeling them right-about-face in a square yard. The type of face and character of bearing are surprisingly un-American. The first ranged from something like the pure Spanish, to something, in its sad fixity, not unlike the pure Indian, although I do not suppose there was one pure blood of either race in all the country. As for the second, it was a matter of perpetual surprise to find, in that world of absolutely mannerless Americans, a people full of deportment, solemnly courteous, and doing all things with grace and decorum. In dress they ran to colour and bright sashes. Not even the most Americanised could always resist the temptation to stick a red rose into his hatband. Not even the most Americanised would descend to wear the vile dress hat of civilisation. Spanish was the language of the streets. It was difficult to get along without a word or two of that language for an occasion. The only communications in which the population joined were with a view to amusement. A weekly public ball took place with great etiquette, in addition to the numerous fandangoes in private houses. There was a really fair amateur brass band. Night after night serenaders would be going about the street, sometimes in a company and with several instruments and voices together, sometimes severally, each guitar before a different window. It was a strange thing to lie awake in nineteenth-century America, and hear the guitar accompany, and one of these old, heart-breaking Spanish love songs mount into the night air, perhaps in a deep baritone, perhaps in that high-pitched, pathetic, womanish alto which is so common among Mexican men, and which strikes on the unaccustomed ear as something not entirely human but altogether sad.

The town, then, was essentially and wholly Mexican; and yet almost all the land in the neighbourhood was held by Americans, and it was from the same class, numerically so small, that the principal officials were selected. This Mexican and that Mexican would describe to you his old family estates, not one rood of which remained to him. You would ask him how that came about, and elicit some tangled story back-foremost, from which you gathered that the Americans had been greedy like designing men, and the Mexicans greedy like children, but no other certain fact. Their merits and their faults contributed alike to the ruin of the former landholders. It is true they were improvident, and easily dazzled with the sight of ready money; but they were gentlefolk besides, and that in a way which curiously unfitted them to combat Yankee craft. Suppose they have a paper to sign, they would think it a reflection on the other party to examine the terms with any great minuteness; nay, suppose them to observe some doubtful clause, it is ten to one they would refuse from delicacy to object to it. I know I am speaking within the mark, for I have seen such a case occur, and the Mexican, in spite of the advice of his lawyer, has signed the imperfect paper like a lamb. To have spoken in the matter, he said, above all to have let the other party guess that he had seen a lawyer, would have "been like doubting his word." The scruple sounds oddly to one of ourselves, who have been brought up to understand all business as a competition in fraud, and honesty itself to be a virtue which regards the carrying out but not the creation of agreements. This single unworldly trait will account for much of that revolution of which we are speaking. The Mexicans have the name of being great swindlers, but certainly the accusation cuts both ways. In a contest of this sort, the entire booty would scarcely have passed into the hands of the more scrupulous race.

Physically the Americans have triumphed; but it is not entirely seen how far they have themselves been morally conquered. This is, of course, but a part of a part of an extraordinary problem now in the course of being solved in the various States of the American

Union. I am reminded of an anecdote. Some years ago, at a great sale of wine, all the odd lots were purchased by a grocer in a small way in the old town of Edinburgh. The agent had the curiosity to visit him some time after and inquire what possible use he could have for such material. He was shown, by way of answer, a huge vat where all the liquors, from humble Gladstone to imperial Tokay, were fermenting together. "And what," he asked, "do you propose to call this?" "I'm no very sure," replied the grocer, "but I think it's going to turn out port." In the older Eastern States, I think we may say that this hotch-potch of races is going to turn out English, or thereabout. But the problem is indefinitely varied in other zones. The elements are differently mingled in the south, in what we may call the Territorial belt, and in the group of States on the Pacific coast. Above all, in these last, we may look to see some monstrous hybrid — whether good or evil, who shall forecast? but certainly original and all their own. In my little restaurant at Monterey, we have sat down to table day after day, a Frenchman, two Portuguese, an Italian, a Mexican, and a Scotchman: we had for common visitors an American from Illinois, a nearly pure blood Indian woman, and a naturalised Chinese; and from time to time a Switzer and a German came down from country ranches for the night. No wonder that the Pacific coast is a foreign land to visitors from the Eastern States, for each race contributes something of its own. Even the despised Chinese have taught the youth of California, none indeed of their virtues, but the debasing use of opium. And chief among these influences is that of the Mexicans.

The Mexicans although in the State are out of it. They still preserve a sort of international independence, and keep their affairs snug to themselves. Only four or five years ago Vasquez, the bandit, his troops being dispersed and the hunt too hot for him in other parts of California, returned to his native Monterey, and was seen publicly in her streets and saloons, fearing no man. The year that I was there there occurred two reputed murders. As the Montereyans are exceptionally vile speakers of each other and of every one behind his back, it is not possible for me to judge how much truth there may have been in these reports; but in the one case every one believed, and in the other some suspected, that there had been foul play; and nobody dreamed for an instant of taking the authorities into their counsel. Now this is, of course, characteristic enough of the Mexicans; but it is a noteworthy feature that all the Americans in Monterey acquiesced without a word in this inaction. Even when I spoke to them upon the subject, they seemed not to understand my surprise; they had forgotten the traditions of their own race and upbringing, and become, in a word, wholly Mexicanised.

Again, the Mexicans, having no ready money to speak of, rely almost entirely in their business transactions upon each other's worthless paper. Pedro the penniless pays you with an I O U from the equally penniless Miguel. It is a sort of local currency by courtesy. Credit in these parts has passed into a superstition. I have seen a strong, violent man struggling for months to recover a debt, and getting nothing but an exchange of waste paper. The very storekeepers are averse to asking for cash payments, and are more surprised than pleased when they are offered. They fear there must be something under it, and that you mean to withdraw your custom from them. I have seen the enterprising chemist and stationer begging me with fervour to let my account run on, although I had my purse open in my hand; and partly from the commonness of the case, partly from some remains of that generous old Mexican tradition which made all men welcome to their tables, a person may be notoriously both unwilling and unable to pay, and still find credit for the necessaries of life in the stores of Monterey. Now this villainous habit of living upon "tick" has grown into Californian nature. I do not mean that the American and European storekeepers of Monterey are as lax as Mexicans; I mean that American farmers in many parts of the State expect unlimited credit, and profit by it in the meanwhile, without a thought for consequences. Jew storekeepers have already learned the advantage to be gained from this; they lead on the farmer into irretrievable indebtedness, and keep him ever after as their bond-slave hopelessly grinding in the mill. So the whirligig of time brings in its revenges, and except that the Jew knows better than to foreclose, you may see Americans bound in the same chains with which they themselves had formerly bound the Mexican. It seems as if certain sorts of follies, like certain sorts of grain, were natural to the soil rather than to the race that holds and tills it for the moment.

In the meantime, however, the Americans rule in Monterey County. The new county seat, Salinas City, in the bald, corn-bearing plain under the Gabelano Peak, is a town of a purely American character. The land is held, for the most part, in those enormous tracts which are another legacy of Mexican days, and form the present chief danger and disgrace of California; and the holders are mostly of American or British birth. We have here in England no idea of the troubles and inconveniences which flow from the existence of these large landholders — land-thieves, land-sharks, or land-grabbers, they are more commonly and plainly called. Thus the town-lands of Monterey are all in the hands of a single man. How they came there is an obscure, vexatious question, and, rightly or wrongly, the man is hated with a great hatred. His life has been repeatedly in danger. Not very long ago, I was told, the stage was stopped and examined three evenings in succession by disguised horsemen thirsting for his blood. A certain house on the Salinas road, they say, he always passes in his buggy at full speed, for the squatter sent him warning long ago. But a year since he was publicly pointed out for death by no less a man than Mr. Dennis Kearney. Kearney is a man too well known in California, but a word of explanation is required for English readers. Originally an Irish drayman, he rose, by his command of bad language, to almost dictatorial authority in the State; throned it there for six months or so, his mouth full of oaths, gallowses, and conflagrations; was first snuffed out last winter by Mr. Coleman, backed by his San Francisco Vigilantes and three gatling guns; completed his own ruin by throwing in his lot with the grotesque Greenbacker party; and had at last to be rescued by his old enemies, the police, out of the hands of his rebellious followers. It was while he was at the top of his fortune that Kearney visited Monterey with his battle-cry against Chinese labour, the railroad monopolists, and the land-thieves; and his one articulate counsel to the Montereyans was to "hang David Jacks." Had the town been American, in my private opinion, this would have been done years ago. Land is a subject on which there is no jesting in the West, and I have seen my friend the lawyer drive out of Monterey to adjust a competition of titles with the face of a captain going into battle and his Smith-and-Wesson convenient to his hand.

On the ranche of another of these landholders you may find our old friend, the truck system, in full operation. Men live there, year in year out, to cut timber for a nominal wage, which is all consumed in supplies. The longer they remain in this desirable service the deeper they will fall in debt — a burlesque injustice in a new country, where labour should be precious, and one of those typical instances which explains the prevailing discontent and the success of the demagogue Kearney.

In a comparison between what was and what is in California, the praisers of times past will fix upon the Indians of Carmel. The valley drained by the river so named is a true Californian valley, bare, dotted with chaparral, overlooked by quaint, unfinished hills. The Carmel runs by many pleasant farms, a clear and shallow river, loved by wading kine; and at last, as it is falling towards a quicksand and the great Pacific, passes a ruined mission on a hill. From the mission church the eye embraces a great field of ocean, and the ear is filled with a continuous sound of distant breakers on the shore. But the day of the Jesuit has gone by, the day of the Yankee has succeeded, and there is no one left to care for the converted savage. The church is roofless and ruinous, sea-breezes and sea-fogs, and the alternation of the rain and sunshine, daily widening the breaches and casting the crockets from the wall. As an antiquity in this new land, a quaint specimen of missionary architecture, and a memorial of good deeds, it had a triple claim to preservation from all thinking people; but neglect and abuse have been its portion. There is no sign of American interference, save where a headboard has been torn from a grave to be a mark for pistol bullets. So it is with the Indians for whom it was erected. Their lands, I was told, are being yearly encroached upon by the neighbouring American proprietor, and with that exception no man troubles his head for the Indians of Carmel. Only one day in the year, the day before our Guy Fawkes, the *padre* drives over the hill from Monterey; the little sacristy, which is the only covered portion of the church, is filled with seats and decorated for the service; the Indians troop together, their bright dresses contrasting with their dark and melancholy faces; and there, among a crowd of somewhat unsympathetic holiday-makers, you may hear God served with perhaps more touching circumstances than in any other temple under heaven. An Indian, stone-blind and about eighty years of age, conducts the singing; other Indians compose the choir; yet they have the Gregorian music at their finger ends, and pronounce the Latin so correctly that I could follow the meaning as they sang. The pronunciation was odd and nasal, the singing hurried and staccato. "In sæcula sæculo-ho-horum," they went, with a vigorous aspirate to every additional syllable. I have never seen faces more vividly lit up with joy than the faces of these Indian singers. It was to them not only the worship of God, nor an act by which they recalled and commemorated better days, but was besides an exercise of culture, where all they knew of art and letters was united and expressed. And it made a man's heart sorry for the good fathers of yore who had taught them to dig and to reap, to read and to sing, who had given them European mass-books which they still preserve and study in their cottages, and who had now passed away from all authority and influence in that land — to be succeeded by greedy land-thieves and sacrilegious pistol-shots. So ugly a thing may our Anglo-Saxon Protestantism appear beside the doings of the Society of Jesus.

But revolution in this world succeeds to revolution. All that I say in this paper is in a paulo-past tense. The Monterey of last year exists no longer. A huge hotel has sprung up in the desert by the railway. Three sets of diners sit down successively to table. Invaluable toilettes figure along the beach and between the live oaks; and Monterey is advertised in the newspapers, and posted in the waiting-rooms at railway stations, as a resort for wealth and fashion. Alas for the little town! it is not strong enough to resist the influence of the flaunting caravanserai, and the poor, quaint, penniless native gentlemen of Monterey must perish, like a lower race, before the millionaire vulgarians of the Big Bonanza.

[1880.]

III. FONTAINEBLEAU

VILLAGE COMMUNITIES OF PAINTERS

I

THE charm of Fontainebleau is a thing apart. It is a place that people love even more than they admire. The vigorous forest air, the silence, the majestic avenues of highway, the wilderness of tumbled boulders, the great age and dignity of certain groves — these are but ingredients, they are not the secret of the philtre. The place is sanative; the air, the light, the perfumes, and the shapes of things concord in happy harmony. The artist may be idle and not fear the " blues." He may dally with his life. Mirth, lyric mirth, and a vivacious classical contentment are of the very essence of the better kind of art; and these, in that most smiling forest, he has the chance to learn or to remember. Even on the plain of Bière, where the Angelus of Millet still tolls upon the ear of fancy, a larger air, a higher heaven, something ancient and healthy in the face of nature, purify the mind alike from dulness and hysteria. There is no place where the young are more gladly conscious of their youth, or the old better contented with their age.

The fact of its great and special beauty further recommends this country to the artist. The field was chosen by men in whose blood there still raced some of the gleeful or solemn exultation of great art — Millet who loved dignity like Michelangelo, Rousseau whose modern brush was dipped in the glamour of the ancients. It was chosen before the day of that strange turn in the history of art, of which we now perceive the culmination in impressionistic tales and pictures — that voluntary aversion of the eye from all speciously strong and beautiful effects — that disinterested love of dulness which has set so many Peter Bells to paint the river-side primrose. It was then chosen for its proximity to Paris. And for the same cause, and by the force of tradition, the painter of to-day continues to inhabit and to paint it. There is in France scenery incomparable for romance and harmony. Provence, and the valley of the Rhone from Vienne to Tarascon, are one succession of masterpieces waiting for the brush. The beauty is not merely beauty; it tells, besides, a tale to the imagination, and surprises while it charms. Here you shall see castellated towns that would befit the scenery of dreamland; streets that glow with colour like cathedral windows; hills of the most exquisite proportions; flowers of every precious colour, growing thick like grass. All these, by the grace of railway travel, are brought to the very door of the modern painter; yet he does not seek them; he remains faithful to Fontainebleau, to the eternal bridge of Gretz, to the watering-pot cascade in Cernay valley. Even Fontainebleau was chosen for him; even in Fontainebleau he shrinks from what is sharply charactered. But one thing, at least, is certain, whatever he may choose to paint and in whatever manner, it is good for the artist to dwell among graceful shapes. Fontainebleau, if it be but quiet scenery, is classically graceful; and though the student may look for different qualities, this quality, silently present, will educate his hand and eye.

But, before all its other advantages — charm, loveliness, or proximity to Paris — comes the great fact that it is already colonised. The institution of a painters' colony is a work of time and tact. The population must be conquered. The inn-keeper has to be taught, and he soon learns, the lesson of unlimited credit; he must be taught to welcome as a favoured guest a young gentleman in a very greasy coat, and with little baggage beyond a box of colours and a canvas; and he must learn to preserve his faith in customers who will eat heartily and drink of the best, borrow money to buy tobacco, and perhaps not pay a stiver for a year. A colour merchant has next to be attracted. A certain vogue must be given to the place, lest the painter, most gregarious of animals, should find himself alone. And no sooner are these first difficulties overcome, than fresh perils spring up upon the other side; and the bourgeois and the tourist are knocking at the gate. This is the crucial moment for the colony. If these intruders gain a footing, they not only banish freedom and amenity; pretty soon, by means of their long purses, they will have undone the education of the innkeeper; prices will rise and credit shorten; and the poor painter must fare farther on and find another hamlet. "Not here, O Apollo!" will become his song. Thus Trouville and, the other day, St. Raphael were lost to the arts. Curious and not always edifying are the shifts that the French student uses to defend his lair; like the cuttlefish, he must sometimes blacken the waters of his chosen pool;

but at such a time and for so practical a purpose Mrs. Grundy must allow him licence. Where his own purse and credit are not threatened, he will do the honours of his village generously. Any artist is made welcome, through whatever medium he may seek expression; science is respected; even the idler, if he prove, as he so rarely does, a gentleman, will soon begin to find himself at home. And when that essentially modern creature, the English or American girl-student, began to walk calmly into his favourite inns as if into a drawing-room at home, the French painter owned himself defenceless; he submitted or he fled. His French respectability, quite as precise as ours, though covering different provinces of life, recoiled aghast before the innovation. But the girls were painters; there was nothing to be done; and Barbizon, when I last saw it and for the time at least, was practically ceded to the fair invader. Paterfamilias, on the other hand, the common tourist, the holiday shopman, and the cheap young gentleman upon the spree, he hounded from his villages with every circumstance of contumely.

This purely artistic society is excellent for the young artist. The lads are mostly fools; they hold the latest orthodoxy in its crudeness; they are at that stage of education, for the most part, when a man is too much occupied with style to be aware of the necessity for any matter; and this, above all for the Englishman, is excellent. To work grossly at the trade, to forget sentiment, to think of his material and nothing else, is, for awhile at least, the king's highway of progress. Here, in England, too many painters and writers dwell dispersed, unshielded, among the intelligent bourgeois.

These, when they are not merely indifferent, prate to him about the lofty aims and moral influence of art. And this is the lad's ruin. For art is, first of all and last of all, a trade. The love of words and not a desire to publish new discoveries, the love of form and not a novel reading of historical events, mark the vocation of the writer and the painter. The arabesque, properly speaking, and even in literature, is the first fancy of the artist; he first plays with his material as a child plays with a kaleidoscope; and he is already in a second stage when he begins to use his pretty counters for the end of representation. In that, he must pause long and toil faithfully; that is his apprenticeship; and it is only the few who will really grow beyond it, and go forward, fully equipped, to do the business of real art — to give life to abstractions and significance and charm to facts. In the meanwhile, let him dwell much among his fellow-craftsmen. They alone can take a serious interest in the childish tasks and pitiful successes of these years. They alone can behold with equanimity this fingering of the dumb keyboard, this polishing of empty sentences, this dull and literal painting of dull and insignificant subjects. Outsiders will spur him on. They will say, "Why do you not write a great book? paint a great picture?" If his guardian angel fail him, they may even persuade him to the attempt, and, ten to one, his hand is coarsened and his style falsified for life.

And this brings me to a warning. The life of the apprentice to any art is both unstrained and pleasing; it is strewn with small successes in the midst of a career of failure, patiently supported; the heaviest scholar is conscious of a certain progress; and if he come not appreciably nearer to the art of Shakespeare, grows letter-perfect in the domain of A-B, ab. But the time comes when a man should cease prelusory gymnastic, stand up, put a violence upon his will, and for better or worse, begin the business of creation. This evil day there is a tendency continually to postpone: above all with painters. They have made so many studies that it has become a habit; they make more, the walls of exhibitions blush with them; and death finds these aged students still busy with their horn-book. This class of man finds a congenial home in artist villages; in the slang of the English colony at Barbizon we used to call them "Snoozers." Continual returns to the city, the society of men farther advanced, the study of great works, a sense of humour or, if such a thing is to be had, a little religion or philosophy, are the means of treatment. It will be time enough to think of curing the malady after it has been caught; for to catch it is the very thing for which you seek that dream-land of the painters' village. "Snoozing" is a part of the artistic education; and the rudiments must be learned stupidly, all else being forgotten, as if they were an object in themselves.

Lastly, there is something, or there seems to be something, in the very air of France that communicates the love of style. Precision, clarity, the cleanly and crafty employment of material, a grace in the handling, apart from any value in the thought, seem to be acquired by the mere residence; or if not acquired, become at least the more appreciated. The air of Paris is alive with this technical inspiration. And to leave that airy city and awake next day upon the borders of the forest is but to change externals. The same spirit of dexterity and finish breathes from the long alleys and the lofty groves, from the wildernesses that are still pretty in their confusion, and the great plain that contrives to be decorative in its emptiness.

II

In spite of its really considerable extent, the forest of Fontainebleau is hardly anywhere tedious. I know the whole western side of it with what, I suppose, I may call thoroughness; well enough at least to testify that there is no square mile without some special character and charm. Such quarters, for instance, as the Long Rocher, the Bas-Bréau, and the Reine Blanche, might be a hundred miles apart; they have scarce a point in common beyond the silence of the birds. The two last are really conterminous; and in both are tall and ancient trees that have outlived a thousand political vicissitudes. But in the one the great oaks prosper placidly upon an even floor; they beshadow a great field; and the air and the light are very free below their stretching boughs. In the other the trees find difficult footing; castles of white rock lie tumbled one upon another, the foot slips, the crooked viper slumbers, the moss clings in the crevice; and above it all the great beech goes spiring and casting forth her arms, and, with a grace beyond church architecture, canopies this rugged chaos. Meanwhile, dividing the two cantons, the broad white causeway of the Paris road runs in an avenue: a road conceived for pageantry and for triumphal marches, an avenue for an army; but, its days of glory over, it now lies grilling in the sun between cool groves, and only at intervals the vehicle of the cruising tourist is seen far away and faintly audible along its ample sweep. A little upon one side, and you find a district of sand and birch and boulder; a little upon the other lies the valley of Apremont, all juniper and heather; and close beyond that you may walk into a zone of pine trees. So artfully are the ingredients mingled. Nor must it be forgotten that, in all this part, you come continually forth upon a hill-top, and behold the plain, northward and westward, like an unrefulgent sea; nor that all day long the shadows keep changing; and at last, to the red fires of sunset, night succeeds, and with the night a new forest, full of whisper, gloom, and fragrance. There are few things more renovating than to leave Paris, the lamplit arches of the Carrousel, and the long alignment of the glittering streets, and to bathe the senses in this fragrant darkness of the wood.

In this continual variety the mind is kept vividly alive. It is a changeful place to paint, a stirring place to live in. As fast as your foot carries you, you pass from scene to scene, each vigorously painted in the colours of the sun, each endeared by that hereditary spell of forests on the mind of man who still remembers and salutes the ancient refuge of his race.

And yet the forest has been civilised throughout. The most savage corners bear a name, and have been cherished like antiquities; in the most remote, Nature has prepared and balanced her effects as if with conscious art; and man, with his guiding arrows of blue paint, has countersigned the picture. After your farthest wandering, you are never surprised to come forth upon the vast avenue of highway, to strike the centre point of branching alleys, or to find the aqueduct trailing, thousand-footed, through the brush. It is not a wilderness; it is rather a preserve. And, fitly enough, the centre of the maze is not a hermit's cavern. In the midst, a little mirthful town lies sunlit, humming with the business of pleasure; and the palace, breathing distinction and peopled by historic names, stands smokeless among gardens.

Perhaps the last attempt at savage life was that of the harmless humbug who called himself the hermit. In a great tree, close by the high-road, he had built himself a little cabin after the manner of the Swiss Family Robinson; thither he mounted at night, by the romantic aid of a rope ladder; and if dirt be any proof of sincerity, the man was savage as a Sioux. I had the pleasure of his acquaintance; he appeared grossly stupid, not in his perfect wits, and interested in nothing but small change; for that he had a great avidity. In the course of time he proved to be a chicken-stealer, and vanished from his perch; and perhaps from the first he was no true votary of forest freedom, but an ingenious, theatrically-minded beggar, and his cabin in the tree was only stock-in-trade to beg withal. The choice of his position would seem to indicate so much; for if in the forest there are no places still to be discovered, there are many that have been forgotten, and that lie unvisited. There, to be sure, are the blue arrows waiting to reconduct you, now blazed upon a tree, now posted in the corner of a rock. But your security from interruption is complete; you might camp for weeks, if there were only water, and not a soul suspect your presence; and if I may suppose the reader to have committed some great crime and come to me for aid, I think I could still find my way to a small cavern, fitted with a hearth and chimney, where he might lie perfectly concealed. A confederate landscape-painter might daily supply him with food; for water, he would have to make a nightly tramp as far as to the nearest pond; and at last, when the hue and cry began to blow over, he might get gently on the train at some side station, work round by a series of junctions, and be quietly captured at the frontier.

Thus Fontainebleau, although it is truly but a pleasure-ground, and although, in favourable weather, and in the more celebrated quarters, it literally buzzes with the tourist, yet has some of the immunities and offers some of the repose of natural forests. And the solitary, although he must return at night to his frequented inn, may yet pass the day with his own thoughts in the companionable silence of the trees. The demands of the imagination vary; some can be alone in a back garden looked upon by windows; others, like the ostrich, are content with a solitude that meets the eye; and others, again, expand in fancy to the very borders of their desert, and are irritably conscious of a hunter's camp in an adjacent county. To these last, of course, Fontainebleau will seem but an extended tea-garden: a Rosherville on a by-day. But to the plain man it offers solitude: an excellent thing in itself, and a good whet for company.

III

I was for some time a consistent Barbizonian; *et ego in Arcadia vixi,* it was a pleasant season; and that noiseless hamlet lying close among the borders of the wood is for me, as for so many others, a green spot in memory. The great Millet was just dead, the green shutters of his modest house were closed; his daughters were in mourning. The date of my first visit was thus an epoch in the history of art: in a lesser way, it was an epoch in the history of the Latin Quarter. The *Petit Cénacle* was dead and buried; Murger and his crew of sponging vagabonds were all at rest from their expedients; the tradition of their real life was nearly lost; and the petrified legend of the *Vie de Bohème* had become a sort of gospel, and still gave the cue to zealous imitators. But if the book be written in rose-water, the imitation was still farther expurgated; honesty was the rule; the innkeepers gave, as I have said, almost unlimited credit; they suffered the seediest painter to depart, to take all his belongings, and to leave his bill unpaid; and if they sometimes lost, it was by English and Americans alone. At the same time, the great influx of Anglo-Saxons had begun to affect the life of the studious. There had been disputes; and, in one instance at least, the English and the Americans had made common cause to prevent a cruel pleasantry. It would be well if nations and races could communicate their qualities; but in practice when they look upon each other, they have an eye to nothing but defects. The Anglo-Saxon is essentially dishonest; the French is devoid by nature of the principle that we call "Fair Play." The Frenchman marvelled at the scruples of his guest, and, when that defender of innocence retired over-seas and left his bills unpaid, he marvelled once again; the good and evil were, in his eyes, part and parcel of the same eccentricity; a shrug expressed his judgment upon both.

At Barbizon there was no master, no pontiff in the arts. Palizzi bore rule at Gretz — urbane, superior rule — his memory rich in anecdotes of the great men of yore, his mind fertile in theories; sceptical, composed, and venerable to the eye; and yet beneath these outworks, all twittering with Italian superstition, his eye scouting for omens, and the whole fabric of his manners giving way on the appearance of a hunchback. Cernay had Pelouse, the admirable, placid Pelouse, smilingly critical of youth, who, when a full-blown commercial traveller, suddenly threw down his samples, bought a colour-box, and became the master whom we have all admired. Marlotte, for a central figure, boasted Olivier de Penne. Only Barbizon, since the death of Millet, was a headless commonwealth. Even its secondary lights, and those who in my day made the stranger welcome, have since deserted it. The good Lachèvre has departed, carrying his household gods; and long before that Gaston Lafenestre was taken from our midst by an untimely death. He died before he had deserved success; it may be, he would never have deserved it; but his kind, comely, modest countenance still haunts the memory of all who knew him. Another — whom I will not name — has moved farther on, pursuing the strange Odyssey of his decadence. His days of royal favour had departed even then; but he still retained, in his narrower life at Barbizon, a certain stamp of conscious importance, hearty, friendly, filling the room, the occupant of several chairs; nor had he yet ceased his losing battle, still labouring upon great canvases that none would buy, still waiting the return of fortune. But these days also were too good to last; and the former favourite of two sovereigns fled, if I heard the truth, by night. There was a time when he was counted a great man, and Millet but a dauber; behold, how the whirligig of time brings in his revenges! To pity Millet is a piece of arrogance; if life be hard for such resolute and pious spirits, it is harder still for us, had we the wit to understand it; but we may pity his unhappier rival, who, for no apparent merit, was raised to opulence and momentary fame, and, through no apparent fault, was suffered step by step to sink again to nothing. No misfortune can exceed the bitterness of such back-foremost progress, even bravely supported as it was; but to those also who were taken early from the easel, a regret is due. From all the young men of this period, one stood out by the vigour of his promise; he was in the age of fermentation, enamoured of eccentricities. "Il faut faire de la peinture nouvelle," was his watchword; but if time and experience had continued his education, if he had been granted health to return from these excursions to the steady and the central, I must believe that the name of Hills had become famous.

Siron's inn, that excellent artists' barrack, was managed upon easy principles. At any hour of the night, when you returned from wandering in the forest, you went to the billiard-room and helped yourself to liquors, or descended to the cellar and returned laden with beer or wine. The Sirons were all locked in slumber; there was none to check your inroads; only at the week's end a computation was made, the gross sum was divided, and a varying share set down to every lodger's name under the rubric: *estrats*. Upon the more long-suffering the larger tax was levied; and your bill lengthened in a direct proportion to the easiness of your disposition. At any hour of the morning, again, you could get your coffee or cold milk, and set forth into the forest. The doves had perhaps wakened you, fluttering into your chamber; and on the threshold of the inn you were met by the aroma of the forest. Close by were the great aisles, the mossy boulders, the interminable field of forest shadow. There you were free to dream and wander. And at noon, and again at six o'clock, a good meal awaited you on Siron's table. The whole of your accommodation, set aside that varying item of the *estrats,* cost you five francs a day; your bill was never offered you until you asked it; and if you were out of luck's way, you might depart for where you pleased and leave it pending.

IV

Theoretically, the house was open to all comers; practically, it was a kind of club. The guests protected themselves, and, in so doing, they protected Siron. Formal manners being laid aside, essential courtesy was the more rigidly exacted; the new arrival had to feel the pulse of the society; and a breach of its undefined observances was promptly punished. A man might be as plain, as dull, as slovenly, as free of speech as he desired; but to a touch of presumption or a word of hectoring these free Barbizonians were as sensitive as a tea-party of maiden ladies. I have seen people driven forth from Barbizon; it would be difficult to say in words what they had done, but they deserved their fate. They had shown themselves unworthy to enjoy these corporate freedoms; they had pushed themselves; they had "made their head;" they wanted tact to appreciate the "fine shades" of Barbizonian etiquette. And once they were condemned, the process of extrusion was ruthless in its cruelty; after one evening with the formidable Bodmer, the Baily of our commonwealth, the erring stranger was beheld no more; he rose exceeding early the next day, and the first coach conveyed him from the scene of his discomfiture. These sentences of banishment were never, in my knowledge, delivered against an artist; such would, I believe, have been illegal; but the odd and pleasant fact is this, that they were never needed. Painters, sculptors, writers, singers, I have seen all of these in Barbizon; and some were sulky, and some blatant and inane; but one and all entered at once into the spirit of the association. This singular society is purely French, a creature of French virtues, and possibly of French defects. It cannot be imitated by the English. The roughness, the impatience, the more obvious selfishness, and even the more ardent friendships of the Anglo-Saxon, speedily dismember such a commonwealth. But this random gathering of young French painters, with neither apparatus nor parade of government, yet kept the life of the place upon a certain footing, insensibly imposed their etiquette upon the docile, and by caustic speech enforced their edicts against the unwelcome. To think of it is to wonder the more at the strange failure of their race upon the larger theatre. This inbred civility — to use the word in its completest meaning — this natural and facile adjustment of contending liberties, seems all that is required to make a governable nation and a just and prosperous country.

Our society, thus purged and guarded, was full of high spirits, of laughter, and of the initiative of youth. The few elder men who joined us were still young at heart, and took the key from their companions. We returned from long stations in the fortifying air, our blood renewed by the sunshine, our spirits refreshed by the silence of the forest; the Babel of loud voices sounded good; we fell to eat and play like the natural man; and in the high inn chamber, panelled with indifferent pictures and lit by candles guttering in the night air, the talk and laughter sounded far into the night. It was a good place and a good life for any naturally-minded youth; better yet for the student of painting, and perhaps best of all for the student of letters. He, too, was saturated in this atmosphere of style; he was shut out from the disturbing currents of the world, he might forget that there existed other and more pressing interests than that of art. But, in such a place, it was hardly possible to write; he could not drug his conscience, like the painter, by the production of listless studies; he saw himself idle among many who were apparently, and some who were really, employed; and what with the impulse of increasing health and the continual provocation of romantic scenes, he became tormented with the desire to work. He enjoyed a strenuous idleness full of visions, hearty meals, long, sweltering walks, mirth among companions; and still floating like music through his brain, foresights of great works that Shakespeare might be proud to have conceived, headless epics, glorious torsos of dramas, and words that were alive with import. So in youth, like Moses from the mountain, we have sights of that House Beautiful of art which we shall never enter. They are dreams and unsubstantial; visions of style that repose upon no base of human meaning; the last heart-throbs of that excited amateur who has to die in all of us before the artist can be born. But they come to us in such a rainbow of glory that all subsequent achievement appears dull and earthly in comparison. We were all artists; almost all in the age of illusion, cultivating an imaginary genius, and walking to the strains of some deceiving Ariel; small wonder, indeed, if we were happy! But art, of whatever nature, is a kind mistress; and though these dreams of youth fall by their own baselessness, others succeed, graver and more substantial; the symptoms change, the amiable malady endures; and still, at an equal distance, the House Beautiful shines upon its hill-top.

V

Gretz lies out of the forest, down by the bright river. It boasts a mill, an ancient church, a castle, and a bridge of many sterlings. And the bridge is a piece of public property; anonymously famous; beaming on the incurious dilettante from the walls of a hundred exhibitions. I have seen it in the Salon; I have seen it in the Academy; I have seen it in the last French Exposition, excellently done by Bloomer; in a black-and-white, by Mr. A. Henley, it once adorned this essay in the pages of the *Magazine of Art*. Long-suffering bridge! And if you visit Gretz to-morrow, you shall find another generation, camped at the bottom of Chevillon's garden under their white umbrellas, and doggedly painting it again.

The bridge taken for granted, Gretz is a less inspiring place than Barbizon. I give it the palm over Cernay. There is something ghastly in the great empty village square of Cernay, with the inn tables standing in one corner, as though the stage were set for rustic opera, and in the early morning all the painters breaking their fast upon white wine under the windows of the villagers. It is vastly different to awake in Gretz, to go down the green inn-garden, to find the river streaming through the bridge, and to see the dawn begin across the poplared level. The meals are laid in the cool arbour, under fluttering leaves. The splash of oars and bathers, the bathing costumes out to dry, the trim canoes beside the jetty, tell of a society that has an eye to pleasure. There is "something to do" at Gretz. Perhaps, for that very reason, I can recall no such enduring ardours, no such glories of exhilaration, as among the solemn groves and uneventful hours of Barbizon. This "something to do" is a great enemy to joy; it is a way out of it; you wreak your high spirits on some cut-and-dry employment, and behold them gone! But Gretz is a merry place after its kind: pretty to see, merry to inhabit. The course of its pellucid river, whether up or down, is full of gentle attractions for the navigator: islanded reed-mazes where, in autumn, the red berries cluster; the mirrored and inverted images of trees; lilies, and mills, and the foam and thunder of weirs. And of all noble sweeps of roadway, none is nobler, on a windy dusk, than the high road to Nemours between its lines of talking poplar.

But even Gretz is changed. The old inn, long shored and trussed and buttressed, fell at length under the mere weight of years, and the place as it was is but a fading image in the memory of former guests. They, indeed, recall the ancient wooden stair; they recall the rainy evening, the wide hearth, the blaze of the twig fire, and the company that gathered round the pillar in the kitchen. But the material fabric is now dust; soon, with the last of its inhabitants, its very memory shall follow; and they, in their turn, shall suffer the same law, and, both in name and lineament, vanish from the world of men. "For remembrance of the old house' sake," as Pepys once quaintly put it, let me tell one story. When the tide of invasion swept over France, two foreign painters were left stranded and penniless in Gretz; and there, until the war was over, the Chevillons ungrudgingly harboured them. It was difficult to obtain supplies; but the two waifs were still welcome to the best, sat down daily with the family to table, and at the due intervals were supplied with clean napkins, which they scrupled to employ. Madame Chevillon observed the fact and reprimanded them. But they stood firm; eat they must, but having no money they would soil no napkins.

VI

Nemours and Moret, for all they are so picturesque, have been little visited by painters. They are, indeed, too populous; they have manners of their own, and might resist the drastic process of colonisation. Montigny has been somewhat strangely neglected; I never knew it inhabited but once, when Will H. Low installed himself there with a barrel of *piquette*, and entertained his friends in a leafy trellis above the weir, in sight of the green country and to the music of the falling water. It was a most airy, quaint, and pleasant place of residence, just too rustic to be stagey; and from my memories of the place in general, and that garden trellis in particular — at morning, visited by birds, or at night, when the dew fell and the stars were of the party — I am inclined to think perhaps too favourably of the future of Montigny. Chailly-en-Bière has outlived all things, and lies dustily slumbering in the plain — the cemetery of itself. The great road remains to testify of its former bustle of postilions and carriage bells; and, like memorial tablets, there still hang in the inn room the paintings of a former generation, dead or decorated long ago. In my time, one man only, greatly daring, dwelt there. From time to time he would walk over to Barbizon, like a shade revisiting the glimpses of the moon, and after some communication with flesh and blood return to his austere hermitage. But even he, when I last revisited the forest, had come to Barbizon for good, and closed the roll of Chaillyites. It may revive — but I much doubt it. Achères and Recloses still wait a pioneer; Bourron is out of the question, being merely Gretz over again, without the river, the bridge, or the beauty; and of all the possible places on the western side, Marlotte alone remains to be discussed. I scarcely know Marlotte, and, very likely for that reason, am not much in love with it. It seems a glaring and unsightly hamlet. The inn of Mother Antonie is unattractive; and its more reputable rival, though comfortable enough, is commonplace. Marlotte has a name; it is famous; if I were the young painter I would leave it alone in its glory.

VII

These are the words of an old stager; and though time is a good conservative in forest places, much may be untrue to-day. Many of us have passed Arcadian days there and moved on, but yet left a portion of our souls behind us buried in the woods. I would not dig for these reliquiæ; they are incommunicable treasures that will not enrich the finder; and yet there may lie, interred below great oaks or scattered along forest paths, stores of youth's dynamite and dear remembrances. And as one generation passes on and renovates the field of tillage for the next, I entertain a fancy that when the young men of to-day go forth into the forest, they shall find the air still vitalised by the spirits of their predecessors, and, like those "unheard melodies" that are the sweetest of all, the memory of our laughter shall still haunt the field of trees. Those merry voices that in woods call the wanderer farther, those thrilling silences and whispers of the groves, surely in Fontainebleau they must be vocal of me and my companions? We are not content to pass away entirely from the scenes of our delight; we would leave, if but in gratitude, a pillar and a legend.

One generation after another fall like honey-bees upon this memorable forest, rifle its sweets, pack themselves with vital memories, and when the theft is consummated depart again into life richer, but poorer also. The forest, indeed, they have possessed, from that day forward it is theirs indissolubly, and they will return to walk in it at night in the fondest of their dreams, and use it for ever in their books and pictures. Yet when they made their packets, and put up their notes and sketches, something, it should seem, had been forgotten. A projection of themselves shall appear to haunt unfriended these scenes of happiness, a natural child of fancy, begotten and forgotten unawares. Over the whole field of our wanderings such fetches are still travelling like indefatigable bagmen; but the imps of Fontainebleau, as of all beloved spots, are very long of life, and memory is piously unwilling to forget their orphanage. If anywhere about that wood you meet my airy bantling, greet him with tenderness. He was a pleasant lad, though now abandoned. And when it comes to your own turn to quit the forest may you leave behind you such another; no Antony or Werther, let us hope, no tearful whipster, but, as becomes this not uncheerful and most active age in which we figure, the child of happy hours.

No art, it may be said, was ever perfect, and not many noble, that has not been mirthfully conceived. And no man, it may be added, was ever anything but a wet blanket and a cross to his companions who boasted not a copious spirit of enjoyment. Whether as man or artist, let the youth make haste to Fontainebleau, and once there let him address himself to the spirit of the place; he will learn more from exercise than from studies, although both are necessary; and if he can get into his heart the gaiety and inspiration of the woods he will have gone far to undo the evil of his sketches. A spirit once well strung up to the concert-pitch of the primeval out-of-doors will hardly dare to finish a study and magniloquently ticket it a picture. The incommunicable thrill of things, that is the tuning-fork by which we test the flatness of our art. Here it is that Nature teaches and condemns, and still spurs up to further effort and new failure. Thus it is that she sets us blushing at our ignorant and tepid works; and the more we find of these inspiring shocks the less shall we be apt to love the literal in our productions. In all sciences and senses the letter kills; and to-day, when cackling human geese express their ignorant condemnation of all studio pictures, it is a lesson most useful to be learnt. Let the young painter go to Fontainebleau, and while he stupefies himself with studies that teach him the mechanical side of his trade, let him walk in the great air, and be a servant of mirth, and not pick and botanise, but wait upon the moods of nature. So he will learn — or learn not to forget — the poetry of life and earth, which, when he has acquired his track, will save him from joyless reproduction. .

[1882.]

IV. EPILOGUE TO "AN INLAND VOYAGE"[1]

THE country where they journeyed, that green, breezy valley of the Loing, is one very attractive to cheerful and solitary people. The weather was superb; all night it thundered and lightened, and the rain fell in sheets; by day, the heavens were cloudless, the sun fervent, the air vigorous and pure. They walked separate: the Cigarette plodding behind with some philosophy, the lean Arethusa posting on ahead. Thus each enjoyed his own reflections by the way; each had perhaps time to tire of them before he met his comrade at the designated inn; and the pleasures of society and solitude combined to fill the day. The Arethusa carried in his knapsack the works of Charles of Orleans, and employed some of the hours of travel in the concoction of English rondels. In this path, he must thus have preceded Mr. Lang, Mr. Dobson, Mr. Henley, and all contemporary roundeleers; but for good reasons, he will be the last to publish the result. The Cigarette walked burthened with a volume of Michelet. And both these books, it will be seen, played a part in the subsequent adventure.

The Arethusa was unwisely dressed. He is no precisian in attire; but by all accounts, he was never so ill-

[1] See An Inland Voyage, by Robert Louis Stevenson, 1878.

inspired as on that tramp; having set forth indeed, upon
a moment's notice, from the most unfashionable spot in
Europe, Barbizon. On his head, he wore a smoking-
cap of Indian work, the gold lace pitifully frayed and
tarnished. A flannel shirt of an agreeable dark hue,
which the satirical called black; a light tweed coat made
by a good English tailor; ready-made cheap linen trousers and leathern gaiters completed his array. In person,
he is exceptionally lean; and his face is not like those of
happier mortals, a certificate. For years he could not
pass a frontier or visit a bank without suspicion; the
police everywhere, but in his native city, looked askance upon him; and (though I am sure it will not be
credited) he is actually denied admittance to the casino
of Monte Carlo. If you will imagine him, dressed as
above, stooping under his knapsack, walking nearly
five miles an hour with the folds of the ready-made
trousers fluttering about his spindle shanks, and still
looking eagerly round him as if in terror of pursuit —
the figure, when realised, is far from reassuring. When
Villon journeyed (perhaps by the same pleasant valley)
to his exile at Roussillon, I wonder if he had not something of the same appearance. Something of the same
preoccupation he had beyond a doubt, for he too must
have tinkered verses as he walked, with more success
than his successor. And if he had anything like the
same inspiring weather, the same nights of uproar, men
in armour rolling and resounding down the stairs of
heaven, the rain hissing on the village streets, the wild
bull's-eye of the storm flashing all night long into the
bare inn-chamber — the same sweet return of day, the
same unfathomable blue of noon, the same high-col-

oured, halcyon eves — and above all if he had anything like as good a comrade, anything like as keen a relish for what he saw, and what he ate, and the rivers that he bathed in, and the rubbish that he wrote, I would exchange estates to-day with the poor exile, and count myself a gainer.

But there was another point of similarity between the two journeys, for which the Arethusa was to pay dear: both were gone upon in days of incomplete security. It was not long after the Franco-Prussian war. Swiftly as men forget, that country-side was still alive with tales of uhlans, and outlying sentries, and hairbreadth 'scapes from the ignominious cord, and pleasant momentary friendships between invader and invaded. A year, at the most two years later, you might have tramped all that country over and not heard one anecdote. And a year or two later, you would — if you were a rather ill-looking young man in nondescript array — have gone your rounds in greater safety; for along with more interesting matter, the Prussian spy would have somewhat faded from men's imaginations.

For all that, our voyager had got beyond Château Renard before he was conscious of arousing wonder. On the road between that place and Châtillon-sur-Loing, however, he encountered a rural postman; they fell together in talk, and spoke of a variety of subjects; but through one and all, the postman was still visibly preoccupied, and his eyes were faithful to the Arethusa's knapsack. At last, with mysterious roguishness, he inquired what it contained, and on being answered, shook his head with kindly incredulity. "*Non,*" said he, "*non, vous avez des portraits.*" And then with a

languishing appeal, "*Voyons,* show me the portraits!"
It was some little while before the Arethusa, with a
shout of laughter, recognised his drift. By portraits he
meant indecent photographs; and in the Arethusa, an
austere and rising author, he thought to have identified
a pornographic colporteur. When countryfolk in France
have made up their minds as to a person's calling, argument is fruitless. Along all the rest of the way, the
postman piped and fluted meltingly to get a sight of the
collection; now he would upbraid, now he would reason — "*Voyons,* I will tell nobody"; then he tried cor-
ruption, and insisted on paying for a glass of wine;
and, at last, when their ways separated — "*Non,*" said
he, "*ce n'est pas bien de votre part. O non, ce n'est
pas bien.*" And shaking his head with quite a sentimental sense of injury, he departed unrefreshed.

On certain little difficulties encountered by the Arethusa at Châtillon-sur-Loing, I have not space to dwell;
another Châtillon, of grislier memory, looms too near
at hand. But the next day, in a certain hamlet called
La Jussière, he stopped to drink a glass of syrup in a
very poor, bare drinking shop. The hostess, a comely
woman, suckling a child, examined the traveller with
kindly and pitying eyes. "You are not of this department?" she asked. The Arethusa told her he was
English. "Ah!" she said, surprised. "We have no
English. We have many Italians, however, and they
do very well; they do not complain of the people of
hereabouts. An Englishman may do very well also; it
will be something new." Here was a dark saying, over
which the Arethusa pondered as he drank his grena-
dine; but when he rose and asked what was to pay,

the light came upon him in a flash. *"O, pour vous,"* replied the landlady, "a halfpenny!" *Pour vous?* By heaven, she took him for a beggar! He paid his half-penny, feeling that it were ungracious to correct her. But when he was forth again upon the road, he became vexed in spirit. The conscience is no gentleman, he is a rabbinical fellow; and his conscience told him he had stolen the syrup.

That night the travellers slept in Gien; the next day they passed the river and set forth (severally, as their custom was) on a short stage through the green plain upon the Berry side, to Châtillon-sur-Loire. It was the first day of the shooting; and the air rang with the report of firearms and the admiring cries of sports-men. Overhead the birds were in consternation, wheel-ing in clouds, settling and re-arising. And yet with all this bustle on either hand, the road itself lay solitary. The Arethusa smoked a pipe beside a milestone, and I remember he laid down very exactly all he was to do at Châtillon: how he was to enjoy a cold plunge, to change his shirt, and to await the Cigarette's arrival, in sublime inaction, by the margin of the Loire. Fired by these ideas, he pushed the more rapidly forward, and came, early in the afternoon and in a breathing heat, to the entering-in of that ill-fated town. Childe Roland to the dark tower came.

A polite gendarme threw his shadow on the path. "*Monsieur est voyageur?*" he asked.

And the Arethusa, strong in his innocence, forgetful of his vile attire, replied — I had almost said with gaiety: "So it would appear."

"His papers are in order?" said the gendarme. And

when the Arethusa, with a slight change of voice, admitted he had none, he was informed (politely enough) that he must appear before the Commissary.

The Commissary sat at a table in his bedroom, stripped to the shirt and trousers, but still copiously perspiring; and when he turned upon the prisoner a large meaningless countenance, that was (like Bardolph's) "all whelks and bubuckles," the dullest might have been prepared for grief. Here was a stupid man, sleepy with the heat and fretful at the interruption, whom neither appeal nor argument could reach.

THE COMMISSARY. You have no papers?

THE ARETHUSA. Not here.

THE COMMISSARY. Why?

THE ARETHUSA. I have left them behind in my valise.

THE COMMISSARY. You know, however, that it is forbidden to circulate without papers?

THE ARETHUSA. Pardon me: I am convinced of the contrary. I am here on my rights as an English subject by international treaty.

THE COMMISSARY (*with scorn*). You call yourself an Englishman?

THE ARETHUSA. I do.

THE COMMISSARY. Humph.— What is your trade?

THE ARETHUSA. I am a Scotch Advocate.

THE COMMISSARY (*with singular annoyance*). A Scotch advocate! Do you then pretend to support yourself by that in this department?

The Arethusa modestly disclaimed the pretension. The Commissary had scored a point.

THE COMMISSARY. Why, then, do you travel?

THE ARETHUSA. I travel for pleasure.

197

THE COMMISSARY (*pointing to the knapsack, and with sublime incredulity*). *Avec ça? Voyez-vous, je suis un homme intelligent!* (With that? Look here, I am a person of intelligence!)

The culprit remaining silent under this home thrust, the Commissary relished his triumph for a while, and then demanded (like the postman, but with what different expectations!) to see the contents of the knapsack. And here the Arethusa, not yet sufficiently awake to his position, fell into a grave mistake. There was little or no furniture in the room except the Commissary's chair and table; and to facilitate matters, the Arethusa (with all the innocence on earth) leant the knapsack on a corner of the bed. The Commissary fairly bounded from his seat; his face and neck flushed past purple, almost into blue; and he screamed to lay the desecrating object on the floor.

The knapsack proved to contain a change of shirts, of shoes, of socks, and of linen trousers, a small dressing-case, a piece of soap in one of the shoes, two volumes of the *Collection Jannet* lettered *Poésies de Charles d'Orléans,* a map, and a version book containing divers notes in prose and the remarkable English roundels of the voyager, still to this day unpublished: the Commissary of Châtillon is the only living man who has clapped an eye on these artistic trifles. He turned the assortment over with a contumelious finger; it was plain from his daintiness that he regarded the Arethusa and all his belongings as the very temple of infection. Still there was nothing suspicious about the map, nothing really criminal except the roundels; as for Charles of Orleans, to the ignorant mind of the prisoner, he seemed as good as a certificate; and it was supposed the farce was nearly over.

The inquisitor resumed his seat.

THE COMMISSARY (*after a pause*). *Eh bien, je vais vous dire ce que vous êtes. Vous êtes allemand et vous venez chanter à la foire.* (Well, then, I will tell you what you are. You are a German and have come to sing at the fair.)

THE ARETHUSA. Would you like to hear me sing? I believe I could convince you of the contrary.

THE COMMISSARY. *Pas de plaisanterie, monsieur!*

THE ARETHUSA. Well, sir, oblige me at least by looking at this book. Here, I open it with my eyes shut. Read one of these songs — read this one — and tell me, you who are a man of intelligence, if it would be possible to sing it at a fair?

THE COMMISSARY (*critically*). *Mais oui. Très bien.*

THE ARETHUSA. *Comment, monsieur!* What! But you do not observe it is antique. It is difficult to understand, even for you and me; but for the audience at a fair, it would be meaningless.

THE COMMISSARY (*taking a pen*). *Enfin, il faut en finir.* What is your name?

THE ARETHUSA (*speaking with the swallowing vivacity of the English*). Robert-Louis-Stev'ns'n.

THE COMMISSARY (*aghast*). *Hé! Quoi?*

THE ARETHUSA (*perceiving and improving his advantage*). Rob'rt-Lou's-Stev'ns'n.

THE COMMISSARY (*after several conflicts with his pen*). *Eh bien, il faut se passer du nom. Ça ne s'écrit pas.* (Well, we must do without the name: it is unspellable.)

The above is a rough summary of this momentous conversation, in which I have been chiefly careful to preserve the plums of the Commissary; but the remainder of the scene, perhaps because of his rising anger, has left but little definite in the memory of the Arethusa. The Commissary was not, I think, a practised literary man; no sooner, at least, had he taken pen in hand and embarked on the composition of the *procès-verbal,* than he became distinctly more uncivil and began to show a predilection for that simplest of all forms of repartee: "You lie!" Several times the Arethusa let it pass, and then suddenly flared up, refused to accept more insults or to answer further questions, defied the Commissary to do his worst, and promised him, if he did, that he should bitterly repent it. Perhaps if he had worn this proud front from the first, instead of beginning with a sense of entertainment and then going on to argue, the thing might have turned otherwise; for even at this eleventh hour the Commissary was visibly staggered. But it was too late; he had been challenged; the *procès-verbal* was begun; and he again squared his elbows over his writing, and the Arethusa was led forth a prisoner.

A step or two down the hot road stood the gendarmerie. Thither was our unfortunate conducted, and there he was bidden to empty forth the contents of his pockets. A handkerchief, a pen, a pencil, a pipe and tobacco, matches, and some ten francs of change: that was all. Not a file, not a cipher, not a scrap of writing whether to identify or to condemn. The very gendarme was appalled before such destitution.

"I regret," he said, "that I arrested you, for I see

that you are no *voyou*." And he promised him every indulgence.

The Arethusa, thus encouraged, asked for his pipe. That he was told was impossible, but if he chewed, he might have some tobacco. He did not chew, however, and asked instead to have his handkerchief.

"*Non,*" said the gendarme. "*Nous avons eu des histoires de gens qui se sont pendus.*" (No, we have had histories of people who hanged themselves.)

"What," cried the Arethusa. "And is it for that you refuse me my handkerchief? But see how much more easily I could hang myself in my trousers!"

The man was struck by the novelty of the idea; but he stuck to his colours, and only continued to repeat vague offers of service.

"At least," said the Arethusa, "be sure that you arrest my comrade; he will follow me ere long on the same road, and you can tell him by the sack upon his shoulders."

This promised, the prisoner was led round into the back court of the building, a cellar door was opened, he was motioned down the stair, and bolts grated and chains clanged behind his descending person.

The philosophic and still more the imaginative mind is apt to suppose itself prepared for any mortal accident. Prison, among other ills, was one that had been often faced by the undaunted Arethusa. Even as he went down the stairs, he was telling himself that here was a famous occasion for a roundel, and that like the committed linnets of the tuneful cavalier, he too would make his prison musical. I will tell the truth at once: the roundel was never written, or it should be printed in this place, to raise a smile. Two reasons interfered: the first moral, the second physical.

It is one of the curiosities of human nature, that although all men are liars, they can none of them bear to be told so of themselves. To get and take the lie with equanimity is a stretch beyond the stoic; and the Arethusa, who had been surfeited upon that insult, was blazing inwardly with a white heat of smothered wrath. But the physical had also its part. The cellar in which he was confined was some feet underground, and it was only lighted by an unglazed, narrow aperture high up in the wall and smothered in the leaves of a green vine. The walls were of naked masonry, the floor of bare earth; by way of furniture there was an earthenware basin, a water-jug, and a wooden bedstead with a blue-gray cloak for bedding. To be taken from the hot air of a summer's afternoon, the reverberation of the road and the stir of rapid exercise, and plunged into the gloom and damp of this receptacle for vagabonds, struck an instant chill upon the Arethusa's blood. Now see in how small a matter a hardship may consist: the floor was exceedingly uneven underfoot, with the very spade-marks, I suppose, of the labourers who dug the foundations of the barrack; and what with the poor twilight and the irregular surface, walking was impossible. The caged author resisted for a good while; but the chill of the place struck deeper and deeper; and at length, with such reluctance as you may fancy, he was driven to climb upon the bed and wrap himself in the public covering. There, then, he lay upon the verge of shivering, plunged in semi-darkness, wound in a garment whose touch he dreaded like the plague, and (in a spirit far removed from resignation) telling the roll of the insults he had just received. These are not circumstances favourable to the muse.

Meantime (to look at the upper surface where the sun was still shining and the guns of sportsmen were still noisy through the tufted plain) the Cigarette was drawing near at his more philosophic pace. In those days of liberty and health he was the constant partner of the Arethusa, and had ample opportunity to share in that gentleman's disfavour with the police. Many a bitter bowl had he partaken of with that disastrous comrade. He was himself a man born to float easily through life, his face and manner artfully recommending him to all. There was but one suspicious circumstance he could not carry off, and that was his companion. He will not readily forget the Commissary in what is ironically called the free town of Frankfort-on-the-Main; nor the Franco-Belgian frontier; nor the inn at La Fère; last, but not least, he is pretty certain to remember Châtillon-sur-Loire.

At the town entry, the gendarme culled him like a wayside flower; and a moment later, two persons, in a high state of surprise, were confronted in the Commissary's office. For if the Cigarette was surprised to be arrested, the Commissary was no less taken aback by the appearance and appointments of his captive. Here was a man about whom there could be no mistake: a man of an unquestionable and unassailable manner, in apple-pie order, dressed not with neatness merely but elegance, ready with his passport, at a word, and well supplied with money: a man the Commissary would have doffed his hat to on chance upon the highway; and this *beau*

cavalier unblushingly claimed the Arethusa for his comrade! The conclusion of the interview was foregone;
of its humours, I remember only one. "Baronet?" demanded the magistrate, glancing up from the passport.
" Alors, monsieur, vous êtes le fils d'un baron?" And
when the Cigarette (his one mistake throughout the interview) denied the soft impeachment, *"Alors,"* from
the Commissary, *" ce n'est pas votre passeport!"* But
these were ineffectual thunders; he never dreamed of
laying hands upon the Cigarette; presently he fell into
a mood of unrestrained admiration, gloating over the
contents of the knapsack, commending our friend's
tailor. Ah, what an honoured guest was the Commissary entertaining! what suitable clothes he wore for the
warm weather! what beautiful maps, what an attractive
work of history he carried in his knapsack! You are to
understand there was now but one point of difference
between them: what was to be done with the Arethusa?
the Cigarette demanding his release, the Commissary
still claiming him as the dungeon's own. Now it chanced
that the Cigarette had passed some years of his life in
Egypt, where he had made acquaintance with two very
bad things, cholera morbus and pashas; and in the eye
of the Commissary, as he fingered the volume of Michelet, it seemed to our traveller there was something
Turkish. I pass over this lightly; it is highly possible
there was some misunderstanding, highly possible that
the Commissary (charmed with his visitor) supposed
the attraction to be mutual and took for an act of growing friendship what the Cigarette himself regarded as a
bribe. And at any rate, was there ever a bribe more
singular than an odd volume of Michelet's history? The

work was promised him for the morrow, before our departure; and presently after, either because he had his price, or to show that he was not the man to be behind in friendly offices—*" Eh bien,"* he said, *" je suppose qu'il faut lâcher votre camarade."* And he tore up that feast of humour, the unfinished *procès-verbal.* Ah, if he had only torn up instead the Arethusa's roundels! There were many works burnt at Alexandria, there are many treasured in the British Museum, that I could better spare than the *procès-verbal* of Châtillon. Poor bubuckled Commissary! I begin to be sorry that he never had his Michelet: perceiving in him fine human traits, a broad-based stupidity, a gusto in his magisterial functions, a taste for letters, a ready admiration for the admirable. And if he did not admire the Arethusa, he was not alone in that.

To the imprisoned one, shivering under the public covering, there came suddenly a noise of bolts and chains. He sprang to his feet, ready to welcome a companion in calamity; and instead of that, the door was flung wide, the friendly gendarme appeared above in the strong daylight, and with a magnificent gesture (being probably a student of the drama) — *"Vous êtes libre !"* he said. None too soon for the Arethusa. I doubt if he had been half an hour imprisoned; but by the watch in a man's brain (which was the only watch he carried) he should have been eight times longer; and he passed forth with ecstasy up the cellar stairs into the healing warmth of the afternoon sun; and the breath of the earth came as sweet as a cow's into his nostril; and he heard again (and could have laughed for pleasure) the concord of delicate noises that we call the hum of life.

And here it might be thought that my history ended; but not so, this was an act-drop and not the curtain. Upon what followed in front of the barrack, since there was a lady in the case, I scruple to expatiate. The wife of the Maréchal-des-logis was a handsome woman, and yet the Arethusa was not sorry to be gone from her society. Something of her image, cool as a peach on that hot afternoon, still lingers in his memory: yet more of her conversation. "You have there a very fine parlour," said the poor gentleman. —"Ah," said Madame la Maréchale (des-logis), "you are very well acquainted with such parlours!" And you should have seen with what a hard and scornful eye she measured the vagabond before her! I do not think he ever hated the Commissary; but before that interview was at an end, he hated Madame la Maréchale. His passion (as I am led to understand by one who was present) stood confessed in a burning eye, a pale cheek, and a trembling utterance; Madame meanwhile tasting the joys of the matador, goading him with barbed words and staring him coldly down.

It was certainly good to be away from this lady, and better still to sit down to an excellent dinner in the inn. Here, too, the despised travellers scraped acquaintance with their next neighbour, a gentleman of these parts, returned from the day's sport, who had the good taste to find pleasure in their society. The dinner at an end, the gentleman proposed the acquaintance should be ripened in the café.

The café was crowded with sportsmen conclamantly explaining to each other and the world the smallness of their bags. About the centre of the room, the Cigarette and the Arethusa sat with their new acquaintance; a trio very well pleased, for the travellers (after their late experience) were greedy of consideration, and their sportsman rejoiced in a pair of patient listeners. Suddenly the glass door flew open with a crash; the Maréchal-des-logis appeared in the interval, gorgeously belted and befrogged, entered without salutation, strode up the room with a clang of spurs and weapons, and disappeared through a door at the far end. Close at his heels followed the Arethusa's gendarme of the afternoon, imitating, with a nice shade of difference, the imperial bearing of his chief; only, as he passed, he struck lightly with his open hand on the shoulder of his late captive, and with that ringing, dramatic utterance of which he had the secret—" *Suivez!* " said he.

The arrest of the members, the oath of the Tennis Court, the signing of the declaration of independence, Mark Antony's oration, all the brave scenes of history, I conceive as having been not unlike that evening in the café at Châtillon. Terror breathed upon the assembly. A moment later, when the Arethusa had followed his recaptors into the farther part of the house, the Cigarette found himself alone with his coffee in a ring of empty chairs and tables, all the lusty sportsmen huddled into corners, all their clamorous voices hushed in whispering, all their eyes shooting at him furtively as at a leper.

And the Arethusa? Well, he had a long, sometimes a trying, interview in the back kitchen. The Maréchal-des-logis, who was a very handsome man, and I believe both intelligent and honest, had no clear opinion on the case. He thought the Commissary had done wrong, but he did not wish to get his subordinates into trouble; and he proposed this, that, and the other, to all of which the Arethusa (with a growing sense of his position) demurred.

"In short," suggested the Arethusa, "you want to wash your hands of further responsibility? Well, then, let me go to Paris."

The Maréchal-des-logis looked at his watch.

"You may leave," said he, "by the ten o'clock train for Paris."

And at noon the next day the travellers were telling their misadventure in the dining-room at Siron's.

V. RANDOM MEMORIES

I. THE COAST OF FIFE

MANY writers have vigorously described the pains of the first day or the first night at school; to a boy of any enterprise, I believe, they are more often agreeably exciting. Misery — or at least misery unrelieved — is confined to another period, to the days of suspense and the " dreadful looking-for" of departure; when the old life is running to an end, and the new life, with its new interests, not yet begun; and to the pain of an imminent parting, there is added the unrest of a state of conscious pre-existence. The area-railings, the beloved shop-window, the smell of semi-suburban tanpits, the song of the church-bells upon a Sunday, the thin, high voices of compatriot children in a playing-field — what a sudden, what an overpowering pathos breathes to him from each familiar circumstance! The assaults of sorrow come not from within, as it seems to him, but from without. I was proud and glad to go to school; had I been let alone, I could have borne up like any hero; but there was around me, in all my native town, a conspiracy of lamentation: " Poor little boy, he is going away — unkind little boy, he is going to leave us "; so the unspoken burthen followed me as I went, with yearning and reproach. And at length, one melancholy afternoon in the early autumn, and at a place where it seems to me, looking back, it must be always autumn and generally Sunday, there came suddenly upon the face of all I saw — the long empty road, the lines of the tall houses, the church upon the hill, the woody hillside garden — a look of such a piercing sadness that my heart died; and seating myself on a door-step, I shed tears of miserable sympathy. A benevolent cat cumbered me the while with consolations — we two were alone in all that was visible of the London Road: two poor waifs who had each tasted sorrow — and she fawned upon the weeper, and gambolled for his entertainment, watching the effect, it seemed, with motherly eyes.

For the sake of the cat, God bless her! I confessed at home the story of my weakness; and so it comes about that I owed a certain journey, and the reader owes the present paper, to a cat in the London Road. It was judged, if I had thus brimmed over on the public highway, some change of scene was (in the medical sense) indicated; my father at the time was visiting the harbour lights of Scotland; and it was decided he should take me along with him around a portion of the shores of Fife; my first professional tour, my first journey in the complete character of man, without the help of petticoats.

The Kingdom of Fife (that royal province) may be observed by the curious on the map, occupying a tongue of land between the firths of Forth and Tay. It may be continually seen from many parts of Edinburgh (among the rest, from the windows of my father's house) dying away into the distance and the easterly *haar* with one smoky seaside town beyond another, or in winter printing on the gray heaven some glittering hill-tops. It has no beauty to recommend it, being a low, sea-salted, wind-vexed promontory; trees very rare, except (as common on the east coast) along the dens of rivers; the fields well cultivated, I understand, but not lovely to the eye. It is of the coast I speak: the interior may be the garden of Eden. History broods over that part of the world like the easterly haar. Even on the map, its long row of Gaelic place-names bear testimony to an old and settled race. Of these little towns, posted along the shore as close as sedges, each with its bit of harbour, its old weather-beaten church or public building, its flavour of decayed prosperity and decaying fish, not one but has its legend, quaint or tragic: Dunfermline, in whose royal towers the king may be still observed (in the ballad) drinking the blood-red wine; somnolent Inverkeithing, once the quarantine of Leith; Aberdour, hard by the monastic islet of Inchcolm, hard by Donibristle where the "bonny face was spoiled"; Burntisland where, when Paul Jones was off the coast, the Reverend Mr. Shirra had a table carried between tide-marks, and publicly prayed against the rover at the pitch of his voice and his broad lowland dialect; Kinghorn, where Alexander "brak's neckbane" and left Scotland to the English wars; Kirkcaldy, where the witches once prevailed extremely and sank tall ships and honest mariners in the North Sea; Dysart, famous —well famous at least to me for the Dutch ships that lay in its harbour, painted like toys and with pots of flowers and cages of song-birds in the cabin windows, and for one particular Dutch skipper who would sit all day in slippers on the break of the poop, smoking a

long German pipe; Wemyss (pronounce Weems) with
its bat-haunted caves, where the Chevalier Johnstone,
on his flight from Culloden, passed a night of superstitious terrors; Leven, a bald, quite modern place, sacred
to summer visitors, whence there has gone but yesterday the tall figure and the white locks of the last Englishman in Delhi, my uncle Dr. Balfour, who was still
walking his hospital rounds, while the troopers from
Meerut clattered and cried "Deen Deen" along the streets
of the imperial city, and Willoughby mustered his handful of heroes at the magazine, and the nameless brave
one in the telegraph office was perhaps already fingering his last despatch; and just a little beyond Leven,
Largo Law and the smoke of Largo town mounting
about its feet, the town of Alexander Selkirk, better
known under the name of Robinson Crusoe. So on,
the list might be pursued (only for private reasons,
which the reader will shortly have an opportunity to
guess) by St. Monance, and Pittenweem, and the two
Anstruthers, and Cellardyke, and Crail, where Primate
Sharpe was once a humble and innocent country minister: on to the heel of the land, to Fife Ness, overlooked
by a sea wood of matted elders and the quaint old man-
sion of Balcomie, itself overlooking but the breach or
the quiescence of the deep — the Carr Rock beacon rising close in front, and as night draws in, the star of the
Inchcape reef springing up on the one hand, and the
star of the May Island on the other, and farther off yet
a third and a greater on the craggy foreland of St. Abb's.
And but a little way round the corner of the land, imminent itself above the sea, stands the gem of the
province and the light of mediæval Scotland, St. An-

drews, where the great Cardinal Beaton held garrison against the world, and the second of the name and title perished (as you may read in Knox's jeering narrative) under the knives of true-blue Protestants, and to this day (after so many centuries) the current voice of the professor is not hushed.

Here it was that my first tour of inspection began, early on a bleak easterly morning. There was a crashing run of sea upon the shore, I recollect, and my father and the man of the harbour light must sometimes raise their voices to be audible. Perhaps it is from this circumstance, that I always imagine St. Andrews to be an ineffectual seat of learning, and the sound of the east wind and the bursting surf to linger in its drowsy classrooms and confound the utterance of the professor, until teacher and taught are alike drowned in oblivion, and only the sea-gull beats on the windows and the draught of the sea-air rustles in the pages of the open lecture. But upon all this, and the romance of St. Andrews in general, the reader must consult the works of Mr. Andrew Lang; who has written of it but the other day in his dainty prose and with his incommunicable humour, and long ago in one of his best poems, with grace, and local truth and a note of unaffected pathos. Mr. Lang knows all about the romance, I say, and the educational advantages, but I doubt if he had turned his attention to the harbour lights; and it may be news even to him, that in the year 1863 their case was pitiable. Hanging about with the east wind humming in my teeth, and my hands (I make no doubt) in my pockets, I looked for the first time upon that tragi-comedy of the visiting engineer which I have seen so often re-enacted on a more important stage. Eighty years ago, I find my grandfather writing: "It is the most painful thing that can occur to me to have a correspondence of this kind with any of the keepers, and when I come to the Light House, instead of having the satisfaction to meet them with approbation and welcome their Family, it is distressing when one is obliged to put on a most angry countenance and demeanour." This painful obligation has been hereditary in my race. I have myself, on a perfectly amateur and unauthorised inspection of Turnberry Point, bent my brows upon the keeper on the question of storm-panes; and felt a keen pang of self-reproach, when we went down stairs again and I found he was making a coffin for his infant child; and then regained my equanimity with the thought that I had done the man a service, and when the proper inspector came, he would be readier with his panes. The human race is perhaps credited with more duplicity than it deserves. The visitation of a lighthouse at least is a business of the most transparent nature. As soon as the boat grates on the shore, and the keepers step forward in their uniformed coats, the very slouch of the fellows' shoulders tells their story, and the engineer may begin at once to assume his "angry countenance." Certainly the brass of the handrail will be clouded; and if the brass be not immaculate, certainly all will be to match — the reflectors scratched, the spare lamp unready, the storm-panes in the storehouse. If a light is not rather more than middling good, it will be radically bad. Mediocrity (except in literature) appears to be unattainable by man. But of course the unfortunate of St. Andrews was only an amateur, he was not in the Service, he had no uniform coat, he was (I believe) a plumber by his trade and stood (in the mediæval phrase) quite out of the danger of my father; but he had a painful interview for all that, and perspired extremely.

From St. Andrews, we drove over Magus Muir. My father had announced we were "to post," and the phrase called up in my hopeful mind visions of topboots and the pictures in Rowlandson's *Dance of Death;* but it was only a jingling cab that came to the inn door, such as I had driven in a thousand times at the low price of one shilling on the streets of Edinburgh. Beyond this disappointment, I remember nothing of that drive. It is a road I have often travelled, and of not one of these journeys do I remember any single trait. The fact has not been suffered to encroach on the truth of the imagination. I still see Magus Muir two hundred years ago; a desert place, quite uninclosed; in the midst, the primate's carriage fleeing at the gallop; the assassins loose-reined in pursuit, Burley Balfour, pistol in hand, among the first. No scene of history has ever written itself so deeply on my mind; not because Balfour, that questionable zealot, was an ancestral cousin of my own; not because of the pleadings of the victim and his daughter; not even because of the live bum-bee that flew out of Sharpe's 'bacco-box, thus clearly indicating his complicity with Satan; nor merely because, as it was after all a crime of a fine religious flavour, it figured in Sunday books and afforded a grateful relief from *Ministering Children* or the *Memoirs of Mrs. Katharine Winslowe.* The figure that always fixed my attention is that of Hackston of Rathillet, sitting in the saddle with his cloak about his mouth, and through all that long, bungling, vociferous hurly-burly, revolving privately a case of conscience. He would take no hand in the deed, because he had a private spite against the victim, and "that action" must be sullied with no suggestion of a worldly motive; on the other hand, "that action," in itself was highly justified, he had cast in his lot with "the actors," and he must stay there, inactive but publicly sharing the responsibility. "You are a gentleman — you will protect me!" cried the wounded old man, crawling towards him. "I will never lay a hand on you," said Hackston, and put his cloak about his mouth. It is an old temptation with me, to pluck away that cloak and see the face — to open that bosom and to read the heart. With incomplete romances about Hackston, the drawers of my youth were lumbered. I read him up in every printed book that I could lay my hands on. I even dug among the Wodrow manuscripts, sitting shame-faced in the very room where my hero had been tortured two centuries before, and keenly conscious of my youth in the midst of other and (as I fondly thought) more gifted students. All was vain: that he had passed a riotous nonage, that he was a zealot, that he twice displayed (compared with his grotesque companions) some tincture of soldierly resolution and even of military common sense, and that he figured memorably in the scene on Magus Muir, so much and no more could I make out. But whenever I cast my eyes backward, it is to see him like a landmark on the plains of history, sitting with his cloak about his mouth, inscrutable. How small a thing creates an immortality! I do not think he can have been a man entirely commonplace; but had he not thrown his cloak about his mouth, or had the witnesses forgot to chronicle the action, he would not thus have haunted the imagination of my boyhood, and to-day he would scarce delay me for a paragraph. An incident, at once romantic and dramatic, which at once awakes the judgment and makes a picture for the eye, how little do we realise its perdurable power! Perhaps no one does so but the author, just as none but he appreciates the influence of jingling words; so that he looks on upon life, with something of a covert smile, seeing people led by what they fancy to be thoughts and what are really the accustomed artifices of his own trade, or roused by what they take to be principles and are really picturesque effects. In a pleasant book about a school-class club, Colonel Fergusson has recently told a little anecdote. A "Philosophical Society" was formed by some Academy boys — among them, Colonel Fergusson himself, Fleeming Jenkin, and Andrew Wilson, the Christian Buddhist and author of *The Abode of Snow*. Before these learned pundits, one member laid the following ingenious problem: "What would be the result of putting a pound of potassium in a pot of porter?" "I should think there would be a number of interesting bi-products," said a smatterer at my elbow; but for me the tale itself has a bi-product, and stands as a type of much that is most human. For this inquirer who conceived himself to burn with a zeal entirely chemical, was really immersed in a design of a quite different nature; unconsciously to his own recently breeched intelligence, he was engaged in literature. Putting, pound, potassium, pot, porter; initial p, mediant t — that was his idea, poor little boy! So with politics and that which

excites men in the present, so with history and that
which rouses them in the past: there lie at the root of
what appears, most serious unsuspected elements.

The triple town of Anstruther Wester, Anstruther
Easter, and Cellardyke, all three Royal Burghs — or two
Royal Burghs and a less distinguished suburb, I forget
which — lies continuously along the seaside, and boasts
of either two or three separate parish churches, and
either two or three separate harbours. These ambigui-
ties are painful; but the fact is (although it argue me
uncultured), I am but poorly posted upon Cellardyke.
My business lay in the two Anstruthers. A tricklet of
a stream divides them, spanned by a bridge; and over
the bridge at the time of my knowledge, the celebrated
Shell House stood outpost on the west. This had been
the residence of an agreeable eccentric; during his fond
tenancy, he had illustrated the outer walls, as high (if I
remember rightly) as the roof, with elaborate patterns
and pictures, and snatches of verse in the vein of *exegi
monumentum ;* shells and pebbles, artfully contrasted
and conjoined, had been his medium; and I like to think
of him standing back upon the bridge, when all was
finished, drinking in the general effect and (like Gibbon)
already lamenting his employment.

The same bridge saw another sight in the seven-
teenth century. Mr. Thomson, the "curat" of Anstruther Easter, was a man highly obnoxious to the
devout: in the first place, because he was a "curat";
in the second place, because he was a person of irregular
and scandalous life; and in the third place, because he
was generally suspected of dealings with the Enemy of
Man. These three disqualifications, in the popular lit-

erature of the time, go hand in hand; but the end of
Mr. Thomson was a thing quite by itself, and in the
proper phrase, a manifest judgment. He had been at a
friend's house in Anstruther Wester, where (and elsewhere, I suspect,) he had partaken of the bottle; indeed, to put the thing in our cold modern way, the
reverend gentleman was on the brink of *delirium tre-
mens.* It was a dark night, it seems; a little lassie
came carrying a lantern to fetch the curate home; and
away they went down the street of Anstruther Wester,
the lantern swinging a bit in the child's hand, the barred
lustre tossing up and down along the front of slumbering houses, and Mr. Thomson not altogether steady on
his legs nor (to all appearance) easy in his mind. The
pair had reached the middle of the bridge when (as I
conceive the scene) the poor tippler started in some base-
less fear and looked behind him; the child, already
shaken by the minister's strange behaviour, started also;
in so doing, she would jerk the lantern; and for the
space of a moment the lights and the shadows would
be all confounded. Then it was that to the unhinged
toper and the twittering child, a huge bulk of blackness
seemed to sweep down, to pass them close by as they
stood upon the bridge, and to vanish on the farther side
in the general darkness of the night. "Plainly the devil
came for Mr. Thomson!" thought the child. What
Mr. Thomson thought himself, we have no ground of
knowledge; but he fell upon his knees in the midst of
the bridge like a man praying. On the rest of the journey to the manse, history is silent; but when they came
to the door, the poor caitiff, taking the lantern from the
child, looked upon her with so lost a countenance that

her little courage died within her, and she fled home screaming to her parents. Not a soul would venture out; all that night, the minister dwelt alone with his terrors in the manse; and when the day dawned, and men made bold to go about the streets, they found the devil had come indeed for Mr. Thomson.

This manse of Anstruther Easter has another and a more cheerful association. It was early in the morning, about a century before the days of Mr. Thomson, that his predecessor was called out of bed to welcome a Grandee of Spain, the Duke of Medina Sidonia, just landed in the harbour underneath. But sure there was never seen a more decayed grandee; sure there was never a duke welcomed from a stranger place of exile. Half-way between Orkney and Shetland, there lies a certain isle; on the one hand the Atlantic, on the other the North Sea, bombard its pillared cliffs; sore-eyed, short-living, inbred fishers and their families herd in its few huts; in the graveyard pieces of wreck-wood stand for monuments; there is nowhere a more inhospitable spot. *Belle-Isle-en-Mer* — Fair-Isle-at-Sea — that is a name that has always rung in my mind's ear like music; but the only "Fair Isle" on which I ever set my foot, was this unhomely, rugged turret-top of submarine sierras. Here, when his ship was broken, my lord Duke joyfully got ashore; here for long months he and certain of his men were harboured; and it was from this durance that he landed at last to be welcomed (as well as such a papist deserved, no doubt) by the godly incumbent of Anstruther Easter; and after the Fair Isle, what a fine city must that have appeared! and after the island diet, what a hospitable spot the minister's table!

220

And yet he must have lived on friendly terms with his
outlandish hosts. For to this day there still survives a
relic of the long winter evenings when the sailors of the
great Armada crouched about the hearths of the Fair-
Islanders, the planks of their own lost galleon perhaps
lighting up the scene, and the gale and the surf that beat
about the coast contributing their melancholy voices.
All the folk of the north isles are great artificers of knitting: the Fair-Islanders alone dye their fabrics in the
Spanish manner. To this day, gloves and nightcaps,
innocently decorated, may be seen for sale in the Shetland warehouse at Edinburgh, or on the Fair Isle itself
in the catechist's house; and to this day, they tell the
story of the Duke of Medina Sidonia's adventure.

It would seem as if the Fair Isle had some attraction
for "persons of quality." When I landed there myself,
an elderly gentleman, unshaved, poorly attired, his
shoulders wrapped in a plaid, was seen walking to and
fro, with a book in his hand, upon the beach. He paid
no heed to our arrival, which we thought a strange thing
in itself; but when one of the officers of the *Pharos,*
passing narrowly by him, observed his book to be a
Greek Testament, our wonder and interest took a higher
flight. The catechist was cross-examined; he said the
gentleman had been put across some time before in Mr.
Bruce of Sumburgh's schooner, the only link between
the Fair Isle and the rest of the world; and that he held
services and was doing "good." So much came glibly
enough; but when pressed a little farther, the catechist
displayed embarrassment. A singular diffidence appeared upon his face: "They tell me," said he, in low
tones, "that he's a lord." And a lord he was; a peer

as soon as dinner was despatched, in a chamber scented with dry rose-leaves, drew in my chair to the table and proceeded to pour forth literature, at such a speed, and with such intimations of early death and immortality, as I now look back upon with wonder. Then it was that I wrote *Voces Fidelium,* a series of dramatic monologues in verse; then that I indited the bulk of a covenanting novel — like so many others, never finished. Late I sat into the night, toiling (as I thought) under the very dart of death, toiling to leave a memory behind me. I feel moved to thrust aside the curtain of the years, to hail that poor feverish idiot, to bid him go to bed and clap *Voces Fidelium* on the fire before he goes; so clear does he appear before me, sitting there between his candles in the rose-scented room and the late night; so ridiculous a picture (to my elderly wisdom) does the fool present! But he was driven to his bed at last without miraculous intervention; and the manner of his driving sets the last touch upon this eminently youthful business. The weather was then so warm that I must keep the windows open; the night without was populous with moths. As the late darkness deepened, my literary tapers beaconed forth more brightly; thicker and thicker came the dusty night-fliers, to gyrate for one brilliant instant round the flame and fall in agonies upon my paper. Flesh and blood could not endure the spectacle; to capture immortality was doubtless a noble enterprise, but not to capture it at such a cost of suffering; and out would go the candles, and off would I go to bed in the darkness, raging to think that the blow might fall on the morrow, and there was *Voces Fidelium* still incomplete. Well, the moths are all gone, and *Voces Fidelium* along with them; only the fool is still on hand and practises new follies.

Only one thing in connection with the harbour tempted me, and that was the diving, an experience I burned to taste of. But this was not to be, at least in Anstruther; and the subject involves a change of scene to the sub-arctic town of Wick. You can never have dwelt in a country more unsightly than that part of Caithness, the land faintly swelling, faintly falling, not a tree, not a hedgerow, the fields divided by single slate stones set upon their edge, the wind always singing in your ears and (down the long road that led nowhere) thrumming in the telegraph wires. Only as you approached the coast was there anything to stir the heart. The plateau broke down to the North Sea in formidable cliffs, the tall out-stacks rose like pillars ringed about with surf, the coves were over-brimmed with clamorous froth, the sea-birds screamed, the wind sang in the thyme on the cliff's edge; here and there, small ancient castles toppled on the brim; here and there, it was possible to dip into a dell of shelter, where you might lie and tell yourself you were a little warm, and hear (near at hand) the whin-pods bursting in the afternoon sun, and (farther off) the rumour of the turbulent sea. As for Wick itself, it is one of the meanest of man's towns, and situate certainly on the baldest of God's bays. It lives for herring, and a strange sight it is to see (of an afternoon) the heights of Pulteney blackened by seaward-looking fishers, as when a city crowds to a review — or, as when bees have swarmed, the ground is horrible with lumps and clusters; and a strange sight, and a beautiful, to see the fleet put silently out against a rising moon, fellow-men; standing there in their midst, but quite divorced from intercourse: a creature deaf and dumb, pathetically looking forth upon them from a climate of his own. Except that I could move and feel, I was like a man fallen in a catalepsy. But time was scarce given me to realise my isolation; the weights were hung upon my back and breast, the signal rope was thrust into my unresisting hand; and setting a twenty-pound foot upon the ladder, I began ponderously to descend.

Some twenty rounds below the platform, twilight fell. Looking up, I saw a low green heaven mottled with vanishing bells of white; looking around, except for the weedy spokes and shafts of the ladder, nothing but a green gloaming, somewhat opaque but very restful and delicious. Thirty rounds lower, I stepped off on the *pierres perdues* of the foundation; a dumb helmeted figure took me by the hand, and made a gesture (as I read it) of encouragement; and looking in at the creature's window, I beheld the face of Bain. There we were, hand to hand and (when it pleased us) eye to eye; and either might have burst himself with shouting, and not a whisper come to his companion's hearing. Each, in his own little world of air, stood incommunicably separate.

Bob had told me ere this a little tale, a five minutes' drama at the bottom of the sea, which at that moment possibly shot across my mind. He was down with another, settling a stone of the sea-wall. They had it well adjusted, Bob gave the signal, the scissors were slipped, the stone set home; and it was time to turn to something else. But still his companion remained bowed over the block like a mourner on a tomb, or only raised

228

himself to make absurd contortions and mysterious signs unknown to the vocabulary of the diver. There, then, these two stood for awhile, like the dead and the living; till there flashed a fortunate thought into Bob's mind, and he stooped, peered through the window of that other world, and beheld the face of its inhabitant wet with streaming tears. Ah! the man was in pain! And Bob, glancing downward, saw what was the trouble: the block had been lowered on the foot of that unfortunate — he was caught alive at the bottom of the sea under fifteen tons of rock.

That two men should handle a stone so heavy, even swinging in the scissors, may appear strange to the inexpert. These must bear in mind the great density of the water of the sea, and the surprising results of transplantation to that medium. To understand a little what these are, and how a man's weight, so far from being an encumbrance, is the very ground of his agility, was the chief lesson of my submarine experience. The knowledge came upon me by degrees. As I began to go forward with the hand of my estranged companion, a world of tumbled stones was visible, pillared with the weedy uprights of the staging: overhead, a flat roof of green: a little in front, the sea-wall, like an unfinished rampart. And presently in our upward progress, Bob motioned me to leap upon a stone; I looked to see if he were possibly in earnest, and he only signed to me the more imperiously. Now the block stood six feet high; it would have been quite a leap to me unencumbered; with the breast and back weights, and the twenty pounds upon each foot, and the staggering load of the helmet, the thing was out of reason. I laughed aloud in my tomb; and to prove to Bob how far he was astray, I gave a little impulse from my toes. Up I soared like a bird, my companion soaring at my side. As high as to the stone, and then higher, I pursued my impotent and empty flight. Even when the strong arm of Bob had checked my shoulders, my heels continued their ascent; so that I blew out sideways like an autumn leaf, and must be hauled in, hand over hand, as sailors haul in the slack of a sail, and propped upon my feet again like an intoxicated sparrow. Yet a little higher on the foundation, and we began to be affected by the bottom of the swell, running there like a strong breeze of wind. Or so I must suppose; for, safe in my cushion of air, I was conscious of no impact; only swayed idly like a weed, and was now borne helplessly abroad, and now swiftly — and yet with dream-like gentleness — impelled against my guide. So does a child's balloon divagate upon the currents of the air, and touch and slide off again from every obstacle. So must have ineffectually swung, so resented their inefficiency, those light crowds that followed the Star of Hades, and uttered exiguous voices in the land beyond Cocytus.

There was something strangely exasperating, as well as strangely wearying, in these uncommanded evolutions. It is bitter to return to infancy, to be supported, and directed, and perpetually set upon your feet, by the hand of someone else. The air besides, as it is supplied to you by the busy millers on the platform, closes the eustachian tubes and keeps the neophyte perpetually swallowing, till his throat is grown so dry that he can swallow no longer. And for all these reasons — although I had a fine, dizzy, muddle-headed joy in my surround-

ings, and longed, and tried, and always failed, to lay
hands on the fish that darted here and there about me,
swift as humming-birds—yet I fancy I was rather relieved than otherwise when Bain brought me back to
the ladder and signed to me to mount. And there was
one more experience before me even then. Of a sudden, my ascending head passed into the trough of a
swell. Out of the green, I shot at once into a glory of
rosy, almost of sanguine light—the multitudinous seas
incarnadined, the heaven above a vault of crimson.
And then the glory faded into the hard, ugly daylight
of a Caithness autumn, with a low sky, a gray sea, and
a whistling wind.

Bob Bain had five shillings for his trouble, and I had
done what I desired. It was one of the best things I
got from my education as an engineer: of which however, as a way of life, I wish to speak with sympathy.
It takes a man into the open air; it keeps him hanging
about harbour-sides, which is the richest form of idling;
it carries him to wild islands; it gives him a taste of the
genial dangers of the sea; it supplies him with dexteri-
ties to exercise; it makes demands upon his ingenuity;
it will go far to cure him of any taste (if ever he had
one) for the miserable life of cities. And when it has
done so, it carries him back and shuts him in an office!
From the roaring skerry and the wet thwart of the
tossing boat, he passes to the stool and desk; and with
a memory full of ships, and seas, and perilous head-
lands, and the shining pharos, he must apply his long-
sighted eyes to the petty niceties of drawing, or measure
his inaccurate mind with several pages of consecutive
figures. He is a wise youth, to be sure, who can bal-

ance one part of genuine life against two parts of drudgery between four walls, and for the sake of the one, manfully accept the other.

Wick was scarce an eligible place of stay. But how much better it was to hang in the cold wind upon the pier, to go down with Bob Bain among the roots of the staging, to be all day in a boat coiling a wet rope and shouting orders — not always very wise — than to be warm and dry, and dull, and dead-alive, in the most comfortable office. And Wick itself had in those days a note of originality. It may have still, but I misdoubt it much. The old minister of Keiss would not preach, in these degenerate times, for an hour and a half upon the clock. The gipsies must be gone from their caverns; where you might see, from the mouth, the women tending their fire, like Meg Merrilies, and the men sleeping off their coarse potations; and where in winter gales, the surf would beleaguer them closely, bursting in their very door. A traveller to-day upon the Thurso coach would scarce observe a little cloud of smoke among the moorlands, and be told, quite openly, it marked a private still. He would not indeed make that journey, for there is now no Thurso coach. And even if he could, one little thing that happened to me could never happen to him, or not with the same trenchancy of contrast.

We had been upon the road all evening; the coach-top was crowded with Lews fishers going home, scarce anything but Gaelic had sounded in my ears; and our way had lain throughout over a moorish country very northern to behold. Latish at night, though it was still broad day in our subarctic latitude, we came down upon the shores of the roaring Pentland Firth, that grave of mariners; on one hand, the cliffs of Dunnet Head ran seaward; in front was the little bare, white town of Castleton, its streets full of blowing sand; nothing beyond, but the North Islands, the great deep, and the perennial ice-fields of the Pole. And here, in the last imaginable place, there sprang up young outlandish voices and a chatter of some foreign speech; and I saw, pursuing the coach with its load of Hebridean fishers — as they had pursued *vetturini* up the passes of the Apennines or perhaps along the grotto under Virgil's tomb — two little dark-eyed, white-toothed Italian vagabonds, of twelve to fourteen years of age, one with a hurdy-gurdy, the other with a cage of white mice. The coach passed on, and their small Italian chatter died in the distance; and I was left to marvel how they had wandered into that country, and how they fared in it, and what they thought of it, and when (if ever) they should see again the silver wind-breaks run among the olives, and the stone-pine stand guard upon Etruscan sepulchres.

Upon any American, the strangeness of this incident is somewhat lost. For as far back as he goes in his own land, he will find some alien camping there; the Cornish miner, the French or Mexican half-blood, the negro in the South, these are deep in the woods and far among the mountains. But in an old, cold, and rugged country such as mine, the days of immigration are long at an end; and away up there, which was at that time far beyond the northernmost extreme of railways, hard upon the shore of that ill-omened strait of whirlpools, in a land of moors where no stranger came, unless it should be a sportsman to shoot grouse or an antiquary to decipher runes, the presence of these small pedestrians struck the mind as though a bird-of-paradise had risen from the heather or an albatross come fishing in the bay of Wick. They were as strange to their surroundings as my lordly evangelist or the old Spanish grandee on the Fair Isle.

VII. THE LANTERN-BEARERS

I

THESE boys congregated every autumn about a certain easterly fisher-village, where they tasted in a high degree the glory of existence. The place was created seemingly on purpose for the diversion of young gentlemen. A street or two of houses, mostly red and many of them tiled; a number of fine trees clustered about the manse and the kirkyard, and turning the chief street into a shady alley; many little gardens more than usually bright with flowers; nets a-drying, and fisher-wives scolding in the backward parts; a smell of fish, a genial smell of seaweed; whiffs of blowing sand at the street-corners; shops with golf-balls and bottled lollipops; another shop with penny pickwicks (that remarkable cigar) and the *London Journal,* dear to me for its startling pictures, and a few novels, dear for their suggestive names: such, as well as memory serves me, were the ingredients of the town. These, you are to conceive posted on a spit between two sandy bays, and sparsely flanked with villas — enough for the boys to lodge in with their subsidiary parents, not enough (not yet enough) to cocknify the scene: a haven in the rocks in front: in front of that, a file of gray islets: to the left, endless links and sand wreaths, a wilderness of hiding-holes, alive with popping rabbits and soaring gulls: to the right, a range of seaward crags, one rugged brow beyond another; the ruins of a mighty and ancient fortress on the brink of one; coves between — now charmed into sunshine quiet, now whistling with wind and clamorous with bursting surges; the dens and sheltered hollows redolent of thyme and southernwood, the air at the cliff's edge brisk and clean and pungent of the sea — in front of all, the Bass Rock, tilted seaward like a doubtful bather, the surf ringing it with white, the solan-geese hanging round its summit like a great and glittering smoke. This choice piece of seaboard was sacred, besides, to the wrecker; and the Bass, in the eye of fancy, still flew the colours of King James; and in the ear of fancy the arches of Tantallon still rang with horseshoe iron, and echoed to the commands of Bell-the-Cat.

There was nothing to mar your days, if you were a boy summering in that part, but the embarrassment of pleasure. You might golf if you wanted; but I seem to have been better employed. You might secrete yourself in the Lady's Walk, a certain sunless dingle of elders, all mossed over by the damp as green as grass, and dotted here and there by the streamside with roofless walls, the cold homes of anchorites. To fit themselves for life, and with a special eye to acquire the art of smoking, it was even common for the boys to harbour there; and you might have seen a single penny pickwick, honestly shared in lengths with a blunt knife, bestrew the glen with these apprentices. Again, you might join our fishing parties, where we sat perched as thick as solan-geese, a covey of little anglers, boy and

girl, angling over each other's heads, to the much entan-
glement of lines and loss of podleys and consequent shrill
recrimination — shrill as the geese themselves. Indeed,
had that been all, you might have done this often; but
though fishing be a fine pastime, the podley is scarce
to be regarded as a dainty for the table; and it was a
point of honour that a boy should eat all that he had
taken. Or again, you might climb the Law, where the
whale's jawbone stood landmark in the buzzing wind,
and behold the face of many counties, and the smoke
and spires of many towns, and the sails of distant ships.
You might bathe, now in the flaws of fine weather,
that we pathetically call our summer, now in a gale of
wind, with the sand scourging your bare hide, your
clothes thrashing abroad from underneath their guardian stone, the froth of the great breakers casting you
headlong ere it had drowned your knees. Or you might
explore the tidal rocks, above all in the ebb of springs,
when the very roots of the hills were for the nonce
discovered; following my leader from one group to
another, groping in slippery tangle for the wreck of
ships, wading in pools after the abominable creatures of
the sea, and ever with an eye cast backward on the
march of the tide and the menaced line of your retreat.
And then you might go Crusoeing, a word that covers
all extempore eating in the open air: digging perhaps a
house under the margin of the links, kindling a fire of
the sea-ware, and cooking apples there — if they were
truly apples, for I sometimes suppose the merchant must
have played us off with some inferior and quite local
fruit, capable of resolving, in the neighbourhood of
fire, into mere sand and smoke and iodine; or per-

haps pushing to Tantallon, you might lunch on sandwiches and visions in the grassy court, while the wind
hummed in the crumbling turrets; or clambering along
the coast, eat geans[1] (the worst, I must suppose, in
Christendom) from an adventurous gean tree that had
taken root under a cliff, where it was shaken with an
ague of east wind, and silvered after gales with salt,
and grew so foreign among its bleak surroundings that
to eat of its produce was an adventure in itself.

There are mingled some dismal memories with so
many that were joyous. Of the fisher-wife, for instance,
who had cut her throat at Canty Bay; and of how I ran
with the other children to the top of the Quadrant, and
beheld a posse of silent people escorting a cart, and on
the cart, bound in a chair, her throat bandaged, and the
bandage all bloody — horror! — the fisher-wife herself,
who continued thenceforth to hag-ride my thoughts,
and even to-day (as I recall the scene) darkens daylight.
She was lodged in the little old jail in the chief street;
but whether or no she died there, with a wise terror of
the worst, I never inquired. She had been tippling; it
was but a dingy tragedy; and it seems strange and hard
that, after all these years, the poor crazy sinner should
be still pilloried on her cart in the scrap-book of my
memory. Nor shall I readily forget a certain house in
the Quadrant where a visitor died, and a dark old woman continued to dwell alone with the dead body; nor
how this old woman conceived a hatred to myself and
one of my cousins, and in the dread hour of the dusk,
as we were clambering on the garden-walls, opened a
window in that house of mortality and cursed us in a

---

[1] Wild cherries.

shrill voice and with a marrowy choice of language. It was a pair of very colourless urchins that fled down the lane from this remarkable experience! But I recall with a more doubtful sentiment, compounded out of fear and exultation, the coil of equinoctial tempests; trumpeting squalls, scouring flaws of rain; the boats with their reefed lugsails scudding for the harbour mouth, where danger lay, for it was hard to make when the wind had any east in it; the wives clustered with blowing shawls at the pier-head, where (if fate was against them) they might see boat and husband and sons — their whole wealth and their whole family — engulfed under their eyes; and (what I saw but once) a troop of neighbours forcing such an unfortunate homeward, and she squalling and battling in their midst, a figure scarcely human, a tragic Mænad.

These are things that I recall with interest; but what my memory dwells upon the most, I have been all this while withholding. It was a sport peculiar to the place, and indeed to a week or so of our two months' holiday there. Maybe it still flourishes in its native spot; for boys and their pastimes are swayed by periodic forces inscrutable to man; so that tops and marbles reappear in their due season, regular like the sun and moon; and the harmless art of knucklebones has seen the fall of the Roman empire and the rise of the United States. It may still flourish in its native spot, but nowhere else, I am persuaded; for I tried myself to introduce it on Tweedside, and was defeated lamentably; its charm being quite local, like a country wine that cannot be exported.

The idle manner of it was this:—

Toward the end of September, when school-time was drawing near and the nights were already black, we would begin to sally from our respective villas, each equipped with a tin bull's-eye lantern. The thing was so well known that it had worn a rut in the commerce of Great Britain; and the grocers, about the due time, began to garnish their windows with our particular brand of luminary. We wore them buckled to the waist upon a cricket belt, and over them, such was the rigour of the game, a buttoned top-coat. They smelled noisomely of blistered tin; they never burned aright, though they would always burn our fingers; their use was naught; the pleasure of them merely fanciful; and yet a boy with a bull's-eye under his top-coat asked for nothing more. The fishermen used lanterns about their boats, and it was from them, I suppose, that we had got the hint; but theirs were not bull's-eyes, nor did we ever play at being fishermen. The police carried them at their belts, and we had plainly copied them in that; yet we did not pretend to be policemen. Burglars, indeed, we may have had some haunting thoughts of; and we had certainly an eye to past ages when lanterns were more common, and to certain story-books in which we had found them to figure very largely. But take it for all in all, the pleasure of the thing was substantive; and to be a boy with a bull's-eye under his top-coat was good enough for us.

When two of these asses met, there would be an anxious "Have you got your lantern?" and a gratified "Yes!" That was the shibboleth, and very needful too; for, as it was the rule to keep our glory contained, none could recognise a lantern-bearer, unless (like the pole-cat) by the smell. Four or five would sometimes climb into the belly of a ten-man lugger, with nothing but the thwarts above them — for the cabin was usually locked, or choose out some hollow of the links where the wind might whistle overhead. There the coats would be unbuttoned and the bull's-eyes discovered; and in the chequering glimmer, under the huge windy hall of the night, and cheered by a rich steam of toasting tinware, these fortunate young gentlemen would crouch together in the cold sand of the links or on the scaly bilges of the fishing-boat, and delight themselves with inappropriate talk. Woe is me that I may not give some specimens — some of their foresights of life, or deep inquiries into the rudiments of man and nature, these were so fiery and so innocent, they were so richly silly, so romantically young. But the talk, at any rate, was but a condiment; and these gatherings themselves only accidents in the career of the lantern-bearer. The essence of this bliss was to walk by yourself in the black night; the slide shut, the top-coat buttoned; not a ray escaping, whether to conduct your footsteps or to make your glory public: a mere pillar of darkness in the dark; and all the while, deep down in the privacy of your fool's heart, to know you had a bull's-eye at your belt, and to exult and sing over the knowledge.

II

It is said that a poet has died young in the breast of the most stolid. It may be contended, rather, that this (somewhat minor) bard in almost every case survives, and is the spice of life to his possessor. Justice is not

done to the versatility and the unplumbed childishness
of man's imagination. His life from without may seem
but a rude mound of mud; there will be some golden
chamber at the heart of it, in which he dwells delighted;
and for as dark as his pathway seems to the observer,
he will have some kind of a bull's-eye at his belt.

It would be hard to pick out a career more cheerless
than that of Dancer, the miser, as he figures in the " Old
Bailey Reports," a prey to the most sordid persecutions,
the butt of his neighbourhood, betrayed by his hired
man, his house beleaguered by the impish school-boy,
and he himself grinding and fuming and impotently
fleeing to the law against these pin-pricks. You marvel
at first that any one should willingly prolong a life so
destitute of charm and dignity; and then you call to
memory that had he chosen, had he ceased to be a
miser, he could have been freed at once from these
trials, and might have built himself a castle and gone es-
corted by a squadron. For the love of more recondite
joys, which we cannot estimate, which, it may be, we
should envy, the man had willingly foregone both comfort and consideration. "His mind to him a kingdom
was"; and sure enough, digging into that mind, which
seems at first a dust-heap, we unearth some priceless
jewels. For Dancer must have had the love of power
and the disdain of using it, a noble character in itself;
disdain of many pleasures, a chief part of what is commonly called wisdom; disdain of the inevitable end, that
finest trait of mankind; scorn of men's opinions, another
element of virtue; and at the back of all, a conscience just
like yours and mine, whining like a cur, swindling like
a thimble-rigger, but still pointing (there or thereabout)

to some conventional standard. Here were a cabinet portrait to which Hawthorne perhaps had done justice; and yet not Hawthorne either, for he was mildly minded, and it lay not in him to create for us that throb of the miser's pulse, his fretful energy of gusto, his vast arms of ambition clutching in he knows not what: insatiable, insane, a god with a muck-rake. Thus, at least, looking in the bosom of the miser, consideration detects the poet in the full tide of life, with more, indeed, of the poetic fire than usually goes to epics; and tracing that mean man about his cold hearth, and to and fro in his discomfortable house, spies within him a blazing bonfire of delight. And so with others, who do not live by bread alone, but by some cherished and perhaps fantastic pleasure; who are meat salesmen to the external eye, and possibly to themselves are Shakespeares, Napoleons, or Beethovens; who have not one virtue to rub against another in the field of active life, and yet perhaps, in the life of contemplation, sit with the saints. We see them on the street, and we can count their buttons; but heaven knows in what they pride themselves! heaven knows where they have set their treasure!

There is one fable that touches very near the quick of life: the fable of the monk who passed into the woods, heard a bird break into song, hearkened for a trill or two, and found himself on his return a stranger at his convent gates; for he had been absent fifty years, and of all his comrades there survived but one to recognise him. It is not only in the woods that this enchanter carols, though perhaps he is native there. He sings in the most doleful places. The miser hears him and chuckles, and the days are moments. With no more apparatus than an ill-smelling lantern I have evoked him on the naked links. All life that is not merely mechanical is spun out of two strands: seeking for that bird and hearing him. And it is just this that makes life so hard to value, and the delight of each so incommunicable. And just a knowledge of this, and a remembrance of those fortunate hours in which the bird has sung to us, that fills us with such wonder when we turn the pages of the realist. There, to be sure, we find a picture of life in so far as it consists of mud and of old iron, cheap desires and cheap fears, that which we are ashamed to remember and that which we are careless whether we forget; but of the note of that time-devouring nightingale we hear no news.

The case of these writers of romance is most obscure. They have been boys and youths; they have lingered outside the window of the beloved, who was then most probably writing to some one else; they have sat before a sheet of paper, and felt themselves mere continents of congested poetry, not one line of which would flow; they have walked alone in the woods, they have walked in cities under the countless lamps; they have been to sea, they have hated, they have feared, they have longed to knife a man, and maybe done it; the wild taste of life has stung their palate. Or, if you deny them all the rest, one pleasure at least they have tasted to the full — their books are there to prove it — the keen pleasure of successful literary composition. And yet they fill the globe with volumes, whose cleverness inspires me with despairing admiration, and whose consistent falsity to all I care to call existence, with despairing wrath. If I had no better hope than to continue to revolve among the dreary and petty businesses, and to be moved by the

paltry hopes and fears with which they surround and
animate their heroes, I declare I would die now. But
there has never an hour of mine gone quite so dully yet;
if it were spent waiting at a railway junction, I would
have some scattering thoughts, I could count some grains
of memory, compared to which the whole of one of these
romances seems but dross.

These writers would retort (if I take them properly)
that this was very true; that it was the same with themselves and other persons of (what they call) the artistic
temperament; that in this we were exceptional, and
should apparently be ashamed of ourselves; but that our
works must deal exclusively with (what they call) the
average man, who was a prodigious dull fellow, and
quite dead to all but the paltriest considerations. I accept the issue. We can only know others by ourselves.
The artistic temperament (a plague on the expression!)
does not make us different from our fellow-men, or it
would make us incapable of writing novels; and the
average man (a murrain on the word!) is just like you
and me, or he would not be average. It was Whitman
who stamped a kind of Birmingham sacredness upon
the latter phrase; but Whitman knew very well, and
showed very nobly, that the average man was full of
joys and full of a poetry of his own. And this harping
on life's dulness and man's meanness is a loud profession
of incompetence; it is one of two things: the cry of the
blind eye, *I cannot see,* or the complaint of the dumb
tongue, *I cannot utter.* To draw a life without delights
is to prove I have not realised it. To picture a man
without some sort of poetry — well, it goes near to
prove my case, for it shows an author may have little

enough. To see Dancer only as a dirty, old, small-minded, impotently fuming man, in a dirty house, besieged by Harrow boys, and probably beset by small attorneys, is to show myself as keen an observer as . . . the Harrow boys. But these young gentlemen (with a more becoming modesty) were content to pluck Dancer by the coat-tails; they did not suppose they had surprised his secret or could put him living in a book: and it is there my error would have lain. Or say that in the same romance — I continue to call these books romances, in the hope of giving pain — say that in the same romance, which now begins really to take shape, I should leave to speak of Dancer, and follow instead the Harrow boys; and say that I came on some such business as that of my lantern-bearers on the links; and described the boys as very cold, spat upon by flurries of rain, and drearily surrounded, all of which they were; and their talk as silly and indecent, which it certainly was. I might upon these lines, and had I Zola's genius, turn out, in a page or so, a gem of literary art, render the lantern-light with the touches of a master, and lay on the indecency with the ungrudging hand of love; and when all was done, what a triumph would my picture be of shallowness and dulness! how it would have missed the point! how it would have belied the boys! To the ear of the stenographer, the talk is merely silly and indecent; but ask the boys themselves, and they are discussing (as it is highly proper they should) the possibilities of existence. To the eye of the observer they are wet and cold and drearily surrounded; but ask themselves, and they are in the heaven of a recondite pleasure, the ground of which is an ill-smelling lantern.

III •

For, to repeat, the ground of a man's joy is often hard
to hit. It may hinge at times upon a mere accessory,
like the lantern, it may reside, like Dancer's, in the mysterious inwards of psychology. It may consist with
perpetual failure, and find exercise in the continued chase.
It has so little bond with externals (such as the observer
scribbles in his note-book) that it may even touch them
not; and the man's true life, for which he consents to
live, lie altogether in the field of fancy. The clergyman,
in his spare hours, may be winning battles, the farmer
sailing ships, the banker reaping triumph in the arts: all
leading another life, plying another trade from that they
chose; like the poet's housebuilder, who, after all is
cased in stone,

> " By his fireside, as impotent fancy prompts,
> Rebuilds it to his liking."

In such a case the poetry runs underground. The observer (poor soul, with his documents!) is all abroad.
For to look at the man is but to court deception. We shall
see the trunk from which he draws his nourishment;
but he himself is above and abroad in the green dome
of foliage, hummed through by winds and nested in by
nightingales. And the true realism were that of the
poets, to climb up after him like a squirrel, and catch
some glimpse of the heaven for which he lives. And
the true realism, always and everywhere, is that of the
poets: to find out where joy resides, and give it a voice
far beyond singing.

For to miss the joy is to miss all. In the joy of the

actors lies the sense of any action. That is the explanation,
that the excuse. To one who has not the secret of the
lanterns, the scene upon the links is meaningless. And
hence the haunting and truly spectral unreality of re-
alistic books. Hence, when we read the English realists,
the incredulous wonder with which we observe the
hero's constancy under the submerging tide of dulness,
and how he bears up with his jibbing sweetheart, and
endures the chatter of idiot girls, and stands by his
whole unfeatured wilderness of an existence, instead of
seeking relief in drink or foreign travel. Hence in the
French, in that meat-market of middle-aged sensuality,
the disgusted surprise with which we see the hero drift
sidelong, and practically quite untempted, into every
description of misconduct and dishonour. In each, we
miss the personal poetry, the enchanted atmosphere,
that rainbow work of fancy that clothes what is naked
and seems to ennoble what is base; in each, life falls
dead like dough, instead of soaring away like a balloon
into the colours of the sunset; each is true, each inconceivable; for no man lives in the external truth, among
salts and acids, but in the warm, phantasmagoric chamber of his brain, with the painted windows and the
storied walls.

Of this falsity we have had a recent example from a
man who knows far better — Tolstoi's *Powers of Darkness*. Here is a piece full of force and truth, yet quite
untrue. For before Mikita was led into so dire a situation he was tempted, and temptations are beautiful at
least in part; and a work which dwells on the ugliness
of crime and gives no hint of any loveliness in the temptation, sins against the modesty of life, and even when

a Tolstoi writes it, sinks to melodrama. The peasants are not understood; they saw their life in fairer colours; even the deaf girl was clothed in poetry for Mikita, or he had never fallen. And so, once again, even an Old Bailey melodrama, without some brightness of poetry and lustre of existence, falls into the inconceivable and ranks with fairy tales.

IV

In nobler books we are moved with something like the emotions of life; and this emotion is very variously provoked. We are so moved when Levine labours in the field, when André sinks beyond emotion, when Richard Feverel and Lucy Desborough meet beside the river, when Antony, "not cowardly, puts off his helmet," when Kent has infinite pity on the dying Lear, when, in Dostoieffsky's *Despised and Rejected,* the uncomplaining hero drains his cup of suffering and virtue. These are notes that please the great heart of man. Not only love, and the fields, and the bright face of danger, but sacrifice and death and unmerited suffering humbly supported, touch in us the vein of the poetic. We love to think of them, we long to try them, we are humbly hopeful that we may prove heroes also.

We have heard, perhaps, too much of lesser matters. Here is the door, here is the open air. *Itur in antiquam silvam.*

VIII. A CHAPTER ON DREAMS

THE past is all of one texture — whether feigned or
suffered — whether acted out in three dimensions, or
only witnessed in that small theatre of the brain which
we keep brightly lighted all night long, after the jets are
down, and darkness and sleep reign undisturbed in the
remainder of the body.   There is no distinction on the
face of our experiences; one is vivid indeed, and one
dull, and one pleasant, and another agonising to remember; but which of them is what we call true, and which
a dream, there is not one hair to prove.   The past stands
on a precarious footing; another straw split in the field
of metaphysic, and behold us robbed of it.   There is
scarce a family that can count four generations but lays
a claim to some dormant title or some castle and estate:
a claim not prosecutable in any court of law, but flatter-
ing to the fancy and a great alleviation of idle hours.   A
man's claim to his own past is yet less valid.   A paper
might turn up (in proper story-book fashion) in the secret drawer of an old ebony secretary, and restore your
family to its ancient honours, and reinstate mine in a
certain West Indian islet (not far from St. Kitt's, as beloved tradition hummed in my young ears) which was
once ours, and is now unjustly someone else's, and for

that matter (in the state of the sugar trade) is not worth anything to anybody. I do not say that these revolutions are likely; only no man can deny that they are possible; and the past, on the other hand, is lost forever: our old days and deeds, our old selves, too, and the very world in which these scenes were acted, all brought down to the same faint residuum as a last night's dream, to some incontinuous images, and an echo in the chambers of the brain. Not an hour, not a mood, not a glance of the eye, can we revoke; it is all gone, past conjuring. And yet conceive us robbed of it, conceive that little thread of memory that we trail behind us broken at the pocket's edge; and in what naked nullity should we be left! for we only guide ourselves, and only know ourselves, by these air-painted pictures of the past.

Upon these grounds, there are some among us who claimed to have lived longer and more richly than their neighbours; when they lay asleep they claim they were still active; and among the treasures of memory that all men review for their amusement, these count in no second place the harvests of their dreams. There is one of this kind whom I have in my eye, and whose case is perhaps unusual enough to be described. He was from a child an ardent and uncomfortable dreamer. When he had a touch of fever at night, and the room swelled and shrank, and his clothes, hanging on a nail, now loomed up instant to the bigness of a church, and now drew away into a horror of infinite distance and infinite littleness, the poor soul was very well aware of what must follow, and struggled hard against the approaches of that slumber which was the beginning of sorrows. But his struggles were in vain; sooner or later the night-hag would have him by the throat, and pluck him, strangling and screaming, from his sleep. His dreams were at times commonplace enough, at times very strange: at times they were almost formless, he would be haunted, for instance, by nothing more definite than a certain hue of brown, which he did not mind in the least while he was awake, but feared and loathed while he was dreaming; at times, again, they took on every detail of circumstance, as when once he supposed he must swallow the populous world, and awoke screaming with the horror of the thought. The two chief troubles of his very narrow existence — the practical and everyday trouble of school tasks and the ultimate and airy one of hell and judgment — were often confounded together into one appalling nightmare. He seemed to himself to stand before the Great White Throne; he was called on, poor little devil, to recite some form of words, on which his destiny depended; his tongue stuck, his memory was blank, hell gaped for him; and he would awake, clinging to the curtain-rod with his knees to his chin.

These were extremely poor experiences, on the whole; and at that time of life my dreamer would have very willingly parted with his power of dreams. But presently, in the course of his growth, the cries and physical contortions passed away, seemingly forever; his visions were still for the most part miserable, but they were more constantly supported; and he would awake with no more extreme symptom than a flying heart, a freezing scalp, cold sweats, and the speechless midnight fear. His dreams, too, as befitted a mind better stocked with particulars, became more circumstantial, and had more the air and continuity of life. The look of the world beginning to take hold on his attention, scenery came to play a part in his sleeping as well as in his waking thoughts, so that he would take long, uneventful journeys and see strange towns and beautiful places as he lay in bed. And, what is more significant, an odd taste that he had for the Georgian costume and for stories laid in that period of English history, began to rule the features of his dreams; so that he masqueraded there in a three-cornered hat, and was much engaged with Jacobite conspiracy between the hour for bed and that for breakfast. About the same time, he began to read in his dreams — tales, for the most part, and for the most part after the manner of G. P. R. James, but so incredibly more vivid and moving than any printed book, that he has ever since been malcontent with literature.

And then, while he was yet a student, there came to him a dream-adventure which he has no anxiety to repeat; he began, that is to say, to dream in sequence and thus to lead a double life — one of the day, one of the night — one that he had every reason to believe was the true one, another that he had no means of proving to be false. I should have said he studied, or was by way of studying, at Edinburgh College, which (it may be supposed) was how I came to know him. Well, in his dream life, he passed a long day in the surgical theatre, his heart in his mouth, his teeth on edge, seeing monstrous malformations and the abhorred dexterity of surgeons. In a heavy, rainy, foggy evening he came forth into the South Bridge, turned up the High Street, and entered the door of a tall *land,* at the top of which he supposed himself to lodge. All night long, in his low had long been in the custom of setting himself to sleep with tales, and so had his father before him; but these were irresponsible inventions, told for the teller's pleasure, with no eye to the crass public or the thwart reviewer: tales where a thread might be dropped, or one adventure quitted for another, on fancy's least suggestion. So that the little people who manage man's internal theatre had not as yet received a very rigorous training; and played upon their stage like children who should have slipped into the house and found it empty, rather than like drilled actors performing a set piece to a huge hall of faces. But presently my dreamer began to turn his former amusement of story-telling to (what is called) account; by which I mean that he began to write and sell his tales. Here was he, and here were the little people who did that part of his business, in quite new conditions. The stories must now be trimmed and pared and set upon all fours, they must run from a beginning to an end and fit (after a manner) with the laws of life; the pleasure, in one word, had become a business; and that not only for the dreamer, but for the little people of his theatre. These understood the change as well as he. When he lay down to prepare himself for sleep, he no longer sought amusement, but printable and profitable tales; and after he had dozed off in his box-seat, his little people continued their evolutions with the same mercantile designs. All other forms of dream deserted him but two: he still occasionally reads the most delightful books, he still visits at times the most delightful places; and it is perhaps worthy of note that to these same places, and to one in particular, he returns at intervals of months and years, finding new field-paths, visiting new neighbours, beholding that happy valley under new effects of noon and dawn and sunset. But all the rest of the family of visions is quite lost to him: the common, mangled version of yesterday's affairs, the raw-head-and-bloody-bones nightmare, rumoured to be the child of toasted cheese — these and their like are gone; and, for the most part, whether awake or asleep, he is simply occupied — he or his little people — in consciously making stories for the market. This dreamer (like many other persons) has encountered some trifling vicissitudes of fortune. When the bank begins to send letters and the butcher to linger at the back gate, he sets to belabouring his brains after a story, for that is his readiest money-winner; and, behold! at once the little people begin to bestir themselves in the same quest, and labour all night long, and all night long set before him truncheons of tales upon their lighted theatre. No fear of his being frightened now; the flying heart and the frozen scalp are things bygone; applause, growing applause, growing interest, growing exultation in his own cleverness (for he takes all the credit), and at last a jubilant leap to wakefulness, with the cry, "I have it, that'll do!" upon his lips: with such and similar emotions he sits at these nocturnal dramas, with such outbreaks, like Claudius in the play, he scatters the performance in the midst. Often enough the waking is a disappointment: he has been too deep asleep, as I explain the thing; drowsiness has gained his little people, they have gone stumbling and maundering through their parts; and the play, to the awakened mind, is seen to be a tissue of absurdities. And yet how often have these sleepless Brownies done him honest service, and given him, as he away like a man with a disease. Once, indeed, he broke all bounds of decency, seized an occasion when she was abroad, ransacked her room, and at last, hidden away among her jewels, found the damning evidence. There he stood, holding this thing, which was his life, in the hollow of his hand, and marvelling at her inconsequent behaviour, that she should seek, and keep, and yet not use it; and then the door opened, and behold herself. So, once more, they stood, eye to eye, with the evidence between them; and once more she raised to him a face brimming with some communication; and once more he shied away from speech and cut her off. But before he left the room, which he had turned upside down, he laid back his death-warrant where he had found it; and at that, her face lighted up. The next thing he heard, she was explaining to her maid, with some ingenious falsehood, the disorder of her things. Flesh and blood could bear the strain no longer; and I think it was the next morning (though chronology is always hazy in the theatre of the mind) that he burst from his reserve. They had been breakfasting together in one corner of a great, parqueted, sparely-furnished room of many windows; all the time of the meal she had tortured him with sly allusions; and no sooner were the servants gone, and these two protagonists alone together, than he leaped to his feet. She too sprang up, with a pale face; with a pale face, she heard him as he raved out his complaint: Why did she torture him so? she knew all, she knew he was no enemy to her; why did she not denounce him at once? what signified her whole behaviour? why did she torture him? and yet again, why did she torture him? And when he had done, she fell upon her knees, and with outstretched hands: "Do you not understand?" she cried. "I love you!"

Hereupon, with a pang of wonder and mercantile delight, the dreamer awoke. His mercantile delight was not of long endurance; for it soon became plain that in this spirited tale there were unmarketable elements; which is just the reason why you have it here so briefly told. But his wonder has still kept growing; and I think the reader's will also, if he consider it ripely. For now he sees why I speak of the little people as of substantive inventors and performers. To the end they had kept their secret. I will go bail for the dreamer (having excellent grounds for valuing his candour) that he had no guess whatever at the motive of the woman — the hinge of the whole well-invented plot — until the instant of that highly dramatic declaration. It was not his tale; it was the little people's! And observe: not only was the secret kept, the story was told with really guileful craftsmanship. The conduct of both actors is (in the cant phrase) psychologically correct, and the emotion aptly graduated up to the surprising climax. I am awake now, and I know this trade; and yet I cannot better it. I am awake, and I live by this business; and yet I could not outdo — could not perhaps equal — that crafty artifice (as of some old, experienced carpenter of plays, some Dennery or Sardou) by which the same situation is twice presented and the two actors twice brought face to face over the evidence, only once it is in her hand, once in his — and these in their due order, the least dramatic first. The more I think of it, the more I am moved to press upon the world my ques-

tion: Who are the Little People? They are near con-
nections of the dreamer's, beyond doubt; they share
in his financial worries and have an eye to the bank-
book; they share plainly in his training; they have
plainly learned like him to build the scheme of a con-
siderate story and to arrange emotion in progressive
order; only I think they have more talent; and one
thing is beyond doubt, they can tell him a story piece
by piece, like a serial, and keep him all the while in ignorance of where they aim. Who are they, then? and
who is the dreamer?

Well, as regards the dreamer, I can answer that, for
he is no less a person than myself;—as I might have
told you from the beginning, only that the critics murmur over my consistent egotism;—and as I am positively forced to tell you now, or I could advance but
little farther with my story. And for the Little People,
what shall I say they are but just my Brownies, God
bless them! who do one-half my work for me while I
am fast asleep, and in all human likelihood, do the rest
for me as well, when I am wide awake and fondly suppose I do it for myself. That part which is done while
I am sleeping is the Brownies' part beyond contention;
but that which is done when I am up and about is by
no means necessarily mine, since all goes to show the
Brownies have a hand in it even then. Here is a doubt
that much concerns my conscience. For myself—what
I call I, my conscience ego, the denizen of the pineal
gland unless he has changed his residence since Des-
cartes, the man with the conscience and the variable
bank-account, the man with the hat and the boots, and
the privilege of voting and not carrying his candidate at

the general elections — I am sometimes tempted to suppose he is no story-teller at all, but a creature as matter of fact as any cheesemonger or any cheese, and a realist bemired up to the ears in actuality; so that, by that account, the whole of my published fiction should be the single-handed product of some Brownie, some Familiar, some unseen collaborator, whom I keep locked in a back garret, while I get all the praise and he but a share (which I cannot prevent him getting) of the pudding. I am an excellent adviser, something like Molière's servant; I pull back and I cut down; and I dress the whole in the best words and sentences that I can find and make; I hold the pen, too; and I do the sitting at the table, which is about the worst of it; and when all is done, I make up the manuscript and pay for the registration; so that, on the whole, I have some claim to share, though not so largely as I do, in the profits of our common enterprise.

I can but give an instance or so of what part is done sleeping and what part awake, and leave the reader to share what laurels there are, at his own nod, between myself and my collaborators; and to do this I will first take a book that a number of persons have been polite enough to read, the *Strange Case of Dr. Jekyll and Mr. Hyde.* I had long been trying to write a story on this subject, to find a body, a vehicle, for that strong sense of man's double being which must at times come in upon and overwhelm the mind of every thinking creature. I had even written one, *The Travelling Companion,* which was returned by an editor on the plea that it was a work of genius and indecent, and which I burned the other day on the ground that it was not a work of genius, and that *Jekyll* had supplanted it. Then came one of those financial fluctuations to which (with an elegant modesty) I have hitherto referred in the third person. For two days I went about racking my brains for a plot of any sort; and on the second night I dreamed the scene at the window, and a scene afterwards split in two, in which Hyde, pursued for some crime, took the powder and underwent the change in the presence of his pursuers. All the rest was made awake, and consciously, although I think I can trace in much of it the manner of my Brownies. The meaning of the tale is therefore mine, and had long pre-existed in my garden of Adonis, and tried one body after another in vain; indeed, I do most of the morality, worse luck! and my Brownies have not a rudiment of what we call a conscience. Mine, too, is the setting, mine the characters. All that was given me was the matter of three scenes, and the central idea of a voluntary change becoming involuntary. Will it be thought ungenerous, after I have been so liberally ladling out praise to my unseen collaborators, if I here toss them over, bound hand and foot, into the arena of the critics? For the business of the powders, which so many have censured, is, I am relieved to say, not mine at all but the Brownies'. Of another tale, in case the reader should have glanced at it, I may say a word: the not very defensible story of *Olalla*. Here the court, the mother, the mother's niche, Olalla, Olalla's chamber, the meetings on the stair, the broken window, the ugly scene of the bite, were all given me in bulk and detail as I have tried to write them; to this I added only the external scenery (for in my dream I never was beyond the court), the portrait, the characters of Felipe and the priest, the moral, such as it is, and the last pages, such as, alas! they are. And I may even say that in this case the moral itself was given me; for it arose immediately on a comparison of the mother and the daughter, and from the hideous trick of atavism in the first. Sometimes a parabolic sense is still more undeniably present in a dream; sometimes I cannot but suppose my Brownies have been aping Bunyan, and yet in no case with what would possibly be called a moral in a tract; never with the ethical narrowness; conveying hints instead of life's larger limitations and that sort of sense which we seem to perceive in the arabesque of time and space.

For the most part, it will be seen, my Brownies are somewhat fantastic, like their stories hot and hot, full of passion and the picturesque, alive with animating incident; and they have no prejudice against the supernatural. But the other day they gave me a surprise, entertaining me with a love-story, a little April comedy, which I ought certainly to hand over to the author of *A Chance Acquaintance,* for he could write it as it should be written, and I am sure (although I mean to try) that I cannot.—But who would have supposed that a Brownie of mine should invent a tale for Mr. Howells?

IX. BEGGARS

I

In a pleasant, airy, up-hill country, it was my fortune when I was young to make the acquaintance of a certain beggar. I call him beggar, though he usually allowed his coat and his shoes (which were open-mouthed, indeed) to beg for him. He was the wreck of an athletic man, tall, gaunt, and bronzed; far gone in consumption, with that disquieting smile of the mortally stricken on his face; but still active afoot, still with the brisk military carriage, the ready military salute. Three ways led through this piece of country; and as I was inconstant in my choice, I believe he must often have awaited me in vain. But often enough, he caught me; often enough, from some place of ambush by the roadside, he would spring suddenly forth in the regulation attitude, and launching at once into his inconsequential talk, fall into step with me upon my farther course. "A fine morning, sir, though perhaps a trifle inclining to rain. I hope I see you well, sir. Why, no, sir, I don't feel as hearty myself as I could wish, but I am keeping about my ordinary. I am pleased to meet you on the road, sir. I assure you I quite look forward to one of our little conversations." He loved the sound of his own voice inordinately, and though (with something too off-hand to call servility) he would always hasten to agree with anything you said, yet he could never suffer you to say it to an end. By what transition he slid to his favourite subject I have no memory; but we had never been long together on the way before he was dealing, in a very military manner, with the English poets. "Shelley was a fine poet, sir, though a trifle atheistical in his opinions. His Queen Mab, sir, is quite an atheistical work. Scott, sir, is not so poetical a writer. With the works of Shakespeare I am not so well acquainted, but he was a fine poet. Keats—John Keats, sir—he was a very fine poet." With such references, such trivial criticism, such loving parade of his own knowledge, he would beguile the road, striding forward up-hill, his staff now clapped to the ribs of his deep, resonant chest, now swinging in the air with the remembered jauntiness of the private soldier; and all the while his toes looking out of his boots, and his shirt looking out of his elbows, and death looking out of his smile, and his big, crazy frame shaken by accesses of cough.

He would often go the whole way home with me: often to borrow a book, and that book always a poet. Off he would march, to continue his mendicant rounds, with the volume slipped into the pocket of his ragged coat; and although he would sometimes keep it quite a while, yet it came always back again at last, not much the worse for its travels into beggardom. And in this way, doubtless, his knowledge grew and his glib, random criticism took a wider range. But my library was not the first he had drawn upon: at our first en-

counter, he was already brimful of Shelley and the atheistical Queen Mab, and "Keats — John Keats, sir." And
I have often wondered how he came by these acquirements; just as I often wondered how he fell to be a
beggar. He had served through the Mutiny — of which
(like so many people) he could tell practically nothing
beyond the names of places, and that it was "difficult
work, sir," and very hot, or that so-and-so was "a very
fine commander, sir." He was far too smart a man to
have remained a private; in the nature of things, he must
have won his stripes. And yet here he was without
a pension. When I touched on this problem, he would
content himself with diffidently offering me advice.
"A man should be very careful when he is young, sir.
If you'll excuse me saying so, a spirited young gentleman like yourself, sir, should be very careful. I was
perhaps a trifle inclined to atheistical opinions myself."
For (perhaps with a deeper wisdom than we are inclined in these days to admit) he plainly bracketed ag-
nosticism with beer and skittles.

Keats — John Keats, sir, — and Shelley were his favourite bards. I cannot remember if I tried him with
Rossetti; but I know his taste to a hair, and if ever I did,
he must have doted on that author. What took him
was a richness in the speech; he loved the exotic, the
unexpected word; the moving cadence of a phrase; a
vague sense of emotion (about nothing) in the very letters of the alphabet: the romance of language. His
honest head was very nearly empty, his intellect like a
child's; and when he read his favourite authors, he can
almost never have understood what he was reading.
Yet the taste was not only genuine, it was exclusive; I

tried in vain to offer him novels; he would none of them;
he cared for nothing but romantic language that he
could not understand. The case may be commoner
than we suppose. I am reminded of a lad who was
laid in the next cot to a friend of mine in a public hospital, and who was no sooner installed than he sent out
(perhaps with his last pence) for a cheap Shakespeare.
My friend pricked up his ears; fell at once in talk with
his new neighbour, and was ready, when the book arrived, to make a singular discovery. For this lover of
great literature understood not one sentence out of
twelve, and his favourite part was that of which he understood the least — the inimitable, mouth-filling rodomontade of the ghost in *Hamlet*. It was a bright day in
hospital when my friend expounded the sense of this beloved jargon: a task for which I am willing to believe my
friend was very fit, though I can never regard it as an
easy one. I know indeed a point or two, on which I
would gladly question Mr. Shakespeare, that lover of big
words, could he revisit the glimpses of the moon, or
could I myself climb backward to the spacious days of
Elizabeth. But in the second case, I should most likely
pretermit these questionings, and take my place instead
in the pit at the Blackfriars, to hear the actor in his
favourite part, playing up to Mr. Burbage, and rolling
out — as I seem to hear him — with a ponderous gusto —

"Unhousel'd, disappointed, unanel'd."

What a pleasant chance, if we could go there in a party!
and what a surprise for Mr. Burbage, when the ghost
received the honours of the evening!

of experience solidly and livingly built up in words, here was a story created, *teres atque rotundus.*

And to think of the old soldier, that lover of the literary bards! He had visited stranger spots than any seaside cave; encountered men more terrible than any spirit; done and dared and suffered in that incredible, unsung epic of the Mutiny War; played his part with the field force of Delhi, beleaguering and beleaguered; shared in that enduring, savage anger and contempt of death and decency that, for long months together, bedevil'd and inspired the army; was hurled to and fro in the battle-smoke of the assault; was there, perhaps, where Nicholson fell; was there when the attacking column, with hell upon every side, found the soldier's enemy—strong drink, and the lives of tens of thousands trembled in the scale, and the fate of the flag of England staggered. And of all this he had no more to say than "hot work, sir," or "the army suffered a great deal, sir," or "I believe General Wilson, sir, was not very highly thought of in the papers." His life was naught to him, the vivid pages of experience quite blank: in words his pleasure lay—melodious, agitated words—printed words, about that which he had never seen and was connatally incapable of comprehending. We have here two temperaments face to face; both untrained, unsophisticated, surprised (we may say) in the egg; both boldly charactered:—that of the artist, the lover and artificer of words; that of the maker, the seeër, the lover and forger of experience. If the one had a daughter and the other had a son, and these married, might not some illustrious writer count descent from the beggar-soldier and the needy knife-grinder?

III

Every one lives by selling something, whatever be his
right to it. The burglar sells at the same time his own
skill and courage and my silver plate (the whole at the
most moderate figure) to a Jew receiver. The bandit
sells the traveller an article of prime necessity: that traveller's life. And as for the old soldier, who stands for
central mark to my capricious figures of eight, he dealt
in a specialty; for he was the only beggar in the world
who ever gave me pleasure for my money. He had
learned a school of manners in the barracks and had the
sense to cling to it, accosting strangers with a regi-
mental freedom, thanking patrons with a merely regi-
mental difference, sparing you at once the tragedy of his
position and the embarrassment of yours. There was
not one hint about him of the beggar's emphasis, the
outburst of revolting gratitude, the rant and cant, the
"God bless you, Kind, Kind gentleman," which insults
the smallness of your alms by disproportionate vehemence, which is so notably false, which would be so un-
bearable if it were true. I am sometimes tempted to
suppose this reading of the beggar's part, a survival of
the old days when Shakespeare was intoned upon the
stage and mourners keened beside the death-bed; to
think that we cannot now accept these strong emotions
unless they be uttered in the just note of life; nor (save
in the pulpit) endure these gross conventions. They
wound us, I am tempted to say, like mockery; the high
voice of keening (as it yet lingers on) strikes in the face
of sorrow like a buffet; and the rant and cant of the
staled beggar stirs in us a shudder of disgust. But the

own I feel with him. Gratitude without familiarity, gratitude otherwise than as a nameless element in a friendship, is a thing so near to hatred that I do not care to split the difference. Until I find a man who is pleased to receive obligations, I shall continue to question the tact of those who are eager to confer them. What an art it is, to give, even to our nearest friends! and what a test of manners, to receive! How, upon either side, we smuggle away the obligation, blushing for each other; how bluff and dull we make the giver; how hasty, how falsely cheerful, the receiver! And yet an act of such difficulty and distress between near friends, it is supposed we can perform to a total stranger and leave the man transfixed with grateful emotions. The last thing you can do to a man is to burthen him with an obligation, and it is what we propose to begin with! But let us not be deceived: unless he is totally degraded to his trade, anger jars in his inside, and he grates his teeth at our gratuity.

We should wipe two words from our vocabulary: gratitude and charity. In real life, help is given out of friendship, or it is not valued; it is received from the hand of friendship, or it is resented. We are all too proud to take a naked gift: we must seem to pay it, if in nothing else, then with the delights of our society. Here, then, is the pitiful fix of the rich man; here is that needle's eye in which he stuck already in the days of Christ, and still sticks to-day, firmer, if possible, than ever: that he has the money and lacks the love which should make his money acceptable. Here and now, just as of old in Palestine, he has the rich to dinner, it is with the rich that he takes his pleasure: and when

his turn comes to be charitable, he looks in vain for a re-
cipient. His friends are not poor, they do not want; the
poor are not his friends, they will not take. To whom
is he to give? Where to find — note this phrase — the
Deserving Poor? Charity is (what they call) central-
ised; offices are hired; societies founded, with secretaries paid or unpaid: the hunt of the Deserving Poor
goes merrily forward. I think it will take more than
a merely human secretary to disinter that character.
What! a class that is to be in want from no fault of its
own, and yet greedily eager to receive from strangers;
and to be quite respectable, and at the same time quite
devoid of self-respect; and play the most delicate part of
friendship, and yet never be seen; and wear the form
of man, and yet fly in the face of all the laws of human
nature: — and all this, in the hope of getting a belly-god
Burgess through a needle's eye! O, let him stick, by all
means: and let his polity tumble in the dust; and let his
epitaph and all his literature (of which my own works
begin to form no inconsiderable part) be abolished even
from the history of man! For a fool of this monstrosity
of dulness, there can be no salvation: and the fool who
looked for the elixir of life was an angel of reason to the
fool who looks for the Deserving Poor!

V

And yet there is one course which the unfortunate
gentleman may take. He may subscribe to pay the
taxes. There were the true charity, impartial and im-
personal, cumbering none with obligation, helping all.
There were a destination for loveless gifts; there were

the way to reach the pocket of the deserving poor, and yet save the time of secretaries! But, alas! there is no colour of romance in such a course; and people nowhere demand the picturesque so much as in their virtues.

X. LETTER TO A YOUNG GENTLEMAN WHO PRO-POSES TO EMBRACE THE CAREER OF ART

WITH the agreeable frankness of youth, you address me on a point of some practical importance to yourself and (it is even conceivable) of some gravity to the world: Should you or should you not become an artist? It is one which you must decide entirely for yourself; all that I can do is to bring under your notice some of the materials of that decision; and I will begin, as I shall probably conclude also, by assuring you that all depends on the vocation.

To know what you like is the beginning of wisdom and of old age. Youth is wholly experimental. The essence and charm of that unquiet and delightful epoch is ignorance of self as well as ignorance of life. These two unknowns the young man brings together again and again, now in the airiest touch, now with a bitter hug; now with exquisite pleasure, now with cutting pain; but never with indifference, to which he is a total stranger, and never with that near kinsman of indifference, contentment. If he be a youth of dainty senses or a brain easily heated, the interest of this series of experiments grows upon him out of all proportion to the pleasure he receives. It is not beauty that he loves, nor pleasure that he seeks, though he may think so; his design and his sufficient reward is to verify his own existence and taste the variety of human fate. To him, before the razor-edge of curiosity is dulled, all that is not actual living and the hot chase of experience wears a face of a disgusting dryness difficult to recall in later days; or if there be any exception — and here destiny steps in — it is in those moments when, wearied or surfeited of the primary activity of the senses, he calls up before memory the image of transacted pains and pleasures. Thus it is that such an one shies from all cut-and-dry professions, and inclines insensibly toward that career of art which consists only in the tasting and recording of experience.

This, which is not so much a vocation for art as an impatience of all other honest trades, frequently exists alone; and so existing, it will pass gently away in the course of years. Emphatically, it is not to be regarded; it is not a vocation, but a temptation; and when your father the other day so fiercely and (in my view) so properly discouraged your ambition, he was recalling not improbably some similar passage in his own experience. For the temptation is perhaps nearly as common as the vocation is rare. But again we have vocations which are imperfect; we have men whose minds are bound up, not so much in any art, as in the general *ars artium* and common base of all creative work; who will now dip into painting, and now study counterpoint, and anon will be inditing a sonnet: all these with equal interest, all often with genuine knowledge. And of this temper, when it stands alone, I find it difficult to speak; but I should counsel such an one to take to letters, for in literature (which drags with so wide a net) all his information may be found some day useful, and if he should go on as he has begun, and turn at last into the critic, he will have learned to use the necessary tools. Lastly we come to those vocations which are at once decisive and precise; to the men who are born with the love of pigments, the passion of drawing, the gift of music, or the impulse to create with words, just as other and perhaps the same men are born with the love of hunting, or the sea, or horses, or the turning-lathe. These are predestined; if a man love the labour of any trade, apart from any question of success or fame, the gods have called him. He may have the general vocation too: he may have a taste for all the arts, and I think he often has; but the mark of his calling is this laborious partiality for one, this inextinguishable zest in its technical successes, and (perhaps above all) a certain candour of mind, to take his very trifling enterprise with a gravity that would befit the cares of empire, and to think the smallest improvement worth accomplishing at any expense of time and industry. The book, the statue, the sonata, must be gone upon with the unreasoning good faith and the unflagging spirit of children at their play. *Is it worth doing?* — when it shall have occurred to any artist to ask himself that question, it is implicitly answered in the negative. It does not occur to the child as he plays at being a pirate on the dining-room sofa, nor to the hunter as he pursues his quarry; and the candour of the one and the ardour of the other should be united in the bosom of the artist.

If you recognise in yourself some such decisive taste, there is no room for hesitation: follow your bent. And observe (lest I should too much discourage you) that the of the public must be ever blind. To those lost pains, suppose you attain the highest pitch of merit, posterity may possibly do justice; suppose, as is so probable, you fail by even a hair's breadth of the highest, rest certain they shall never be observed. Under the shadow of this cold thought, alone in his studio, the artist must preserve from day to day his constancy to the ideal. It is this which makes his life noble; it is by this that the practice of his craft strengthens and matures his character; it is for this that even the serious countenance of the great emperor was turned approvingly (if only for a moment) on the followers of Apollo, and that sternly gentle voice bade the artist cherish his art.

And here there fall two warnings to be made. First, if you are to continue to be a law to yourself, you must beware of the first signs of laziness. This idealism in honesty can only be supported by perpetual effort; the standard is easily lowered, the artist who says *" It will do,"* is on the downward path; three or four pot-boilers are enough at times (above all at wrong times) to falsify a talent, and by the practice of journalism a man runs the risk of becoming wedded to cheap finish. This is the danger on the one side; there is not less upon the other. The consciousness of how much the artist is (and must be) a law to himself, debauches the small heads. Perceiving recondite merits very hard to attain, making or swallowing artistic formulæ, or perhaps falling in love with some particular proficiency of his own, many artists forget the end of all art: to please. It is doubtless tempting to exclaim against the ignorant bourgeois; yet it should not be forgotten, it is he who is to pay us, and that (surely on the face of it) for services

284

that he shall desire to have performed. Here also, if
properly considered, there is a question of transcendental honesty. To give the public what they do not
want, and yet expect to be supported: we have there
a strange pretension, and yet not uncommon, above all
with painters. The first duty in this world is for a man
to pay his way; when that is quite accomplished, he
may plunge into what eccentricity he likes; but emphatically not till then. Till then, he must pay assid-
uous court to the bourgeois who carries the purse. And
if in the course of these capitulations he shall falsify his
talent, it can never have been a strong one, and he will
have preserved a better thing than talent — character.
Or if he be of a mind so independent that he cannot
stoop to this necessity, one course is yet open: he can
desist from art, and follow some more manly way of
life.

I speak of a more manly way of life, it is a point on
which I must be frank. To live by a pleasure is not a
high calling; it involves patronage, however veiled; it
numbers the artist, however ambitious, along with
dancing girls and billiard markers. The French have a
romantic evasion for one employment, and call its prac-
titioners the Daughters of Joy. The artist is of the same
family, he is of the Sons of Joy, chose his trade to please
himself, gains his livelihood by pleasing others, and has
parted with something of the sterner dignity of man.
Journals but a little while ago declaimed against the
Tennyson peerage; and this Son of Joy was blamed for
condescension when he followed the example of Lord
Lawrence and Lord Cairns and Lord Clyde. The poet
was more happily inspired; with a better modesty he ac-

output. Nor have you the right to look for more; in the wages of the life, not in the wages of the trade, lies your reward; the work is here the wages. It will be seen I have little sympathy with the common lamentations of the artist class. Perhaps they do not remember the hire of the field labourer; or do they think no parallel will lie ? Perhaps they have never observed what is the retiring allowance of a field officer; or do they suppose their contributions to the arts of pleasing more important than the services of a colonel ? Perhaps they forget on how little Millet was content to live; or do they think, because they have less genius, they stand excused from the display of equal virtues ? But upon one point there should be no dubiety: if a man be not frugal, he has no business in the arts. If he be not frugal, he steers directly for that last tragic scene of *le vieux saltimbanque ;* if he be not frugal, he will find it hard to continue to be honest. Some day, when the butcher is knocking at the door, he may be tempted, he may be obliged, to turn out and sell a slovenly piece of work. If the obligation shall have arisen through no wantonness of his own, he is even to be commended; for words cannot describe how far more necessary it is that a man should support his family, than that he should attain to — or preserve — distinction in the arts. But if the pressure comes through his own fault, he has stolen, and stolen under trust, and stolen (which is the worst of all) in such a way that no law can reach him.

And now you may perhaps ask me, if the debutant artist is to have no thought of money, and if (as is implied) he is to expect no honours from the State, he may not at least look forward to the delights of popularity ?

Praise, you will tell me, is a savoury dish. And in so far as you may mean the countenance of other artists, you would put your finger on one of the most essential and enduring pleasures of the career of art. But in so far as you should have an eye to the commendations of the public or the notice of the newspapers, be sure you would but be cherishing a dream. It is true that in certain esoteric journals the author (for instance) is duly criticised, and that he is often praised a great deal more than he deserves, sometimes for qualities which he prided himself on eschewing, and sometimes by ladies and gentlemen who have denied themselves the privilege of reading his work. But if a man be sensitive to this wild praise, we must suppose him equally alive to that which often accompanies and always follows it — wild ridicule. A man may have done well for years, and then he may fail; he will hear of his failure. Or he may have done well for years, and still do well, but the critics may have tired of praising him, or there may have sprung up some new idol of the instant, some " dust a little gilt," to whom they now prefer to offer sacrifice. Here is the obverse and the reverse of that empty and ugly thing called popularity. Will any man suppose it worth the gaining ?

of worms in a piece of ancient turf, or the air of a marsh darkened with insects, will sometimes check our breathing so that we aspire for cleaner places. But none is clean: the moving sand is infected with lice; the pure spring, where it bursts out of the mountain, is a mere issue of worms; even in the hard rock the crystal is forming.

In two main shapes this eruption covers the countenance of the earth: the animal and the vegetable: one in some degree the inversion of the other: the second rooted to the spot; the first coming detached out of its natal mud, and scurrying abroad with the myriad feet of insects or towering into the heavens on the wings of birds: a thing so inconceivable that, if it be well considered, the heart stops. To what passes with the anchored vermin, we have little clue: doubtless they have their joys and sorrows, their delights and killing agonies: it appears not how. But of the locomotory, to which we ourselves belong, we can tell more. These share with us a thousand miracles: the miracles of sight, of hearing, of the projection of sound, things that bridge space; the miracles of memory and reason, by which the present is conceived, and when it is gone, its image kept living in the brains of man and brute; the miracle of reproduction, with its imperious desires and staggering consequences. And to put the last touch upon this mountain mass of the revolting and the inconceivable, all these prey upon each other, lives tearing other lives in pieces, cramming them inside themselves, and by that summary process, growing fat: the vegetarian, the whale, perhaps the tree, not less than the lion of the desert; for the vegetarian is only the eater of the dumb.

Meanwhile our rotatory island loaded with predatory

life, and more drenched with blood, both animal and
vegetable, than ever mutinied ship, scuds through space
with unimaginable speed, and turns alternate cheeks to
the reverberation of a blazing world, ninety million
miles away.

II

What a monstrous spectre is this man, the disease
of the agglutinated dust, lifting alternate feet or lying
drugged with slumber; killing, feeding, growing, bringing forth small copies of himself; grown upon with hair
like grass, fitted with eyes that move and glitter in his
face; a thing to set children screaming;—and yet looked
at nearlier, known as his fellows know him, how surprising are his attributes! Poor soul, here for so little,
cast among so many hardships, filled with desires so in-
commensurate and so inconsistent, savagely surrounded,
savagely descended, irremediably condemned to prey
upon his fellow lives: who should have blamed him had
he been of a piece with his destiny and a being merely
barbarous? And we look and behold him instead filled
with imperfect virtues: infinitely childish, often admira-
bly valiant, often touchingly kind; sitting down, amidst
his momentary life, to debate of right and wrong and the
attributes of the deity; rising up to do battle for an egg
or die for an idea; singling out his friends and his mate
with cordial affection; bringing forth in pain, rearing
with long-suffering solicitude, his young. To touch the
heart of his mystery, we find in him one thought, strange
to the point of lunacy: the thought of duty; the thought
of something owing to himself, to his neighbour, to his
God: an ideal of decency, to which he would rise if it

you this! if I could show you these men and women, all the world over, in every stage of history, under every abuse of error, under every circumstance of failure, without hope, without help, without thanks, still obscurely fighting the lost fight of virtue, still clinging, in the brothel or on the scaffold, to some rag of honour, the poor jewel of their souls! They may seek to escape, and yet they cannot; it is not alone their privilege and glory, but their doom; they are condemned to some nobility; all their lives long, the desire of good is at their heels, the implacable hunter.

Of all earth's meteors, here at least is the most strange and consoling: that this ennobled lemur, this hair-crowned bubble of the dust, this inheritor of a few years and sorrows, should yet deny himself his rare delights, and add to his frequent pains, and live for an ideal, however misconceived. Nor can we stop with man. A new doctrine, received with screams a little while ago by canting moralists, and still not properly worked into the body of our thoughts, lights us a step farther into the heart of this rough but noble universe. For nowadays the pride of man denies in vain his kinship with the original dust. He stands no longer like a thing apart. Close at his heels we see the dog, prince of another genus: and in him too, we see dumbly testified the same cultus of an unattainable ideal, the same constancy in failure. Does it stop with the dog? We look at our feet where the ground is blackened with the swarming ant: a creature so small, so far from us in the hierarchy of brutes, that we can scarce trace and scarce comprehend his doings; and here also, in his ordered polities and rigorous justice, we see confessed the law of duty and the fact

of individual sin. Does it stop, then, with the ant ? Rather
this desire of well-doing and this doom of frailty run
through all the grades of life: rather is this earth, from the
frosty top of Everest to the next margin of the internal
fire, one stage of ineffectual virtues and one temple of
pious tears and perseverance. The whole creation
groaneth and travaileth together. It is the common and
the god-like law of life. The browsers, the biters, the
barkers, the hairy coats of field and forest, the squirrel
in the oak, the thousand-footed creeper in the dust, as
they share with us the gift of life, share with us the love
of an ideal: strive like us — like us are tempted to grow
weary of the struggle — to do well; like us receive at
times unmerited refreshment, visitings of support, returns of courage; and are condemned like us to be cruci-
fied between that double law of the members and the
will. Are they like us, I wonder, in the timid hope of
some reward, some sugar with the drug ? do they, too,
stand aghast at unrewarded virtues, at the sufferings of
those whom, in our partiality, we take to be just, and
the prosperity of such as, in our blindness, we call
wicked ? It may be, and yet God knows what they
should look for. Even while they look, even while they
repent, the foot of man treads them by thousands in the
dust, the yelping hounds burst upon their trail, the bul-
let speeds, the knives are heating in the den of the
vivisectionist; or the dew falls, and the generation of a
day is blotted out. For these are creatures, compared
with whom our weakness is strength, our ignorance
wisdom, our brief span eternity.

And as we dwell, we living things, in our isle of terror and under the imminent hand of death, God forbid

it should be man the erected, the reasoner, the wise in his own eyes — God forbid it should be man that wearies in well-doing, that despairs of unrewarded effort, or utters the language of complaint.   Let it be enough for faith, that the whole creation groans in mortal frailty, strives with unconquerable constancy: Surely not all in vain.

XII. A CHRISTMAS SERMON

By the time this paper appears, I shall have been talking for twelve months;[1] and it is thought I should take my leave in a formal and seasonable manner. Valedictory eloquence is rare, and death-bed sayings have not often hit the mark of the occasion. Charles Second, wit and sceptic, a man whose life had been one long lesson in human incredulity, an easy-going comrade, a manœuvring king—remembered and embodied all his wit and scepticism along with more than his usual good humour in the famous "I am afraid, gentlemen, I am an unconscionable time a-dying."

I

An unconscionable time a-dying—there is the picture ("I am afraid, gentlemen,") of your life and of mine. The sands run out, and the hours are "numbered and imputed," and the days go by; and when the last of these finds us, we have been a long time dying, and what else? The very length is something, if we reach that hour of separation undishonoured; and to have lived at all is doubtless (in the soldierly expression) to have

[1] i. e. in the pages of *Scribner's Magazine* (1888).

served. There is a tale in Tacitus of how the veterans mutinied in the German wilderness; of how they mobbed Germanicus, clamouring to go home; and of how, seizing their general's hand, these old, war-worn exiles passed his finger along their toothless gums. *Sunt lacrymæ rerum:* this was the most eloquent of the songs of Simeon. And when a man has lived to a fair age, he bears his marks of service. He may have never been remarked upon the breach at the head of the army; at least he shall have lost his teeth on the camp bread.

The idealism of serious people in this age of ours is of a noble character. It never seems to them that they have served enough; they have a fine impatience of their virtues. It were perhaps more modest to be singly thankful that we are no worse. It is not only our enemies, those desperate characters— it is we ourselves who know not what we do;— thence springs the glimmering hope that perhaps we do better than we think: that to scramble through this random business with hands reasonably clean, to have played the part of a man or woman with some reasonable fulness, to have often resisted the diabolic, and at the end to be still resisting it, is for the poor human soldier to have done right well. To ask to see some fruit of our endeavour is but a transcendental way of serving for reward; and what we take to be contempt of self is only greed of hire.

And again if we require so much of ourselves, shall we not require much of others? If we do not genially judge our own deficiencies, is it not to be feared we shall be even stern to the trespasses of others? And he who (looking back upon his own life) can see no more than that he has been unconscionably long a-dying, will he not be tempted to think his neighbour unconscionably long of getting hanged? It is probable that nearly all who think of conduct at all, think of it too much; it is certain we all think too much of sin. We are not damned for doing wrong, but for not doing right; Christ would never hear of negative morality; *thou shalt* was ever his word, with which he superseded *thou shalt not*. To make our idea of morality centre on forbidden acts is to defile the imagination and to introduce into our judgments of our fellow-men a secret element of gusto. If a thing is wrong for us, we should not dwell upon the thought of it; or we shall soon dwell upon it with inverted pleasure. If we cannot drive it from our minds —one thing of two: either our creed is in the wrong and we must more indulgently remodel it; or else, if our morality be in the right, we are criminal lunatics and should place our persons in restraint. A mark of such unwholesomely divided minds is the passion for interference with others: the Fox without the Tail was of this breed, but had (if his biographer is to be trusted) a certain antique civility now out of date. A man may have a flaw, a weakness, that unfits him for the duties of life, that spoils his temper, that threatens his integrity, or that betrays him into cruelty. It has to be conquered; but it must never be suffered to engross his thoughts. The true duties lie all upon the farther side, and must be attended to with a whole mind so soon as this preliminary clearing of the decks has been effected. In order that he may be kind and honest, it may be needful he should become a total abstainer; let him become so then, and the next day let him forget the circumstance. Trying to be kind and honest will require all his thoughts; a mortified appetite is never a wise companion; in so far as he has had to mortify an appetite, he will still be the worse man; and of such an one a great deal of cheerfulness will be required in judging life, and a great deal of humility in judging others.

It may be argued again that dissatisfaction with our life's endeavour springs in some degree from dulness. We require higher tasks, because we do not recognise the height of those we have. Trying to be kind and honest seems an affair too simple and too inconsequential for gentlemen of our heroic mould; we had rather set ourselves to something bold, arduous, and conclusive; we had rather found a schism or suppress a heresy, cut off a hand or mortify an appetite. But the task before us, which is to co-endure with our existence, is rather one of microscopic fineness, and the heroism required is that of patience. There is no cutting of the Gordian knots of life; each must be smilingly unravelled.

To be honest, to be kind — to earn a little and to spend a little less, to make upon the whole a family happier for his presence, to renounce when that shall be necessary and not be embittered, to keep a few friends but these without capitulation — above all, on the same grim condition, to keep friends with himself — here is a task for all that a man has of fortitude and delicacy. He has an ambitious soul who would ask more; he has a hopeful spirit who should look in such an enterprise to be successful. There is indeed one element in human destiny that not blindness itself can controvert: whatever else we are intended to do, we are not intended to succeed; failure is the fate allotted. It is so in every art and study; it is so above all in the continent art of living well. Here is a pleasant thought for the year's end or for the end of life: Only self-deception will be satisfied, and there need be no despair for the despairer.

II

But Christmas is not only the mile-mark of another year, moving us to thoughts of self-examination: it is a season, from all its associations, whether domestic or religious, suggesting thoughts of joy. A man dissatisfied with his endeavours is a man tempted to sadness. And in the midst of the winter, when his life runs lowest and he is reminded of the empty chairs of his beloved, it is well he should be condemned to this fashion of the smiling face. Noble disappointment, noble self-denial are not to be admired, not even to be pardoned, if they bring bitterness. It is one thing to enter the kingdom of heaven maim; another to maim yourself and stay without. And the kingdom of heaven is of the childlike, of those who are easy to please, who love and who give pleasure. Mighty men of their hands, the smiters and the builders and the judges, have lived long and done sternly and yet preserved this lovely character; and among our carpet interests and twopenny concerns, the shame were indelible if *we* should lose it. Gentleness and cheerfulness, these come before all morality; they are the perfect duties. And it is the trouble with moral men that they have neither one nor other. It was the moral man, the Pharisee, whom Christ could not away with. If your morals make you dreary, depend upon it they are wrong. I do not say "give them up," for they may be all you have; but conceal them like a vice, lest they should spoil the lives of better and simpler people.

A strange temptation attends upon man: to keep his eye on pleasures, even when he will not share in them; to aim all his morals against them. This very year a lady (singular iconoclast!) proclaimed a crusade against dolls; and the racy sermon against lust is a feature of the age. I venture to call such moralists insincere. At any excess or perversion of a natural appetite, their lyre sounds of itself with relishing denunciations; but for all displays of the truly diabolic — envy, malice, the mean lie, the mean silence, the calumnious truth, the back-biter, the petty tyrant, the peevish poisoner of family life — their standard is quite different. These are wrong, they will admit, yet somehow not so wrong; there is no zeal in their assault on them, no secret element of gusto warms up the sermon; it is for things not wrong in themselves that they reserve the choicest of their indignation. A man may naturally disclaim all moral kinship with the Reverend Mr. Zola or the hobgoblin old lady of the dolls; for these are gross and naked in-stances. And yet in each of us some similar element resides. The sight of a pleasure in which we cannot or else will not share moves us to a particular impatience. It may be because we are envious, or because we are sad, or because we dislike noise and romping — being so refined, or because — being so philosophic — we have an overweighing sense of life's gravity: at least, as we go on in years, we are all tempted to frown upon our neighbour's pleasures. People are nowadays so fond of resisting temptations; here is one to be resisted. They are fond of self-denial; here is a propensity that cannot be too peremptorily denied. There is an idea abroad among moral people that they should make their neighbours good. One person I have to make good: myself. But my duty to my neighbour is much more nearly expressed by saying that I have to make him happy — if I may.

III

Happiness and goodness, according to canting moralists, stand in the relation of effect and cause. There was never anything less proved or less probable: our happiness is never in our own hands; we inherit our constitution; we stand buffet among friends and enemies; we may be so built as to feel a sneer or an aspersion with unusual keenness, and so circumstanced as to be unusually exposed to them; we may have nerves very sensitive to pain, and be afflicted with a disease very painful. Virtue will not help us, and it is not meant to help us. It is not even its own reward, except for the self-centred and — I had almost said — the unamiable. No man can pacify his conscience; if quiet be what he want, he shall do better to let that organ perish from disuse. And to avoid the penalties of the law, and the minor *capitis diminutio* of social ostracism, is an affair of wisdom — of cunning, if you will — and not of virtue.

In his own life, then, a man is not to expect happiness, only to profit by it gladly when it shall arise; he is on duty here; he knows not how or why, and does not need to know; he knows not for what hire, and must not ask. Somehow or other, though he does not know what goodness is, he must try to be good; somehow

305

there need be few illusions left about himself. *Here lies one who meant well, tried a little, failed much:* — surely that may be his epitaph, of which he need not be ashamed. Nor will he complain at the summons which calls a defeated soldier from the field: defeated, ay, if he were Paul or Marcus Aurelius! — but if there is still one inch of fight in his old spirit, undishonoured. The faith which sustained him in his life-long blindness and life-long disappointment will scarce even be required in this last formality of laying down his arms. Give him a march with his old bones; there, out of the glorious sun-coloured earth, out of the day and the dust and the ecstasy — there goes another Faithful Failure!

From a recent book of verse, where there is more than one such beautiful and manly poem, I take this memorial piece: it says better than I can, what I love to think; let it be our parting word.

" A late lark twitters from the quiet skies;
And from the west,
Where the sun, his day's work ended,
Lingers as in content,
There falls on the old, gray city
An influence luminous and serene,
A shining peace.

" The smoke ascends
In a rosy-and-golden haze. The spires
Shine, and are changed. In the valley
Shadows rise. The lark sings on. The sun,
Closing his benediction,
Sinks, and the darkening air
Thrills with a sense of the triumphing night—
Night, with her train of stars
And her great gift of sleep.

308

A CHRISTMAS SERMON

" So be my passing!
   My task accomplished and the long day done,
   My wages taken, and in my heart
   Some late lark singing,
   Let me be gathered to the quiet west,
   The sundown splendid and serene,
   Death." [1]

[1] From *A Book of Verses* by William Ernest Henley.   D. Nutt,
1888.

[1888.]

THE SILVERADO SQUATTERS

THE SILVERADO SQUATTERS

THE scene of this little book is on a high mountain. There are, indeed, many higher; there are many of a nobler outline. It is no place of pilgrimage for the summary globe-trotter; but to one who lives upon its sides, Mount Saint Helena soon becomes a centre of interest. It is the Mont Blanc of one section of the Californian Coast Range, none of its near neighbours rising to one-half its altitude. It looks down on much green, intricate country. It feeds in the spring-time many splashing brooks. From its summit you must have an excellent lesson of geography: seeing, to the south, San Francisco Bay, with Tamalpais on the one hand and Monte Diablo on the other; to the west and thirty miles away, the open ocean; eastward, across the cornlands and thick tule swamps of Sacramento Valley, to where the Central Pacific railroad begins to climb the sides of the Sierras; and northward, for what I know, the white head of Shasta looking down on Oregon. Three counties, Napa County, Lake County, and Sonoma County, march across its cliffy shoulders. Its naked peak stands nearly four thousand five hundred feet above the sea; its sides are fringed with forest; and the soil, where it is bare, glows warm with cinnabar.

Life in its shadow goes rustically forward. Bucks,

and bears, and rattlesnakes, and former mining operations, are the staple of men's talk. Agriculture has only begun to mount above the valley. And though in a few years from now the whole district may be smiling with farms, passing trains shaking the mountain to the heart, many-windowed hotels lighting up the night like factories, and a prosperous city occupying the site of sleepy Calistoga; yet in the meantime, around the foot of that mountain the silence of nature reigns in a great measure unbroken, and the people of hill and valley go sauntering about their business as in the days before the flood.

To reach Mount Saint Helena from San Francisco, the traveller has twice to cross the bay: once by the busy Oakland Ferry, and again, after an hour or so of the railway, from Vallejo junction to Vallejo. Thence he takes rail once more to mount the long green strath of Napa Valley.

In all the contractions and expansions of that inland sea, the Bay of San Francisco, there can be few drearier scenes than the Vallejo Ferry. Bald shores and a low, bald islet inclose the sea; through the narrows the tide bubbles, muddy like a river. When we made the passage (bound, although yet we knew it not, for Silverado) the steamer jumped, and the black buoys were dancing in the jabble; the ocean breeze blew killing chill; and, although the upper sky was still unflecked with vapour, the sea fogs were pouring in from seaward, over the hilltops of Marin County, in one great, shapeless, silver cloud.

South Vallejo is typical of many Californian towns. It was a blunder; the site has proved untenable; and,

although it is still such a young place by the scale of
Europe, it has already begun to be deserted for its neighbour and namesake, North Vallejo. A long pier, a number of drinking saloons, a hotel of a great size, marshy
pools where the frogs keep up their croaking, and even
at high noon the entire absence of any human face or
voice — these are the marks of South Vallejo. Yet there
was a tall building beside the pier, labelled the *Star Flour
Mills;* and sea-going, full-rigged ships lay close along
shore, waiting for their cargo. Soon these would be
plunging round the Horn, soon the flour from the *Star
Flour Mills* would be landed on the wharves of Liverpool. For that, too, is one of England's outposts;
thither, to this gaunt mill, across the Atlantic and Pacific deeps and round about the icy Horn, this crowd
of great, three-masted, deep-sea ships come, bringing
nothing, and return with bread.

The Frisby House, for that was the name of the hotel,
was a place of fallen fortunes, like the town. It was
now given up to labourers, and partly ruinous. At dinner there was the ordinary display of what is called in the
west a *two-bit house:* the tablecloth checked red and
white, the plague of flies, the wire hencoops over the
dishes, the great variety and invariable vileness of the
food and the rough coatless men devouring it in silence.
In our bedroom, the stove would not burn, though it
would smoke; and while one window would not open,
the other would not shut. There was a view on a bit
of empty road, a few dark houses, a donkey wandering
with its shadow on a slope, and a blink of sea, with a
tall ship lying anchored in the moonlight. All about
that dreary inn frogs sang their ungainly chorus.

Early the next morning we mounted the hill along a wooden footway, bridging one marish spot after another. Here and there, as we ascended, we passed a house embowered in white roses. More of the bay became apparent, and soon the blue peak of Tamalpais rose above the green level of the island opposite. It told us we were still but a little way from the city of the Golden Gates, already, at that hour, beginning to awake among the sand-hills. It called to us over the waters as with the voice of a bird. Its stately head, blue as a sapphire on the paler azure of the sky, spoke to us of wider outlooks and the bright Pacific. For Tamalpais stands sentry, like a lighthouse, over the Golden Gates, between the bay and the open ocean, and looks down indifferently on both. Even as we saw and hailed it from Vallejo, seamen, far out at sea, were scanning it with shaded eyes; and, as if to answer to the thought, one of the great ships below began silently to clothe herself with white sails, homeward bound for England.

For some way beyond Vallejo the railway led us through bald green pastures. On the west the rough highlands of Marin shut off the ocean; in the midst, in long, straggling, gleaming arms, the bay died out among the grass; there were few trees and few enclosures; the sun shone wide over open uplands, the displumed hills stood clear against the sky. But by-and-by these hills began to draw nearer on either hand, and first thicket and then wood began to clothe their sides; and soon we were away from all signs of the sea's neighbourhood, mounting an inland, irrigated valley. A great variety of oaks stood, now severally, now in a becoming grove, among the fields and vineyards. The towns were compact, in about equal proportions, of bright, new wooden houses and great and growing forest trees; and the chapel bell on the engine sounded most festally that sunny Sunday, as we drew up at one green town after another, with the townsfolk trooping in their Sunday's best to see the strangers, with the sun sparkling on the clean houses, and great domes of foliage humming overhead in the breeze.

This pleasant Napa Valley is, at its north end, blockaded by our mountain. There, at Calistoga, the railroad ceases, and the traveller who intends faring farther, to the Geysers or to the springs in Lake County, must cross the spurs of the mountain by stage. Thus, Mount Saint Helena is not only a summit, but a frontier; and, up to the time of writing, it has stayed the progress of the iron horse.

IN THE VALLEY

CHAPTER I

CALISTOGA

It is difficult for a European to imagine Calistoga, the whole place is so new, and of such an occidental pattern; the very name, I hear, was invented at a supper-party by the man who found the springs.

The railroad and the highway come up the valley about parallel to one another. The street of Calistoga joins them, perpendicular to both — a wide street, with bright, clean, low houses, here and there a verandah over the sidewalk, here and there a horse-post, here and there lounging townsfolk. Other streets are marked out, and most likely named; for these towns in the New World begin with a firm resolve to grow larger, Washington and Broadway, and then First and Second, and so forth, being boldly plotted out as soon as the community indulges in a plan. But, in the meanwhile, all the life and most of the houses of Calistoga are concentrated upon that street between the railway station and the road. I never heard it called by any name, but I will hazard a guess that it is either Washington or Broadway. Here are the blacksmith's, the chemist's, the general merchant's, and Kong Sam Kee, the Chinese laundry-man's; here, probably, is the office of the local paper (for the place has a paper — they all have papers); and here certainly is one of the hotels, Cheeseborough's, whence the daring Foss, a man dear to legend, starts his horses for the Geysers.

It must be remembered that we are here in a land of stage-drivers and highwaymen: a land, in that sense, like England a hundred years ago. The highway robber — road-agent, he is quaintly called — is still busy in these parts. The fame of Vasquez is still young. Only a few years ago, the Lakeport stage was robbed a mile or two from Calistoga. In 1879, the dentist of Mendocino City, fifty miles away upon the coast, suddenly threw off the garments of his trade, like Grindoff, in *The Miller and his Men,* and flamed forth in his second dress as a captain of banditti. A great robbery was followed by a long chase, a chase of days if not of weeks, among the intricate hill-country; and the chase was followed by much desultory fighting, in which several — and the dentist, I believe, amongst the number — bit the dust. The grass was springing for the first time, nourished upon their blood, when I arrived in Calistoga. I am reminded of another highwayman of that same year. "He had been unwell," so ran his humorous defence, "and the doctor told him to take something, so he took the express box."

The cultus of the stage-coachman always flourishes highest where there are thieves on the road, and where the guard travels armed, and the stage is not only a link between country and city, and the vehicle of news, but has a faint warfaring aroma, like a man who should be brother to a soldier. California boasts her famous stage-drivers, and among the famous Foss is not forgotten.

Along the unfenced, abominable mountain roads, he launches his team with small regard to human life or the doctrine of probabilities. Flinching travellers, who behold themselves coasting eternity at every corner, look with natural admiration at their driver's huge, impassive, fleshy countenance. He has the very face for the driver in Sam Weller's anecdote, who upset the election party at the required point. Wonderful tales are current of his readiness and skill. One in particular, of how one of his horses fell at a ticklish passage of the road, and how Foss let slip the reins, and, driving over the fallen animal, arrived at the next stage with only three. This I relate as I heard it, without guarantee.

I only saw Foss once, though, strange as it may sound, I have twice talked with him. He lives out of Calistoga, at a ranche called Fossville. One evening, after he was long gone home, I dropped into Cheeseborough's, and was asked if I should like to speak with Mr. Foss. Supposing that the interview was impossible, and that I was merely called upon to subscribe the general sentiment, I boldly answered "Yes." Next moment, I had one instrument at my ear, another at my mouth, and found myself, with nothing in the world to say, conversing with a man several miles off among desolate hills. Foss rapidly and somewhat plaintively brought the conversation to an end; and he returned to his night's grog at Fossville, while I strolled forth again on Calistoga high street. But it was an odd thing that here, on what we are accustomed to consider the very skirts of civilisation, I should have used the telephone for the first time in my civilised career. So it goes in these young countries; telephones, and telegraphs, and newspapers, and advertisements running far ahead among the Indians and the grizzly bears.

Alone, on the other side of the railway, stands the Springs Hotel, with its attendant cottages. The floor of the valley is extremely level to the very roots of the hills; only here and there a hillock, crowned with pines, rises like the barrow of some chieftain famed in war; and right against one of these hillocks is the Springs Hotel — is or was; for since I was there the place has been destroyed by fire, and has risen again from its ashes. A lawn runs about the house, and the lawn is in its turn surrounded by a system of little five-roomed cottages, each with a verandah and a weedy palm before the door. Some of the cottages are let to residents, and these are wreathed in flowers. The rest are occupied by ordinary visitors to the hotel; and a very pleasant way this is, by which you have a little country cottage of your own, without domestic burthens, and by the day or week.

The whole neighbourhood of Mount Saint Helena is full of sulphur and of boiling springs. The Geysers are famous; they were the great health resort of the Indians before the coming of the whites. Lake County is dotted with spas; Hot Springs and White Sulphur Springs are the names of two stations on the Napa Valley railroad; and Calistoga itself seems to repose on a mere film above a boiling, subterranean lake. At one end of the hotel enclosure are the springs from which it takes its name, hot enough to scald a child seriously while I was there. At the other end, the tenant of a cottage sank a well, and there also the water came up boiling. It keeps this end of the valley as warm as a toast. I have gone across to the hotel a little after five in the morning, when a sea fog from the Pacific was hanging thick and gray, and dark and dirty overhead, and found the thermometer had been up before me, and had already climbed among the nineties; and in the stress of the day it was sometimes too hot to move about.

But in spite of this heat from above and below, doing one on both sides, Calistoga was a pleasant place to dwell in; beautifully green, for it was then that favoured moment in the Californian year, when the rains are over and the dusty summer has not yet set in; often visited by fresh airs, now from the mountain, now across Sonoma from the sea; very quiet, very idle, very silent but for the breezes and the cattle bells afield. And there was something satisfactory in the sight of that great mountain that enclosed us to the north: whether it stood, robed in sunshine, quaking to its topmost pinnacle with the heat and brightness of the day; or whether it set itself to weaving vapours, wisp after wisp growing, trembling, fleeting, and fading in the blue.

The tangled, woody, and almost trackless foothills that enclose the valley, shutting it off from Sonoma on the west, and from Yolo on the east — rough as they were in outline, dug out by winter streams, crowned by cliffy bluffs and nodding pine trees — were dwarfed into satellites by the bulk and bearing of Mount Saint Helena. She over-towered them by two-thirds of her own stature. She excelled them by the boldness of her profile. Her great bald summit, clear of trees and pasture, a cairn of quartz and cinnabar, rejected kinship with the dark and shaggy wilderness of lesser hilltops.

CHAPTER II

THE PETRIFIED FOREST

WE drove off from the Springs Hotel about three in the afternoon. The sun warmed me to the heart. A broad, cool wind streamed pauselessly down the valley, laden with perfume. Up at the top stood Mount Saint Helena, a bulk of mountain, bare atop, with tree-fringed spurs, and radiating warmth. Once we saw it framed in a grove of tall and exquisitely graceful white oaks, in line and colour a finished composition. We passed a cow stretched by the roadside, her bell slowly beating time to the movement of her ruminating jaws, her big red face crawled over by half a dozen flies, a monument of content.

A little farther, and we struck to the left up a mountain road, and for two hours threaded one valley after another, green, tangled, full of noble timber, giving us every now and again a sight of Mount Saint Helena and the blue hilly distance, and crossed by many streams, through which we splashed to the carriage-step. To the right or the left, there was scarce any trace of man but the road we followed; I think we passed but one ranchero's house in the whole distance, and that was closed and smokeless. But we had the society of these bright streams — dazzlingly clear, as is their wont, splashing from the wheels in diamonds, and striking a lively coolness through the sunshine. And what with the innumerable variety of greens, the masses of foliage tossing in the breeze, the glimpses of distance, the descents into seemingly impenetrable thickets, the continual dodging of the road, which made haste to plunge again into the covert, we had a fine sense of woods, and spring-time, and the open air.

Our driver gave me a lecture by the way on Californian trees — a thing I was much in need of, having fallen among painters who know the name of nothing, and Mexicans who know the name of nothing in English. He taught me the madrona, the manzanita, the buckeye, the maple; he showed me the crested mountain quail; he showed me where some young redwoods were already spiring heavenwards from the ruins of the old; for in this district all had already perished: redwoods and redskins, the two noblest indigenous living things, alike condemned.

At length, in a lonely dell, we came on a huge wooden gate with a sign upon it like an inn. "The Petrified Forest. Proprietor: C. Evans," ran the legend. Within, on a knoll of sward, was the house of the proprietor, and another smaller house hard by to serve as a museum, where photographs and petrifactions were retailed. It was a pure little isle of touristry among these solitary hills.

The proprietor was a brave old whitefaced Swede. He had wandered this way, Heaven knows how, and taken up his acres — I forget how many years ago — all alone, bent double with sciatica, and with six bits in his pocket and an axe upon his shoulder. Long, useless years of seafaring had thus discharged him at the end, penniless and sick. Without doubt he had tried his luck at the diggings, and got no good from that; without doubt he had loved the bottle, and lived the life of Jack ashore. But at the end of these adventures, here he came; and, the place hitting his fancy, down he sat to make a new life cf it, far from crimps and the salt sea. And the very sight of his ranche had done him good. It was " the handsomest spot in the Califorlny mountains." "Isn't it handsome, now?" he said. Every penny he makes goes into that ranche to make it handsomer. Then the climate, with the sea-breeze every afternoon in the hottest summer weather, had gradually cured the sciatica; and his sister and niece were now domesticated with him for company — or, rather, the niece came only once in the two days, teaching music the meanwhile in the valley. And then, for a last piece of luck, "the handsomest spot in the Califorlny mountains" had produced a petrified forest, which Mr. Evans now shows at the modest figure of half a dollar a head, or two-thirds of his capital when he first came there with an axe and a sciatica.

This tardy favourite of fortune — hobbling a little, I think, as if in memory of the sciatica, but with not a trace that I can remember of the sea — thoroughly ruralized from head to foot, proceeded to escort us up the hill behind his house.

"Who first found the forest?" asked my wife.

"The first? I was that man," said he. "I was cleaning up the pasture for my beasts, when I found *this* "—kicking a great redwood, seven feet in diameter, that lay there on its side, hollow heart, clinging lumps of bark, all changed into gray stone, with veins of quartz between what had been the layers of the wood.

"Were you surprised?"

"Surprised? No! What would I be surprised about? What did I know about petrifactions—following the sea? Petrifaction! There was no such word in my language! I knew about putrefaction, though! I thought it was a stone; so would you, if you was cleaning up pasture."

And now he had a theory of his own, which I did not quite grasp, except that the trees had not "grewed" there. But he mentioned, with evident pride, that he differed from all the scientific people who had visited the spot; and he flung about such words as "tufa" and "silica" with careless freedom.

When I mentioned I was from Scotland, "My old country," he said; "my old country"—with a smiling look and a tone of real affection in his voice. I was mightily surprised, for he was obviously Scandinavian, and begged him to explain. It seemed he had learned his English and done nearly all his sailing in Scotch ships. "Out of Glasgow," said he, "or Greenock; but that's all the same—they all hail from Glasgow." And he was so pleased with me for being a Scotsman, and his adopted compatriot, that he made me a present of a very beautiful piece of petrifaction—I believe the most beautiful and portable he had.

Here was a man, at least, who was a Swede, a Scot, and an American, acknowledging some kind allegiance to three lands. Mr. Wallace's Scoto-Circassian will not fail to come before the reader. I have myself met and spoken with a Fifeshire German, whose combination of abominable accents struck me dumb. But, indeed, I think we all belong to many countries. And perhaps this habit of much travel, and the engendering of scattered friendships, may prepare the euthanasia of ancient nations.

And the forest itself? Well, on a tangled, briery hillside — for the pasture would bear a little further cleaning up, to my eyes — there lie scattered thickly various lengths of petrified trunk, such as the one already mentioned. It is very curious, of course, and ancient enough, if that were all. Doubtless, the heart of the geologist beats quicker at the sight; but, for my part, I was mightily unmoved. Sight-seeing is the art of disappointment.

> "There's nothing under heaven so blue,
> That's fairly worth the travelling to."

But, fortunately, Heaven rewards us with many agreeable prospects and adventures by the way; and sometimes, when we go out to see a petrified forest, prepares a far more delightful curiosity in the form of Mr. Evans, whom may all prosperity attend throughout a long and green old age.

CHAPTER III

NAPA WINE

I was interested in Californian wine. Indeed, I am interested in all wines, and have been all my life, from the raisin wine that a schoolfellow kept secreted in his play-box up to my last discovery, those notable Valtellines that once shone upon the board of Cæsar.

Some of us, kind old Pagans, watch with dread the shadows falling on the age: how the unconquerable worm invades the sunny terraces of France, and Bordeaux is no more, and the Rhone a mere Arabia Petræa. Château Neuf is dead, and I have never tasted it; Hermitage — a hermitage indeed from all life's sorrows — lies expiring by the river. And in the place of these imperial elixirs, beautiful to every sense, gem-hued, flower-scented, dream-compellers: — behold upon the quays at Cette the chemicals arrayed; behold the analyst at Marseilles, raising hands in obsecration, attesting god Lyœus, and the vats staved in, and the dishonest wines poured forth among the sea. It is not Pan only; Bacchus, too, is dead.

If wine is to withdraw its most poetic countenance, the sun of the white dinner-cloth, a deity to be invoked by two or three, all fervent, hushing their talk, degusting tenderly, and storing reminiscences — for a bottle

of good wine, like a good act, shines ever in the retro-
spect — if wine is to desert us, go thy ways, old Jack!
Now we begin to have compunctions, and look back
at the brave bottles squandered upon dinner-parties,
where the guests drank grossly, discussing politics the
while, and even the schoolboy "took his whack," like
liquorice water. And at the same time, we look tim-
idly forward, with a spark of hope, to where the new
lands, already weary of producing gold, begin to green
with vineyards. A nice point in human history falls to
be decided by Californian and Australian wines.

Wine in California is still in the experimental stage;
and when you taste a vintage, grave economical questions are involved. The beginning of vine-planting is
like the beginning of mining for the precious metals:
the wine-grower also "prospects." One corner of land
after another is tried with one kind of grape after another. This is a failure; that is better; a third best.
So, bit by bit, they grope about for their Clos Vougeot
and Lafite. Those lodes and pockets of earth, more
precious than the precious ores, that yield inimitable
fragrance and soft fire; those virtuous Bonanzas, where
the soil has sublimated under sun and stars to something finer, and the wine is bottled poetry: these still
lie undiscovered; chaparral conceals, thicket embowers
them; the miner chips the rock and wanders farther,
and the grizzly muses undisturbed. But there they
bide their hour, awaiting their Columbus; and nature
nurses and prepares them. The smack of Californian
earth shall linger on the palate of your grandson.

Meanwhile the wine is merely a good wine; the best
that I have tasted better than a Beaujolais, and not un-

like. But the trade is poor; it lives from hand to mouth, putting its all into experiments, and forced to sell its vintages. To find one properly matured, and bearing its own name, is to be fortune's favourite.

Bearing its own name, I say, and dwell upon the innuendo.

"You want to know why California wine is not drunk in the States?" a San Francisco wine merchant said to me, after he had shown me through his premises. "Well, here's the reason."

And opening a large cupboard, fitted with many little drawers, he proceeded to shower me all over with a great variety of gorgeously tinted labels, blue, red, or yellow, stamped with crown or coronet, and hailing from such a profusion of *clos* and *châteaux,* that a single department could scarce have furnished forth the names. But it was strange that all looked unfamiliar.

"Chateau X——?" said I. "I never heard of that."

"I dare say not," said he. "I had been reading one of X——'s novels."

They were all castles in Spain! But that sure enough is the reason why California wine is not drunk in the States.

Napa valley has been long a seat of the wine-growing industry. It did not here begin, as it does too often, in the low valley lands along the river, but took at once to the rough foothills, where alone it can expect to prosper. A basking inclination, and stones, to be a reservoir of the day's heat, seem necessary to the soil for wine; the grossness of the earth must be evaporated, its marrow daily melted and refined for ages; until at length these clods that break below our footing, and to the eye

332

appear but common earth, are truly and to the perceiving mind, a masterpiece of nature. The dust of Richebourg, which the wind carries away, what an apotheosis of the dust! Not man himself can seem a stranger child of that brown, friable powder, than the blood and sun in that old flask behind the faggots.

A Californian vineyard, one of man's outposts in the wilderness, has features of its own. There is nothing here to remind you of the Rhine or Rhone, of the low *côte d'or,* or the infamous and scabby deserts of Champagne; but all is green, solitary, covert. We visited two of them, Mr. Schram's and Mr. M'Eckron's, sharing the same glen.

Some way down the valley below Calistoga, we turned sharply to the south and plunged into the thick of the wood. A rude trail rapidly mounting; a little stream tinkling by on the one hand, big enough perhaps after the rains, but already yielding up its life; overhead and on all sides a bower of green and tangled thicket, still fragrant and still flower-bespangled by the early season, where thimble-berry played the part of our English hawthorn, and the buck-eyes were putting forth their twisted horns of blossom: through all this, we struggled toughly upwards, canted to and fro by the roughness of the trail, and continually switched across the face by sprays of leaf or blossom. The last is no great inconvenience at home; but here in California it is a matter of some moment. For in all woods and by every wayside there prospers an abominable shrub or weed, called poison-oak, whose very neighbourhood is venomous to some, and whose actual touch is avoided by the most impervious.

The two houses, with their vineyards, stood each in a green niche of its own in this steep and narrow forest dell. Though they were so near, there was already a good difference in level; and Mr. M'Eckron's head must be a long way under the feet of Mr. Schram. No more had been cleared than was necessary for cultivation; close around each oasis ran the tangled wood; the glen enfolds them; there they lie basking in sun and silence, concealed from all but the clouds and the mountain birds.

Mr. M'Eckron's is a bachelor establishment; a little bit of a wooden house, a small cellar hard by in the hillside, and a patch of vines planted and tended single-handed by himself. He had but recently begun; his vines were young, his business young also; but I thought he had the look of the man who succeeds. He hailed from Greenock: he remembered his father putting him inside Mons Meg, and that touched me home; and we exchanged a word or two of Scotch, which pleased me more than you would fancy.

Mr. Schram's, on the other hand, is the oldest vineyard in the valley, eighteen years old, I think; yet he began a penniless barber, and even after he had broken ground up here with his black malvoisies, continued for long to tramp the valley with his razor. Now, his place is the picture of prosperity: stuffed birds in the verandah, cellars far dug into the hillside, and resting on pillars like a bandit's cave: — all trimness, varnish, flowers, and sunshine, among the tangled wildwood. Stout, smiling Mrs. Schram, who has been to Europe and apparently all about the States for pleasure, entertained Fanny in the verandah, while I was tasting wines

in the cellar.   To Mr. Schram this was a solemn office;
his serious gusto warmed my heart; prosperity had not
yet wholly banished a certain neophite and girlish trepi-
dation, and he followed every sip and read my face with
proud anxiety.   I tasted all.   I tasted every variety and
shade of Schramberger, red and white Schramberger,
Burgundy Schramberger, Schramberger Hock, Schramberger Golden Chasselas, the latter with a notable bouquet, and I fear to think how many more.   Much of it
goes to London — most, I think; and Mr. Schram has a
great notion of the English taste.

In this wild spot, I did not feel the sacredness of ancient cultivation.   It was still raw, it was no Marathon,
and no Johannisberg; yet the stirring sunlight, and the
growing vines, and the vats and bottles in the cavern,
made a pleasant music for the mind.   Here, also, earth's
cream was being skimmed and garnered; and the London customers can taste, such as it is, the tang of the
earth in this green valley.   So local, so quintessential is
a wine, that it seems the very birds in the verandah
might communicate a flavour, and that romantic cellar
influence the bottle next to be uncorked in Pimlico, and
the smile of jolly Mr. Schram might mantle in the glass.

But these are but experiments.   All things in this
new land are moving farther on: the wine-vats and the
miner's blasting tools but picket for a night, like Bed-
ouin pavillions; and to-morrow, to fresh woods!   This
stir of change and these perpetual echoes of the moving
footfall, haunt the land.   Men move eternally, still chasing Fortune; and, fortune found, still wander.   As we
drove back to Calistoga, the road lay empty of mere
passengers, but its green side was dotted with the

camps of travelling families: one cumbered with a great waggonful of household stuff, settlers going to occupy a ranche they had taken up in Mendocino, or perhaps Tehama County; another, a party in dust coats, men and women, whom we found camped in a grove on the roadside, all on pleasure bent, with a Chinaman to cook for them, and who waved their hands to us as we drove by.

CHAPTER IV

THE SCOT ABROAD

A FEW pages back, I wrote that a man belonged, in these days, to a variety of countries; but the old land is still the true love, the others are but pleasant infidelities. Scotland is indefinable; it has no unity except upon the map. Two languages, many dialects, innumerable forms of piety, and countless local patriotisms and prejudices, part us among ourselves more widely than the extreme east and west of that great continent of America. When I am at home, I feel a man from Glasgow to be something like a rival, a man from Barra to be more than half a foreigner. Yet let us meet in some far country, and, whether we hail from the braes of Manor or the braes of Mar, some ready-made affection joins us on the instant. It is not race. Look at us. One is Norse, one Celtic, and another Saxon. It is not community of tongue. We have it not among ourselves; and we have it almost to perfection, with English, or Irish, or American. It is no tie of faith, for we detest each other's errors. And yet somewhere, deep down in the heart of each one of us, something yearns for the old land, and the old kindly people.

Of all mysteries of the human heart, this is perhaps the

most inscrutable. There is no special loveliness in that gray country, with its rainy, sea-beat archipelago; its fields of dark mountains; its unsightly places, black with coal; its treeless, sour, unfriendly looking corn-lands; its quaint, gray, castled city, where the bells clash of a Sunday, and the wind squalls, and the salt showers fly and beat. I do not even know if I desire to live there; but let me hear, in some far land, a kindred voice sing out, "Oh, why left I my hame?" and it seems at once as if no beauty under the kind heavens, and no society of the wise and good, can repay me for my absence from my country. And though I think I would rather die elsewhere, yet in my heart of hearts I long to be buried among good Scots clods. I will say it fairly, it grows on me with every year: there are no stars so lovely as Edinburgh street-lamps. When I forget thee, auld Reekie, may my right hand forget its cunning!

The happiest lot on earth is to be born a Scotchman. You must pay for it in many ways, as for all other advantages on earth. You have to learn the paraphrases and the shorter catechism; you generally take to drink; your youth, as far as I can find out, is a time of louder war against society, of more outcry and tears and turmoil, than if you had been born, for instance, in England. But somehow life is warmer and closer; the hearth burns more redly; the lights of home shine softer on the rainy street; the very names, endeared in verse and music, cling nearer round our hearts. An Englishman may meet an Englishman to-morrow, upon Chimborazo, and neither of them care; but when the Scotch wine-grower told me of Mons Meg, it was like magic.

" From the dim shieling on the misty island
Mountains divide us, and a world of seas;
Yet still our hearts are true, our hearts are Highland,
And we, in dreams, behold the Hebrides."

And, Highland and Lowland, all our hearts are Scotch.

Only a few days after I had seen M'Eckron, a message reached me in my cottage. It was a Scotchman who had come down a long way from the hills to market. He had heard there was a countryman in Calistoga, and came round to the hotel to see him. We said a few words to each other; we had not much to say — should never have seen each other had we stayed at home, separated alike in space and in society; and then we shook hands, and he went his way again to his ranche among the hills, and that was all.

Another Scotchman there was, a resident, who for the mere love of the common country, douce, serious, religious man, drove me all about the valley, and took as much interest in me as if I had been his son: more, perhaps; for the son has faults too keenly felt, while the abstract countryman is perfect — like a whiff of peats.

And there was yet another. Upon him I came suddenly, as he was calmly entering my cottage, his mind quite evidently bent on plunder: a man of about fifty, filthy, ragged, roguish, with a chimney-pot hat and a tail coat, and a pursing of his mouth that might have been envied by an elder of the kirk. He had just such a face as I have seen a dozen times behind the plate.

"Hullo, sir!" I cried. "Where are you going?"

He turned round without a quiver.

"You are a Scotchman, sir?" he said gravely. "So am I; I come from Aberdeen. This is my card," presenting me with a piece of pasteboard which he had raked out of some gutter in the period of the rains. "I was just examining this palm," he continued, indicating the misbegotten plant before our door, "which is the largest sp*a*cimen I have yet observed in Califoarnia."

There were four or five larger within sight. But where was the use of argument? He produced a tapeline, made me help him to measure the tree at the level of the ground, and entered the figures in a large and filthy pocket-book, all with the gravity of Solomon. He then thanked me profusely, remarking that such little services were due between countrymen; shook hands with me, "for auld lang syne," as he said; and took himself solemnly away, radiating dirt and humbug as he went.

A month or two after this encounter of mine, there came a Scot to Sacramento — perhaps from Aberdeen. Anyway, there never was any one more Scotch in this wide world. He could sing and dance, and drink, I presume; and he played the pipes with vigour and success. All the Scotch in Sacramento became infatuated with him, and spent their spare time and money, driving him about in an open cab, between drinks, while he blew himself scarlet at the pipes. This is a very sad story. After he had borrowed money from every one, he and his pipes suddenly disappeared from Sacramento, and when I last heard, the police were looking for him.

I cannot say how this story amused me, when I felt myself so thoroughly ripe on both sides to be duped in the same way.

It is at least a curious thing, to conclude, that the races which wander widest, Jews and Scotch, should be the most clannish in the world.   But perhaps these two are cause and effect: "For ye were strangers in the land of Egypt."

WITH THE CHILDREN OF ISRAEL

CHAPTER I

TO INTRODUCE MR. KELMAR

ONE thing in this new country very particularly strikes a stranger, and that is the number of antiquities. Already there have been many cycles of population succeeding each other, and passing away and leaving behind them relics. These, standing on into changed times, strike the imagination as forcibly as any pyramid or feudal tower. The towns, like the vineyards, are experimentally founded: they grow great and prosper by passing occasions; and when the lode comes to an end, and the miners move elsewhere, the town remains behind them, like Palmyra in the desert. I suppose there are, in no country in the world, so many deserted towns as here in California.

The whole neighbourhood of Mount Saint Helena, now so quiet and sylvan, was once alive with mining camps and villages. Here there would be two thousand souls under canvas; there one thousand or fifteen hundred ensconced, as if for ever, in a town of comfortable houses. But the luck had failed, the mines petered out; and the army of miners had departed, and left this quarter of the world to the rattlesnakes and deer and grizzlies, and to the slower but steadier advance of husbandry.

It was with an eye on one of these deserted places, Pine Flat, on the Geysers road, that we had come first to Calistoga. There is something singularly enticing in the idea of going, rent-free, into a ready-made house. And to the British merchant, sitting at home at ease, it may appear that, with such a roof over your head and a spring of clear water hard by, the whole problem of the squatter's existence would be solved. Food, however, has yet to be considered. I will go as far as most people on tinned meats; some of the brightest moments of my life were passed over tinned mulligatawney in the cabin of a sixteen-ton schooner, storm-stayed in Portree Bay; but after suitable experiments, I pronounce authoritatively that man cannot live by tins alone. Fresh meat must be had on an occasion. It is true that the great Foss, driving by along the Geysers road, wooden-faced, but glorified with legend, might have been induced to bring us meat, but the great Foss could hardly bring us milk. To take a cow would have involved taking a field of grass and a milkmaid; after which it would have been hardly worth while to pause, and we might have added to our colony a flock of sheep and an experienced butcher.

It is really very disheartening how we depend on other people in this life. "Mihi est propositum," as you may see by the motto, "id quod regibus;" and behold it cannot be carried out, unless I find a neighbour rolling in cattle.

Now, my principal adviser in this matter was one whom I will call Kelmar. That was not what he called himself, but as soon as I set eyes on him, I knew it was or ought to be his name; I am sure it will be his name

among the angels. Kelmar was the store-keeper, a
Russian Jew, good-natured, in a very thriving way of
business, and, on equal terms, one of the most service-
able of men. He also had something of the expression
of a Scotch country elder, who, by some peculiarity,
should chance to be a Hebrew. He had a projecting
under lip, with which he continually smiled, or rather
smirked. Mrs. Kelmar was a singularly kind woman;
and the oldest son had quite a dark and romantic bearing, and might be heard on summer evenings playing
sentimental airs on the violin.

I had no idea, at the time I made his acquaintance,
what an important person Kelmar was. But the Jew
store-keepers of California, profiting at once by the
needs and habits of the people, have made themselves
in too many cases the tyrants of the rural population.
Credit is offered, is pressed on the new customer, and
when once he is beyond his depth, the tune changes,
and he is from thenceforth a white slave. I believe,
even from the little I saw, that Kelmar, if he choose to
put on the screw, could send half the settlers packing
in a radius of seven or eight miles round Calistoga.
These are continually paying him, but are never suffered
to get out of debt. He palms dull goods upon them,
for they dare not refuse to buy; he goes and dines with
them when he is on an outing, and no man is loudlier
welcomed; he is their family friend, the director of their
business, and, to a degree elsewhere unknown in modern days, their king.

For some reason, Kelmar always shook his head at
the mention of Pine Flat, and for some days I thought
he disapproved of the whole scheme and was propor-

tionately sad. One fine morning, however, he met me, wreathed in smiles. He had found the very place for me — Silverado, another old mining town, right up the mountain. Rufe Hanson, the hunter, could take care of us — fine people the Hansons; we should be close to the Toll House, where the Lakeport stage called daily; it was the best place for my health, besides. Rufe had been consumptive, and was now quite a strong man, ain't it? In short, the place and all its accompaniments seemed made for us on purpose.

He took me to his back door, whence, as from every point of Calistoga, Mount Saint Helena could be seen towering in the air. There, in the nick, just where the eastern foothills joined the mountain, and she herself began to rise above the zone of forest—there was Silverado. The name had already pleased me; the high station pleased me still more. I began to inquire with some eagerness. It was but a little while ago that Silverado was a great place. The mine — a silver mine, of course — had promised great things. There was quite a lively population, with several hotels and boarding-houses; and Kelmar himself had opened a branch store, and done extremely well—"Ain't it?" he said, appealing to his wife. And she said, "Yes; extremely well." Now there was no one living in the town but Rufe the hunter; and once more I heard Rufe's praises by the yard, and this time sung in chorus.

I could not help perceiving at the time that there was something underneath; that no unmixed desire to have us comfortably settled had inspired the Kelmars with this flow of words. But I was impatient to be gone, to be about my kingly project; and when we were offered

345

seats in Kelmar's waggon, I accepted on the spot.   The
plan of their next Sunday's outing took them, by good
fortune, over the border into Lake County.   They would
carry us so far, drop us at the Toll House, present us to
the Hansons, and call for us again on Monday morning
early.

CHAPTER II

WE were to leave by six precisely; that was solemnly pledged on both sides; and a messenger came to us the last thing at night, to remind us of the hour. But it was eight before we got clear of Calistoga: Kelmar, Mrs. Kelmar, a friend of theirs whom we named Abramina, her little daughter, my wife, myself, and, stowed away behind us, a cluster of ship's coffee-kettles. These last were highly ornamental in the sheen of their bright tin, but I could invent no reason for their presence. Our carriageful reckoned up, as near as we could get at it, some three hundred years to the six of us. Four of the six, besides, were Hebrews. But I never, in all my life, was conscious of so strong an atmosphere of holiday. No word was spoken but of pleasure; and even when we drove in silence, nods and smiles went round the party like refreshments.

The sun shone out of a cloudless sky. Close at the zenith rode the belated moon, still clearly visible, and, along one margin, even bright. The wind blew a gale from the north; the trees roared; the corn and the deep grass in the valley fled in whitening surges; the dust towered into the air along the road and dispersed like the smoke of battle. It was clear in our teeth from the

347

first, and for all the windings of the road it managed to keep clear in our teeth until the end.

For some two miles we rattled through the valley, skirting the eastern foothills; then we struck off to the right, through haugh-land, and presently, crossing a dry water-course, entered the Toll road, or, to be more local, entered on "the grade." The road mounts the near shoulder of Mount Saint Helena, bound northward into Lake County. In one place it skirts along the edge of a narrow and deep cañon, filled with trees, and I was glad, indeed, not to be driven at this point by the dashing Foss. Kelmar, with his unvarying smile, jogging to the motion of the trap, drove for all the world like a good, plain, country clergyman at home; and I profess I blessed him unawares for his timidity.

Vineyards and deep meadows, islanded and framed with thicket, gave place more and more as we ascended to woods of oak and madrona, dotted with enormous pines. It was these pines, as they shot above the lower wood, that produced that pencilling of single trees I had so often remarked from the valley. Thence, looking up and from however far, each fir stands separate against the sky no bigger than an eyelash; and all together lend a quaint, fringed aspect to the hills. The oak is no baby; even the madrona, upon these spurs of Mount Saint Helena, comes to a fine bulk and ranks with forest trees; but the pines look down upon the rest for underwood. As Mount Saint Helena among her foot-hills, so these dark giants out-top their fellow-vegetables. Alas! if they had left the redwoods, the pines, in turn, would have been dwarfed. But the redwoods, fallen from their high estate, are serving as family bedsteads, or yet more humbly as field fences, along all Napa Valley.

A rough smack of resin was in the air, and a crystal mountain purity. It came pouring over these green slopes by the oceanful. The wood sang aloud, and gave largely of their healthful breath. Gladness seemed to inhabit these upper zones, and we had left indifference behind us in the valley. "I to the hills will lift mine eyes!" There are days in a life when thus to climb out of the lowlands, seems like scaling heaven.

As we continued to ascend, the wind fell upon us with increasing strength. It was a wonder how the two stout horses managed to pull us up that steep incline and still face the athletic opposition of the wind, or how their great eyes were able to endure the dust. Ten minutes after we went by, a tree fell, blocking the road; and even before us leaves were thickly strewn, and boughs had fallen, large enough to make the passage difficult. But now we were hard by the summit. The road crosses the ridge, just in the nick that Kelmar showed me from below, and then, without pause, plunges down a deep, thickly wooded glen on the farther side. At the highest point a trail strikes up the main hill to the leftward; and that leads to Silverado. A hundred yards beyond, and in a kind of elbow of the glen, stands the Toll House Hotel. We came up the one side, were caught upon the summit by the whole weight of the wind as it poured over into Napa Valley, and a minute after had drawn up in shelter, but all buffetted and breathless, at the Toll House door.

A water-tank, and stables, and a gray house of two stories, with gable ends and a verandah, are jammed hard against the hillside, just where a stream has cut for itself a narrow cañon, filled with pines. The pines go right up overhead; a little more and the stream might have played, like a fire-hose, on the Toll House roof. In front the ground drops as sharply as it rises behind. There is just room for the road and a sort of promontory of croquet ground, and then you can lean over the edge and look deep below you through the wood. I said croquet *ground,* not *green;* for the surface was of brown, beaten earth. The toll-bar itself was the only other note of originality: a long beam, turning on a post, and kept slightly horizontal by a counterweight of stones. Regularly about sundown this rude barrier was swung, like a derrick, across the road and made fast, I think, to a tree upon the farther side.

On our arrival there followed a gay scene in the bar. I was presented to Mr. Corwin, the landlord; to Mr. Jennings, the engineer, who lives there for his health; to Mr. Hoddy, a most pleasant little gentleman, once a member of the Ohio legislature, again the editor of a local paper, and now, with undiminished dignity, keeping the Toll House bar. I had a number of drinks and cigars bestowed on me, and enjoyed a famous opportunity of seeing Kelmar in his glory, friendly, radiant, smiling, steadily edging one of the ship's kettles on the reluctant Corwin. Corwin, plainly aghast, resisted gallantly, and for that bout victory crowned his arms.

At last we set forth for Silverado on foot. Kelmar and his jolly Jew girls were full of the sentiment of Sunday outings, breathed geniality and vagueness, and suffered a little vile boy from the hotel to lead them here and there about the woods. For three people all so old, so bulky in body, and belonging to a race so venerable, they could not but surprise us by their extreme and almost imbecile youthfulness of spirit. They were only going to stay ten minutes at the Toll House; had they not twenty long miles of road before them on the other side? Stay to dinner? Not they! Put up the horses? Never. Let us attach them to the verandah by a wisp of straw rope, such as would not have held a person's hat on that blustering day. And with all these protestations of hurry, they proved irresponsible like children. Kelmar himself, shrewd old Russian Jew, with a smirk that seemed just to have concluded a bargain to its satisfaction, intrusted himself and us devoutly to that boy. Yet the boy was patently fallacious; and for that matter a most unsympathetic urchin, raised apparently on gingerbread. He was bent on his own pleasure, nothing else; and Kelmar followed him to his ruin, with the same shrewd smirk. If the boy said there was "a hole there in the hill"—a hole, pure and simple, neither more nor less—Kelmar and his Jew girls would follow him a hundred yards to look complacently down that hole. For two hours we looked for houses; and for two hours they followed us, smelling trees, picking flowers, foisting false botany on the unwary. Had we taken five, with that vile lad to head them off on idle divagations, for five they would have smiled and stumbled through the woods.

However, we came forth at length, and as by accident, upon a lawn, sparse planted like an orchard, but with forest instead of fruit trees. That was the site of Silverado mining town. A piece of ground was levelled up, where Kelmar's store had been; and facing that we saw Rufe Hanson's house, still bearing on its front the legend *Silverado Hotel*. Not another sign of habitation. Silverado town had all been carted from the scene; one of the houses was now the schoolhouse far down the road; one was gone here, one there, but all were gone away. It was now a sylvan solitude, and the silence was unbroken but by the great, vague voice of the wind. Some days before our visit, a grizzly bear had been sporting round the Hansons' chicken-house.

Mrs. Hanson was at home alone, we found. Rufe had been out after a "bar," had risen late, and was now gone, it did not clearly appear whither. Perhaps he had had wind of Kelmar's coming, and was now ensconced among the underwood, or watching us from the shoulder of the mountain. We, hearing there were no houses to be had, were for immediately giving up all hopes of Silverado. But this, somehow, was not to Kelmar's fancy. He first proposed that we should "camp someveres around, ain't it?" waving his hand cheerily as though to weave a spell; and when that was firmly rejected, he decided that we must take up house with the Hansons. Mrs. Hanson had been, from the first, flustered, subdued, and a little pale; but from this proposition she recoiled with haggard indignation. So did we, who would have preferred, in a manner of speaking, death. But Kelmar was not to be put by. He edged Mrs. Hanson into a corner, where for a long time he threatened her with his forefinger, like a character in Dickens; and the poor woman, driven to her entrenchments, at last remembered with a shriek that there were still some houses at the tunnel.

Thither we went; the Jews, who should already have

been miles into Lake County, still cheerily accompanying us. For about a furlong we followed a good road
along the hillside through the forest, until suddenly that
road widened out and came abruptly to an end. A cañon, woody below, red, rocky, and naked overhead, was
here walled across by a dump of rolling stones, danger-
ously steep, and from twenty to thirty feet in height. A
rusty iron chute on wooden legs came flying, like a
monstrous gargoyle, across the parapet. It was down
this that they poured the precious ore; and below here
the carts stood to wait their lading, and carry it mill-
ward down the mountain.

The whole cañon was so entirely blocked, as if by
some rude guerilla fortification, that we could only
mount by lengths of wooden ladder, fixed in the hillside. These led us round the farther corner of the dump;
and when they were at an end, we still persevered over
loose rubble and wading deep in poison oak, till we
struck a triangular platform, filling up the whole glen,
and shut in on either hand by bold projections of the
mountain. Only in front the place was open like the
proscenium of a theatre, and we looked forth into a great
realm of air, and down upon treetops and hilltops, and
far and near on wild and varied country. The place still
stood as on the day it was deserted: a line of iron rails
with a bifurcation; a truck in working order; a world
of lumber, old wood, old iron; a blacksmith's forge on
one side, half buried in the leaves of dwarf madronas;
and on the other, an old brown wooden house.

Fanny and I dashed at the house. It consisted of three
rooms, and was so plastered against the hill, that one
room was right atop of another, that the upper floor was

more than twice as large as the lower, and that all three apartments must be entered from a different side and level. Not a window-sash remained. The door of the lower room was smashed, and one panel hung in splinters. We entered that, and found a fair amount of rubbish: sand and gravel that had been sifted in there by the mountain winds; straw, sticks, and stones; a table, a barrel; a plate-rack on the wall; two home-made boot-jacks, signs of miners and their boots; and a pair of papers pinned on the boarding, headed respectively "Funnel No. 1," and "Funnel No. 2," but with the tails torn away. The window, sashless of course, was choked with the green and sweetly smelling foliage of a bay; and through a chink in the floor, a spray of poison oak had shot up and was handsomely prospering in the interior. It was my first care to cut away that poison oak, Fanny standing by at a respectful distance. That was our first improvement by which we took possession.

The room immediately above could only be entered by a plank propped against the threshold, along which the intruder must foot it gingerly, clutching for support to sprays of poison oak, the proper product of the country. Herein was, on either hand, a triple tier of beds, where miners had once lain; and the other gable was pierced by a sashless window and a doorless doorway opening on the air of heaven, five feet above the ground. As for the third room, which entered squarely from the ground level, but higher up the hill and further up the cañon, it contained only rubbish and the uprights for another triple tier of beds.

The whole building was overhung by a bold, lion-like, red rock. Poison oak, sweet bay trees, calycanthus, brush, and chaparral, grew freely but sparsely all about it. In front, in the strong sunshine, the platform lay overstrewn with busy litter, as though the labours of the mine might begin again to-morrow in the morning.

Following back into the cañon, among the mass of rotting plant and through the flowering bushes, we came to a great crazy staging, with a wry windlass on the top; and clambering up, we could look into an open shaft, leading edgeways down into the bowels of the mountain, trickling with water, and lit by some stray sun-gleams, whence I know not. In that quiet place the still, far-away tinkle of the water-drops was loudly audible. Close by, another shaft led edgeways up into the superincumbent shoulder of the hill. It lay partly open; and sixty or a hundred feet above our head, we could see the strata propped apart by solid wooden wedges, and a pine, half undermined, precariously nodding on the verge. Here also a rugged, horizontal tunnel ran straight into the unsunned bowels of the rock. This secure angle in the mountain's flank was, even on this wild day, as still as my lady's chamber. But in the tunnel a cold, wet draught tempestuously blew. Nor have I ever known that place otherwise than cold and windy.

Such was our first prospect of Juan Silverado. I own I had looked for something different: a clique of neighbourly houses on a village green, we shall say, all empty to be sure, but swept and varnished; a trout stream brawling by; great elms or chestnuts, humming with bees and nested in by song-birds; and the mountains standing round about, as at Jerusalem. Here, mountain and house and the old tools of industry were all alike rusty and downfalling. The hill was here wedged up, and there poured forth its bowels in a spout of broken mineral; man with his picks and powder, and nature with her own great blasting tools of sun and rain, labouring together at the ruin of that proud mountain. The view up the cañon was a glimpse of devastation; dry red minerals sliding together, here and there a crag, here and there dwarf thicket clinging in the general glissade, and over all a broken outline trenching on the blue of heaven. Downwards indeed, from our rock eyrie, we beheld the greener side of nature; and the bearing of the pines and the sweet smell of bays and nutmegs commended themselves gratefully to our senses. One way and another, now the die was cast. Silverado be it!

After we had got back to the Toll House, the Jews were not long of striking forward. But I observed that one of the Hanson lads came down, before their departure, and returned with a ship's kettle. Happy Hansons! Nor was it until after Kelmar was gone, if I remember rightly, that Rufe put in an appearance to arrange the details of our installation.

The latter part of the day, Fanny and I sat in the verandah of the Toll House, utterly stunned by the uproar of the wind among the trees on the other side of the valley. Sometimes, we would have it it was like a sea, but it was not various enough for that; and again, we thought it like the roar of a cataract, but it was too changeful for the cataract; and then we would decide, speaking in sleepy voices, that it could be compared with nothing but itself. My mind was entirely preoccupied by the noise. I hearkened to it by the hour, gapingly hearkened, and let my cigarette go out. Sometimes the wind would make a sally nearer hand, and send a shrill, whistling crash among the foliage on our side of the glen; and sometimes a backdraught would strike into the elbow where we sat, and cast the gravel and torn leaves into our faces. But for the most part, this great, streaming gale passed unweariedly by us into Napa Valley, not two hundred yards away, visible by the tossing boughs, stunningly audible, and yet not moving a hair upon our heads. So it blew all night long while I was writing up my journal, and after we were in bed, under a cloudless, starset heaven; and so it was blowing still next morning when we rose.

It was a laughable thought to us, what had become of our cheerful, wandering Hebrews. We could not suppose they had reached a destination. The meanest boy could lead them miles out of their way to see a gopher-hole. Boys, we felt to be their special danger; none others were of that exact pitch of cheerful irrelevancy to exercise a kindred sway upon their minds: but before the attractions of a boy their most settled resolutions would be wax. We thought we could follow in fancy these three aged Hebrew truants wandering in and out on hilltop and in thicket, a demon boy trotting far ahead, their will-o'-the-wisp conductor; and at last about midnight, the wind still roaring in the darkness, we had a vision of all three on their knees upon a mountain-top around a glow-worm.

CHAPTER III

THE RETURN

NEXT morning we were up by half-past five, according to agreement, and it was ten by the clock before our Jew boys returned to pick us up: Kelmar, Mrs. Kelmar, and Abramina, all smiling from ear to ear, and full of tales of the hospitality they had found on the other side. It had not gone unrewarded; for I observed with interest that the ship's kettles, all but one, had been "placed." Three Lake County families, at least, endowed for life with a ship's kettle. Come, this was no misspent Sunday. The absence of the kettles told its own story: our Jews said nothing about them; but, on the other hand, they said many kind and comely things about the people they had met. The two women, in particular, had been charmed out of themselves by the sight of a young girl surrounded by her admirers; all evening, it appeared, they had been triumphing together in the girl's innocent successes, and to this natural and unselfish joy they gave expression in language that was beautiful by its simplicity and truth.

Take them for all in all, few people have done my heart more good; they seemed so thoroughly entitled to happiness, and to enjoy it in so large a measure and so

358

free from after-thought; almost they persuaded me to be a Jew. There was, indeed, a chink of money in their talk. They particularly commended people who were well to do. " *He* don't care — ain't it?" was their highest word of commendation to an individual fate; and here I seem to grasp the root of their philosophy — it was to be free from care, to be free to make these Sunday wanderings, that they so eagerly pursued after wealth; and all this carefulness was to be careless. The fine, good humour of all three seemed to declare they had attained their end. Yet there was the other side to it; and the recipients of kettles perhaps cared greatly.

No sooner had they returned, than the scene of yesterday began again. The horses were not even tied with a straw rope this time — it was not worth while; and Kelmar disappeared into the bar, leaving them under a tree on the other side of the road. I had to devote myself. I stood under the shadow of that tree for, I suppose, hard upon an hour, and had not the heart to be angry. Once some one remembered me, and brought me out a half a tumblerful of the playful, innocuous American cocktail. I drank it, and lo! veins of living fire ran down my leg; and then a focus of conflagration remained seated in my stomach, not unpleasantly, for quarter of an hour. I love these sweet, fiery pangs, but I will not court them. The bulk of the time I spent in repeating as much French poetry as I could remember to the horses, who seemed to enjoy it hugely. And now it went —

"O ma vieille Font-georges
Où volent les rouges-gorges: "

and again, to a more trampling measure —

" Et tout tremble, Irun, Coïmbre,
Santander, Almodovar,
Sitôt qu'on entend le timbre
Des cymbales de Bivar."

The redbreasts and the brooks of Europe, in that dry and songless land; brave old names and wars, strong cities, cymbals, and bright armour, in that nook of the mountain, sacred only to the Indian and the bear! This is still the strangest thing in all man's travelling, that he should carry about with him incongruous memories. There is no foreign land; it is the traveller only that is foreign, and now and again, by a flash of recollection, lights up the contrasts of the earth.

But while I was thus wandering in my fancy, great feats had been transacted in the bar. Corwin the bold had fallen, Kelmar was again crowned with laurels, and the last of the ship's kettles had changed hands. If I had ever doubted the purity of Kelmar's motives, if I had ever suspected him of a single eye to business in his eternal dallyings, now at least, when the last kettle was disposed of, my suspicions must have been allayed. I dare not guess how much more time was wasted; nor how often we drove off, merely to drive back again and renew interrupted conversations about nothing, before the Toll House was fairly left behind. Alas! and not a mile down the grade there stands a ranche in a sunny vineyard, and here we must all dismount again and enter.

Only the old lady was at home, Mrs. Guele, a brown old Swiss dame, the picture of honesty; and with her we drank a bottle of wine and had an age-long conversation, which would have been highly delightful if Fanny and I had not been faint with hunger. The ladies each narrated the story of her marriage, our two Hebrews with the prettiest combination of sentiment and financial bathos. Abramina, specially, endeared herself with every word. She was as simple, natural, and engaging as a kid that should have been brought up to the business of a money-changer. One touch was so resplendently Hebraic that I cannot pass it over. When her "old man" wrote home for her from America, her old man's family would not intrust her with the money for the passage, till she had bound herself by an oath — on her knees, I think she said — not to employ it otherwise. This had tickled Abramina hugely, but I think it tickled me fully more.

Mrs. Guele told of her home-sickness up here in the long winters; of her honest, country-woman troubles and alarms upon the journey; how in the bank at Frankfort she had feared lest the banker, after having taken her cheque, should deny all knowledge of it — a fear I have myself every time I go to a bank; and how crossing the Luneburger Heath, an old lady, witnessing her trouble and finding whither she was bound, had given her "the blessing of a person eighty years old, which would be sure to bring her safely to the States. And the first thing I did," added Mrs. Guele, "was to fall downstairs."

At length we got out of the house, and some of us into the trap, when — judgment of Heaven! — here came Mr. Guele from his vineyard. So another quarter of an hour went by; till at length, at our earnest pleading, we set forth again in earnest, Fanny and I white-faced and silent, but the Jews still smiling. The heart fails me. There was yet another stoppage! And we drove at last into Calistoga past two in the afternoon, Fanny and I having breakfasted at six in the morning, eight mortal hours before. We were a pallid couple; but still the Jews were smiling.

So ended our excursion with the village usurers; and, now that it was done, we had no more idea of the nature of the business, nor of the part we had been playing in it, than the child unborn. That all the people we had met were the slaves of Kelmar, though in various degrees of servitude; that we ourselves had been sent up the mountain in the interests of none but Kelmar; that the money we laid out, dollar by dollar, cent by cent, and through the hands of various intermediaries, should all hop ultimately into Kelmar's till; — these were facts that we only grew to recognise in the course of time and by the accumulation of evidence. At length all doubt was quieted, when one of the kettle-holders confessed. Stopping his trap in the moonlight, a little way out of Calistoga, he told me, in so many words, that he dare not show face there with an empty pocket. "You see, I don't mind if it was only five dollars, Mr. Stevens," he said, "but I must give Mr. Kelmar *something*."

Even now, when the whole tyranny is plain to me, I cannot find it in my heart to be as angry as perhaps I should be with the Hebrew tyrant. The whole game of business is beggar my neighbour; and though perhaps that game looks uglier when played at such close quarters and on so small a scale, it is none the more intrinsically inhumane for that. The village usurer is not so sad a feature of humanity and human progress as the millionaire manufacturer, fattening on the toil and loss of thousands, and yet declaiming from the platform against the greed and dishonesty of landlords. If it were fair for Cobden to buy up land from owners whom he thought unconscious of its proper value, it was fair enough for my Russian Jew to give credit to his farmers. Kelmar, if he was unconscious of the beam in his own eye, was at least silent in the matter of his brother's mote.

THE ACT OF SQUATTING

THERE were four of us squatters — myself and my wife, the King and Queen of Silverado; Sam, the Crown Prince; and Chuchu, the Grand Duke. Chuchu, a setter crossed with spaniel, was the most unsuited for a rough life. He had been nurtured tenderly in the society of ladies; his heart was large and soft; he regarded the sofa-cushion as a bed-rock necessary of existence. Though about the size of a sheep, he loved to sit in ladies' laps; he never said a bad word in all his blameless days; and if he had seen a flute, I am sure he could have played upon it by nature. It may seem hard to say it of a dog, but Chuchu was a tame cat.

The king and queen, the grand duke, and a basket of cold provender for immediate use, set forth from Calistoga in a double buggy; the crown prince, on horseback, led the way like an outrider. Bags and boxes and a second-hand stove were to follow close upon our heels by Hanson's team.

It was a beautiful still day; the sky was one field of azure. Not a leaf moved, not a speck appeared in heaven. Only from the summit of the mountain one little snowy wisp of cloud after another kept detaching itself, like smoke from a volcano, and blowing southward in some high stream of air: Mount Saint Helena still at her interminable task, making the weather, like a Lapland witch.

By noon we had come in sight of the mill: a great brown building, half-way up the hill, big as a factory, two stories high, and with tanks and ladders along the roof; which, as a pendicle of Silverado mine, we held to be an outlying province of our own. Thither, then, we went, crossing the valley by a grassy trail; and there lunched out of the basket, sitting in a kind of portico, and wondering, while we ate, at this great bulk of useless building. Through a chink we could look far down into the interior, and see sunbeams floating in the dust and striking on tier after tier of silent, rusty machinery. It cost six thousand dollars, twelve hundred English sovereigns; and now, here it stands deserted, like the temple of a forgotten religion, the busy millers toiling somewhere else. All the time we were there, mill and mill town showed no sign of life; that part of the mountain-side, which is very open and green, was tenanted by no living creature but ourselves and the insects; and nothing stirred but the cloud manufactory upon the mountain summit. It was odd to compare this with the former days, when the engine was in full blast, the mill palpitating to its strokes, and the carts came rattling down from Silverado, charged with ore.

By two we had been landed at the mine, the buggy was gone again, and we were left to our own reflections and the basket of cold provender, until Hanson should arrive. Hot as it was by the sun, there was something chill in such a home-coming, in that world of wreck and rust, splinter and rolling gravel, where for so many years no fire had smoked.

Silverado platform filled the whole width of the cañon. Above, as I have said, this was a wild, red, stony gully in the mountains; but below it was a wooded dingle. And through this, I was told, there had gone a path between the mine and the Toll House — our natural north-west passage to civilization. I found and followed it, clearing my way as I went through fallen branches and dead trees. It went straight down that steep cañon, till it brought you out abruptly over the roofs of the hotel. There was nowhere any break in the descent. It almost seemed as if, were you to drop a stone down the old iron chute at our platform, it would never rest until it hopped upon the Toll House shingles. Signs were not wanting of the ancient greatness of Silverado. The footpath was well marked, and had been well trodden in the old days by thirsty miners. And far down, buried in foliage, deep out of sight of Silverado, I came on a last outpost of the mine — a mound of gravel, some wreck of wooden aqueduct, and the mouth of a tunnel, like a treasure grotto in a fairy story. A stream of water, fed by the invisible leakage from our shaft, and dyed red with cinnabar or iron, ran trippingly forth out of the bowels of the cave; and, looking far under the arch, I could see something like an iron lantern fastened on the rocky wall. It was a promising spot for the imagination. No boy could have left it unexplored.

The stream thenceforward stole along the bottom of the dingle, and made, for that dry land, a pleasant warbling in the leaves. Once, I suppose, it ran splashing down the whole length of the cañon, but now its head waters had been tapped by the shaft at Silverado, and for a great part of its course it wandered sunless among the joints of the mountain. No wonder that it should better its pace when it sees, far before it, daylight whitening in the arch, or that it should come trotting forth into the sunlight with a song.

The two stages had gone by when I got down, and the Toll House stood, dozing in sun and dust and silence, like a place enchanted. My mission was after hay for bedding, and that I was readily promised. But when I mentioned that we were waiting for Rufe, the people shook their heads. Rufe was not a regular man any way, it seemed; and if he got playing poker—— Well, poker was too many for Rufe. I had not yet heard them bracketted together; but it seemed a natural conjunction, and commended itself swiftly to my fears; and as soon as I returned to Silverado and had told my story, we practically gave Hanson up, and set ourselves to do what we could find do-able in our desert-island state.

The lower room had been the assayer's office. The floor was thick with *débris* — part human, from the former occupants; part natural, sifted in by mountain winds. In a sea of red dust there swam or floated sticks, boards, hay, straw, stones, and paper; ancient newspapers, above all — for the newspaper, especially when torn, soon becomes an antiquity — and bills of the Silverado boarding-house, some dated Silverado, some Calistoga Mine. Here is one, verbatim; and if any one can calculate the scale of charges, he has my envious admiration.

Calistoga Mine, May 3rd, 1875.

John Stanley
    To S. Chapman, Cr.

To board from April 1st, to April 30 . . .	$25	75
" " " May 1st, to 3rd . . .	2	00
	27	75

Where is John Stanley mining now? Where is S. Chapman, within whose hospitable walls we were to lodge? The date was but five years old, but in that time the world had changed for Silverado; like Palmyra in the desert, it had outlived its people and its purpose; we camped, like Layard, amid ruins, and these names spoke to us of pre-historic time. A boot-jack, a pair of boots, a dog-hutch, and these bills of Mr. Chapman's were the only speaking relics that we disinterred from all that vast Silverado rubbish-heap; but what would I not have given to unearth a letter, a pocket-book, a diary, only a ledger, or a roll of names, to take me back, in a more personal manner, to the past? It pleases me, besides, to fancy that Stanley or Chapman, or one of their companions, may light upon this chronicle, and be struck by the name, and read some news of their anterior home, coming, as it were, out of a subsequent epoch of history in that quarter of the world.

As we were tumbling the mingled rubbish on the floor, kicking it with our feet, and groping for these written evidences of the past, Sam, with a somewhat whitened face, produced a paper bag. "What's this?" said he. It contained a granulated powder, something the colour of Gregory's Mixture, but rosier; and as there were several of the bags, and each more or less broken, the powder was spread widely on the floor. Had any of us ever seen giant powder? No, nobody had; and instantly there grew up in my mind a shadowy belief, verging with every moment nearer to certitude, that I had somewhere heard somebody describe it as just such a powder as the one around us. I have learnt since that it is a substance not unlike tallow, and is made up in rolls for all the world like tallow candles.

Fanny, to add to our happiness, told us a story of a gentleman who had camped one night, like ourselves, by a deserted mine. He was a handy, thrifty fellow, and looked right and left for plunder, but all he could lay his hands on was a can of oil. After dark he had to see to the horses with a lantern; and not to miss an opportunity, filled up his lamp from the oil can. Thus equipped, he set forth into the forest. A little while after, his friends heard a loud explosion; the mountain echoes bellowed, and then all was still. On examination, the can proved to contain oil, with the trifling addition of nitro-glycerine; but no research disclosed a trace of either man or lantern.

It was a pretty sight, after this anecdote, to see us sweeping out the giant powder. It seemed never to be far enough away. And, after all, it was only some rock pounded for assay.

So much for the lower room. We scraped some of the rougher dirt off the floor, and left it. That was our sitting-room and kitchen, though there was nothing to sit upon but the table, and no provision for a fire except a hole in the roof of the room above, which had once contained the chimney of a stove.

To that upper room we now proceeded. There were the eighteen bunks in a double tier, nine on either hand, where from eighteen to thirty-six miners had once snored together all night long, John Stanley, perhaps, snoring loudest. There was the roof, with a hole in it through which the sun now shot an arrow. There was the floor, in much the same state as the one below, though, perhaps, there was more hay, and certainly there was the added ingredient of broken glass, the man who stole the window-frames having apparently made a miscarriage with this one. Without a broom, without hay or bedding, we could but look about us with a beginning of despair. The one bright arrow of day, in that gaunt and shattered barrack, made the rest look dirtier and darker, and the sight drove us at last into the open.

Here, also, the handiwork of man lay ruined: but the plants were all alive and thriving; the view below was fresh with the colours of nature; and we had exchanged a dim, human garret for a corner, even although it were untidy, of the blue hall of heaven. Not a bird, not a beast, not a reptile. There was no noise in that part of the world, save when we passed beside the staging, and heard the water musically falling in the shaft.

We wandered to and fro. We searched among that drift of lumber — wood and iron, nails and rails, and sleepers and the wheels of trucks. We gazed up the cleft into the bosom of the mountain. We sat by the margin of the dump and saw, far below us, the green treetops standing still in the clear air. Beautiful perfumes, breaths of bay, resin, and nutmeg, came to us more often and grew sweeter and sharper as the afternoon declined. But still there was no word of Hanson.

I set to with pick and shovel, and deepened the pool behind the shaft, till we were sure of sufficient water for the morning; and by the time I had finished, the sun had begun to go down behind the mountain shoulder, the platform was plunged in quiet shadow, and a chill descended from the sky. Night began early in our cleft. Before us, over the margin of the dump, we could see the sun still striking aslant into the wooded nick below, and on the battlemented, pine-bescattered ridges on the farther side.

There was no stove, of course, and no hearth in our lodging, so we betook ourselves to the blacksmith's forge across the platform. If the platform be taken as a stage, and the out-curving margin of the dump to represent the line of the footlights, then our house would be the first wing on the actor's left, and this blacksmith's forge, although no match for it in size, the foremost on the right. It was a low, brown cottage, planted close against the hill, and overhung by the foliage and peeling boughs of a madrona thicket. Within it was full of dead leaves and mountain dust, and rubbish from the mine. But we soon had a good fire brightly blazing, and sat close about it on impromptu seats. Chuchu, the slave of sofa-cushions, whimpered for a softer bed; but the rest of us were greatly revived and comforted by that good creature — fire, which gives us warmth and light and companionable sounds, and colours up the emptiest building with better than frescoes. For a while it was even pleasant in the forge, with the blaze in the midst, and a look over our shoulders on the woods and mountains where the day was dying like a dolphin.

It was between seven and eight before Hanson arrived, with a waggonful of our effects and two of his wife's relatives to lend him a hand. The elder showed surprising strength. He would pick up a huge packing-case, full of books of all things, swing it on his shoulder, and away up the two crazy ladders and the breakneck spout of rolling mineral, familiarly termed a

path, that led from the cart-track to our house. Even
for a man unburthened, the ascent was toilsome and
precarious; but Irvine scaled it with a light foot, carrying box after box, as the hero whisks the stage child
up the practicable footway beside the waterfall of
the fifth act. With so strong a helper, the business
was speedily transacted. Soon the assayer's office
was thronged with our belongings, piled higgledy-pig-
gledy, and upside down, about the floor. There were
our boxes, indeed, but my wife had left her keys in Calistoga. There was the stove, but, alas! our carriers had
forgot the chimney, and lost one of the plates along the
road. The Silverado problem was scarce solved.

Rufe himself was grave and good-natured over his
share of blame; he even, if I remember right, expressed
regret. But his crew, to my astonishment and anger,
grinned from ear to ear, and laughed aloud at our distress. They thought it "real funny" about the stove-
pipe they had forgotten; "real funny" that they should
have lost a plate. As for hay, the whole party refused
to bring us any till they should have supped. See how
late they were! Never had there been such a job as
coming up that grade! Nor often, I suspect, such a
game of poker as that before they started. But about
nine, as a particular favour, we should have some hay.

So they took their departure, leaving me still staring,
and we resigned ourselves to wait for their return. The
fire in the forge had been suffered to go out, and we
were one and all too weary to kindle another. We
dined, or, not to take that word in vain, we ate after a
fashion, in the nightmare disorder of the assayer's office,
perched among boxes. A single candle lighted us. It

could scarce be called a house-warming; for there was, of course, no fire, and with the two open doors and the open window gaping on the night, like breaches in a fortress, it began to grow rapidly chill. Talk ceased; nobody moved but the unhappy Chuchu, still in quest of sofa-cushions, who tumbled complainingly among the trunks. It required a certain happiness of disposition to look forward hopefully, from so dismal a beginning, across the brief hours of night, to the warm shining of to-morrow's sun.

But the hay arrived at last, and we turned, with our last spark of courage, to the bedroom. We had improved the entrance, but it was still a kind of rope-walking; and it would have been droll to see us mounting, one after another, by candle-light, under the open stars.

The western door—that which looked up the cañon, and through which we entered by our bridge of flying plank—was still entire, a handsome, panelled door, the most finished piece of carpentry in Silverado. And the two lowest bunks next to this we roughly filled with hay for that night's use. Through the opposite, or eastern-looking gable, with its open door and window, a faint, diffused starshine came into the room like mist; and when we were once in bed, we lay, awaiting sleep, in a haunted, incomplete obscurity. At first the silence of the night was utter. Then a high wind began in the distance among the treetops, and for hours continued to grow higher. It seemed to me much such a wind as we had found on our visit; yet here in our open chamber we were fanned only by gentle and refreshing draughts, so deep was the cañon, so close our house was planted under the overhanging rock.

THE HUNTER'S FAMILY

THERE is quite a large race or class of people in America, for whom we scarcely seem to have a parallel in England. Of pure white blood, they are unknown or unrecognisable in towns; inhabit the fringe of settlements and the deep, quiet places of the country; rebellious to all labour, and pettily thievish, like the English gipsies; rustically ignorant, but with a touch of woodlore and the dexterity of the savage. Whence they came is a moot point. At the time of the war, they poured north in crowds to escape conscription; lived during summer on fruits, wild animals, and petty theft; and at the approach of winter, when these supplies failed, built great fires in the forest, and there died stoically by starvation. They are widely scattered, however, and easily recognised. Loutish, but not ill-looking, they will sit all day, swinging their legs on a field fence, the mind seemingly as devoid of all reflection as a Suffolk peasant's, careless of politics, for the most part incapable of reading, but with a rebellious vanity and a strong sense of independence. Hunting is their most congenial business, or, if the occasion offers, a little amateur detection. In tracking a criminal, following a particular horse along a beaten highway, and drawing

374

inductions from a hair or a footprint, one of those somnolent, grinning Hodges will suddenly display activity
of body and finesse of mind. By their names ye may
know them, the women figuring as Loveina, Larsenia,
Serena, Leanna, Orreana; the men answering to Alvin,
Alva, or Orion, pronounced Orrion, with the accent on
the first. Whether they are indeed a race, or whether
this is the form of degeneracy common to all back-
woodsmen, they are at least known by a generic by-
word, as Poor Whites or Low-downers.

I will not say that the Hanson family was Poor White,
because the name savours of offence; but I may go as
far as this — they were, in many points, not unsimilar
to the people usually so-called. Rufe himself combined
two of the qualifications, for he was both a hunter and
an amateur detective. It was he who pursued Russel
and Dollar, the robbers of the Lake Port stage, and captured them the very morning after the exploit, while
they were still sleeping in a hayfield. Russel, a drunken
Scotch carpenter, was even an acquaintance of his own,
and he expressed much grave commiseration for his fate.
In all that he said and did, Rufe was grave. I never
saw him hurried. When he spoke, he took out his pipe
with ceremonial deliberation, looked east and west, and
then, in quiet tones and few words, stated his business
or told his story. His gait was to match; it would never
have surprised you if, at any step, he had turned round
and walked away again, so warily and slowly, and
with so much seeming hesitation did he go about. He
lay long in bed in the morning — rarely indeed, rose before noon; he loved all games, from poker to clerical
croquet; and in the Toll House croquet ground I have

seen him toiling at the latter with the devotion of a
curate. He took an interest in education, was an active
member of the local school-board, and when I was there,
he had recently lost the schoolhouse key. His waggon
was broken, but it never seemed to occur to him to
mend it. Like all truly idle people, he had an artistic
eye. He chose the print stuff for his wife's dresses,
and counselled her in the making of a patchwork quilt,
always, as she thought, wrongly, but to the more educated eye, always with bizarre and admirable taste—
the taste of an Indian. With all this, he was a perfect,
unoffending gentleman in word and act. Take his clay
pipe from him, and he was fit for any society but that
of fools. Quiet as he was, there burned a deep, permanent excitement in his dark blue eyes; and when
this grave man smiled, it was like sunshine in a shady
place.

Mrs. Hanson (*née,* if you please, Lovelands) was more
commonplace than her lord. She was a comely woman,
too, plump, fair-coloured, with wonderful white teeth;
and in her print dresses (chosen by Rufe) and with a
large sun-bonnet shading her valued complexion, made,
I assure you, a very agreeable figure. But she was on
the surface, what there was of her, out-spoken and loud-
spoken. Her noisy laughter had none of the charm of
one of Hanson's rare, slow-spreading smiles; there was
no reticence, no mystery, no manner about the woman:
she was a first-class dairymaid, but her husband was an
unknown quantity between the savage and the noble-
man. She was often in and out with us, merry, and
healthy, and fair; he came far seldomer — only, indeed,
when there was business, or now and again, to pay a

visit of ceremony, brushed up for the occasion, with his wife on his arm, and a clean clay pipe in his teeth. These visits, in our forest state, had quite the air of an event, and turned our red cañon into a salon.

Such was the pair who ruled in the old Silverado Hotel, among the windy trees, on the mountain shoulder overlooking the whole length of Napa Valley, as the man aloft looks down on the ship's deck. There they kept house, with sundry horses and fowls, and a family of sons, Daniel Webster, and I think George Washington, among the number. Nor did they want visitors. An old gentleman, of singular stolidity, and called Breedlove — I think he had crossed the plains in the same caravan with Rufe — housed with them for awhile during our stay; and they had besides a permanent lodger, in the form of Mrs. Hanson's brother, Irvine Lovelands. I spell Irvine by guess; for I could get no information on the subject, just as I could never find out, in spite of many inquiries, whether or not Rufe was a contraction for Rufus. They were all cheerfully at sea about their names in that generation. And this is surely the more notable where the names are all so strange, and even the family names appear to have been coined. At one time, at least, the ancestors of all these Alvins and Alvas, Loveinas, Lovelands, and Breedloves, must have taken serious council and found a certain poetry in these denominations; that must have been, then, their form of literature. But still times change; and their next descendants, the George Washingtons and Daniel Websters, will at least be clear upon the point. And anyway, and however his name should be spelt, this Irvine Lovelands was the most unmitigated Caliban I ever knew.

Our very first morning at Silverado, when we were full of business, patching up doors and windows, making beds and seats, and getting our rough lodging into shape, Irvine and his sister made their appearance together, she for neighbourliness and general curiosity; he, because he was working for me, to my sorrow, cutting firewood at I forget how much a day. The way that he set about cutting wood was characteristic. We were at that moment patching up and unpacking in the kitchen. Down he sat on one side, and down sat his sister on the other. Both were chewing pine-tree gum, and he, to my annoyance, accompanied that simple pleasure with profuse expectoration. She rattled away, talking up hill and down dale, laughing, tossing her head, showing her brilliant teeth. He looked on in silence, now spitting heavily on the floor, now putting his head back and uttering a loud, discordant, joyless laugh. He had a tangle of shock hair, the colour of wool; his mouth was a grin; although as strong as a horse, he looked neither heavy nor yet adroit, only leggy, coltish, and in the road. But it was plain he was in high spirits, thoroughly enjoying his visit; and he laughed frankly whenever we failed to accomplish what we were about. This was scarcely helpful: it was even, to amateur carpenters, embarrassing; but it lasted until we knocked off work and began to get dinner. Then Mrs. Hanson remembered she should have been gone an hour ago; and the pair retired, and the lady's laughter died away among the nutmegs down the path. That was Irvine's first day's work in my employment — the devil take him!

The next morning he returned and, as he was this time alone, he bestowed his conversation upon us with great liberality. He prided himself on his intelligence; asked us if we knew the school ma'am. *He* didn't think much of her, anyway. He had tried her, he had. He had put a question to her. If a tree a hundred feet high were to fall a foot a day, how long would it take to fall right down ? She had not been able to solve the problem. " She don't know nothing," he opined. He told us how a friend of his kept a school with a revolver, and chuckled mightily over that; his friend could teach school, he could. All the time he kept chewing gum and spitting. He would stand a while looking down; and then he would toss back his shock of hair, and laugh hoarsely, and spit, and bring forward a new subject. A man, he told us, who bore a grudge against him, had poisoned his dog. "That was a low thing for a man to do now, wasn't it ? It wasn't like a man, that, nohow. But I got even with him: I pisoned *his* dog." His clumsy utterance, his rude embarrassed manner, set a fresh value on the stupidity of his remarks. I do not think I ever appreciated the meaning of two words until I knew Irvine — the verb, loaf, and the noun, oaf; between them, they complete his portrait. He could lounge, and wriggle, and rub himself against the wall, and grin, and be more in everybody's way than any other two people that I ever set my eyes on. Nothing that he did became him; and yet you were conscious that he was one of your own race, that his mind was cumbrously at work, revolving the problem of existence like a quid of gum, and in his own cloudy manner enjoying life, and passing judgment on his fellows. Above all things, he was delighted with himself. You would not have thought it, from his uneasy manners and troubled, struggling utterance; but he loved himself to the marrow, and was happy and proud like a peacock on a rail.

His self-esteem was, indeed, the one joint in his harness. He could be got to work, and even kept at work, by flattery. As long as my wife stood over him, crying out how strong he was, so long exactly he would stick to the matter in hand; and the moment she turned her back, or ceased to praise him, he would stop. His physical strength was wonderful; and to have a woman stand by and admire his achievements, warmed his heart like sunshine. Yet he was as cowardly as he was powerful, and felt no shame in owning to the weakness. Something was once wanted from the crazy platform over the shaft, and he at once refused to venture there — "did not like," as he said, "foolen' round them kind o' places," and let my wife go instead of him, looking on with a grin. Vanity, where it rules, is usually more heroic: but Irvine steadily approved himself, and expected others to approve him; rather looked down upon my wife, and decidedly expected her to look up to him, on the strength of his superior prudence.

Yet the strangest part of the whole matter was perhaps this, that Irvine was as beautiful as a statue. His features were, in themselves, perfect; it was only his cloudy, uncouth, and coarse expression that disfigured them. So much strength residing in so spare a frame was proof sufficient of the accuracy of his shape. He must have been built somewhat after the pattern of Jack Sheppard; but the famous housebreaker, we may be certain, was no lout. It was by the extraordinary powers of his mind no less than by the vigour of his body, that he broke his strong prison with such imperfect implements, turning the very obstacles to service. Irvine, in the same case, would have sat down and spat, and grumbled curses. He had the soul of a fat sheep, but, regarded as an artist's model, the exterior of a Greek God. It was a cruel thought to persons less favoured in their birth, that this creature, endowed — to use the language of theatres — with extraordinary "means," should so manage to misemploy them that he looked ugly and almost deformed. It was only by an effort of abstraction, and after many days, that you discovered what he was.

By playing on the oaf's conceit, and standing closely over him, we got a path made round the corner of the dump to our door, so that we could come and go with decent ease; and he even enjoyed the work, for in that there were boulders to be plucked up bodily, bushes to be uprooted, and other occasions for athletic display: but cutting wood was a different matter. Anybody could cut wood; and, besides, my wife was tired of supervising him, and had other things to attend to. And, in short, days went by, and Irvine came daily, and talked and lounged and spat; but the firewood remained intact as sleepers on the platform or growing trees upon the mountain-side. Irvine, as a woodcutter, we could tolerate; but Irvine as a friend of the family, at so much a day, was too bald an imposition, and at length, on the afternoon of the fourth or fifth day of our connection, I explained to him, as clearly as I could, the light in which I had grown to regard his presence. I pointed out to him that I could not continue to give him a salary for spitting on the floor; and this expression, which came after a good many others, at last penetrated his obdurate wits. He rose at once, and said if that was the way he was going to be spoke to, he reckoned he would quit. And, no one interposing, he departed.

So far, so good. But we had no firewood. The next afternoon, I strolled down to Rufe's and consulted him on the subject. It was a very droll interview, in the large, bare north room of the Silverado Hotel, Mrs. Hanson's patchwork on a frame, and Rufe, and his wife, and I, and the oaf himself, all more or less embarrassed. Rufe announced there was nobody in the neighbourhood but Irvine who could do a day's work for anybody. Irvine, thereupon, refused to have any more to do with my service; he "wouldn't work no more for a man as had spoke to him 's I had done." I found myself on the point of the last humiliation — driven to beseech the creature whom I had just dismissed with insult: but I took the high hand in despair, said there must be no talk of Irvine coming back unless matters were to be differently managed; that I would rather chop firewood for myself than be fooled; and, in short, the Hansons being eager for the lad's hire, I so imposed upon them with merely affected resolution, that they ended by begging me to re-employ him again, on a solemn promise that he should be more industrious. The promise, I am bound to say, was kept. We soon had a fine pile of firewood at our door; and if Caliban gave me the cold shoulder and spared me his conversation, I thought none the worse of him for that, nor did I find my days much longer for the deprivation.

The leading spirit of the family was, I am inclined to fancy, Mrs. Hanson. Her social brilliancy somewhat dazzled the others, and she had more of the small change of sense. It was she who faced Kelmar, for instance; and perhaps, if she had been alone, Kelmar would have had no rule within her doors. Rufe, to be sure, had a fine, sober, open-air attitude of mind, seeing the world without exaggeration — perhaps, we may even say, without enough; for he lacked, along with the others, that commercial idealism which puts so high a value on time and money. Sanity itself is a kind of convention. Perhaps Rufe was wrong; but, looking on life plainly, he was unable to perceive that croquet or poker were in any way less important than, for instance, mending his waggon. Even his own profession, hunting, was dear to him mainly as a sort of play; even that he would have neglected, had it not appealed to his imagination. His hunting-suit, for instance, had cost I should be afraid to say how many bucks — the currency in which he paid his way: it was all befringed, after the Indian fashion, and it was dear to his heart. The pictorial side of his daily business was never forgotten. He was even anxious to stand for his picture in those buckskin hunting clothes; and I remember how he once warmed almost into enthusiasm, his dark blue eyes growing perceptibly larger, as he planned the composition in which he should appear, "with the horns of some real big bucks, and dogs, and a camp on a crick" (creek, stream).

There was no trace in Irvine of this woodland poetry. He did not care for hunting, nor yet for buckskin suits. He had never observed scenery. The world, as it appeared to him, was almost obliterated by his own great grinning figure in the foreground: Caliban Malvolio. And it seems to me as if, in the persons of these brothers-in-law, we had the two sides of rusticity fairly well represented: the hunter living really in nature; the clodhopper living merely out of society: the one bent up in every corporal agent to capacity in one pursuit, doing at least one thing keenly and thoughtfully, and thoroughly alive to all that touches it; the other in the inert and bestial state, walking in a faint dream, and taking so dim an impression of the myriad sides of life that he is truly conscious of nothing but himself. It is only in the fastnesses of nature, forests, mountains, and the back of man's beyond, that a creature endowed with five senses can grow up into the perfection of this crass and earthy vanity. In towns or the busier country sides, he is roughly reminded of other men's existence; and if he learns no more, he learns at least to fear contempt. But Irvine had come scatheless through life, conscious only of himself, of his great strength and intelligence; and in the silence of the universe, to which he did not listen, dwelling with delight on the sound of his own thoughts.

THE SEA FOGS

A CHANGE in the colour of the light usually called me in the morning. By a certain hour, the long, vertical chinks in our western gable, where the boards had shrunk and separated, flashed suddenly into my eyes as stripes of dazzling blue, at once so dark and splendid that I used to marvel how the qualities could be combined. At an earlier hour, the heavens in that quarter were still quietly coloured, but the shoulder of the mountain which shuts in the cañon already glowed with sunlight in a wonderful compound of gold and rose and green; and this too would kindle, although more mildly and with rainbow tints, the fissures of our crazy gable. If I were sleeping heavily, it was the bold blue that struck me awake; if more lightly, then I would come to myself in that earlier and fairier light.

One Sunday morning, about five, the first brightness called me. I rose and turned to the east, not for my devotions, but for air. The night had been very still. The little private gale that blew every evening in our cañon, for ten minutes or perhaps a quarter of an hour, had swiftly blown itself out; in the hours that followed not a sigh of wind had shaken the treetops; and our barrack, for all its breaches, was less fresh that morning than of wont. But I had no sooner reached the window than I forgot all else in the sight that met my eyes, and I made but two bounds into my clothes, and down the crazy plank to the platform.

The sun was still concealed below the opposite hilltops, though it was shining already, not twenty feet above my head, on our own mountain slope. But the scene, beyond a few near features, was entirely changed. Napa valley was gone; gone were all the lower slopes and woody foothills of the range; and in their place, not a thousand feet below me, rolled a great level ocean. It was as though I had gone to bed the night before, safe in a nook of inland mountains, and had awakened in a bay upon the coast. I had seen these inundations from below; at Calistoga I had risen and gone abroad in the early morning, coughing and sneezing, under fathoms on fathoms of gray sea vapour, like a cloudy sky — a dull sight for the artist, and a painful experience for the invalid. But to sit aloft one's self in the pure air and under the unclouded dome of heaven, and thus look down on the submergence of the valley, was strangely different and even delightful to the eyes. Far away were hilltops like little islands. Nearer, a smoky surf beat about the foot of precipices and poured into all the coves of these rough mountains. The colour of that fog ocean was a thing never to be forgotten. For an instant, among the Hebrides and just about sundown, I have seen something like it on the sea itself. But the white was not so opaline; nor was there, what surprisingly increased the effect, that breathless, crystal stillness over all. Even in its gentlest moods the salt sea travails, moaning among the weeds or lisping on the sand; but that vast fog ocean lay in a trance of silence, nor did the sweet air of the morning tremble with a sound.

As I continued to sit upon the dump, I began to observe that this sea was not so level as at first sight it appeared to be. Away in the extreme south, a little hill of fog arose against the sky above the general surface, and as it had already caught the sun, it shone on the horizon like the topsails of some giant ship. There were huge waves, stationary, as it seemed, like waves in a frozen sea; and yet, as I looked again, I was not sure but they were moving after all, with a slow and august advance. And while I was yet doubting, a promontory of the hills some four or five miles away, conspicuous by a bouquet of tall pines, was in a single instant overtaken and swallowed up. It reappeared in a little, with its pines, but this time as an islet, and only to be swallowed up once more and then for good. This set me looking nearer, and I saw that in every cove along the line of mountains the fog was being piled in higher and higher, as though by some wind that was inaudible to me. I could trace its progress, one pine tree first growing hazy and then disappearing after another; although sometimes there was none of this fore-running haze, but the whole opaque white ocean gave a start and swallowed a piece of mountain at a gulp. It was to flee these poisonous fogs that I had left the seaboard, and climbed so high among the mountains. And now, behold, here came the fog to besiege me in my chosen altitudes, and yet came so beautifully that my first thought was of welcome.

The sun had now gotten much higher, and through

387

all the gaps of the hills it cast long bars of gold across that white ocean.   An eagle, or some other very great bird of the mountain, came wheeling over the nearer pine-tops, and hung, poised and something sideways, as if to look abroad on that unwonted desolation, spying, perhaps with terror, for the eyries of her comrades. Then, with a long cry, she disappeared again towards Lake County and the clearer air.   At length it seemed to me as if the flood were beginning to subside.   The old landmarks, by whose disappearance I had measured its advance, here a crag, there a brave pine tree, now began, in the inverse order, to make their reappearance into daylight.   I judged all danger of the fog was over. This was not Noah's flood; it was but a morning spring, and would now drift out seaward whence it came.   So, mightily relieved, and a good deal exhilarated by the sight, I went into the house to light the fire.

I suppose it was nearly seven when I once more mounted the platform to look abroad.   The fog ocean had swelled up enormously since last I saw it; and a few hundred feet below me, in the deep gap where the Toll House stands and the road runs through into Lake County, it had already topped the slope, and was pouring over and down the other side like driving smoke. The wind had climbed along with it; and though I was still in calm air, I could see the trees tossing below me, and their long, strident sighing mounted to me where I stood.

Half an hour later, the fog had surmounted all the ridge on the opposite side of the gap, though a shoulder of the mountain still warded it out of our canyon.   Napa valley and its bounding hills were now utterly blotted

out. The fog, sunny white in the sunshine, was pouring over into Lake County in a huge, ragged cataract,
tossing treetops appearing and disappearing in the spray.
The air struck with a little chill, and set me coughing.
It smelt strong of the fog, like the smell of a washing-
house, but with a shrewd tang of the sea salt.

Had it not been for two things — the sheltering spur
which answered as a dyke, and the great valley on the
other side which rapidly engulfed whatever mounted —
our own little platform in the cañon must have been
already buried a hundred feet in salt and poisonous air.
As it was, the interest of the scene entirely occupied
our minds. We were set just out of the wind, and but
just above the fog; we could listen to the voice of the
one as to music on the stage; we could plunge our eyes
down into the other, as into some flowing stream from
over the parapet of a bridge; thus we looked on upon
a strange, impetuous, silent, shifting exhibition of the
powers of nature, and saw the familiar landscape changing from moment to moment like figures in a dream.

The imagination loves to trifle with what is not. Had
this been indeed the deluge, I should have felt more
strongly, but the emotion would have been similar in
kind. I played with the idea, as the child flees in delighted terror from the creations of his fancy. The look
of the thing helped me. And when at last I began to
flee up the mountain, it was indeed partly to escape
from the raw air that kept me coughing, but it was also
part in play.

As I ascended the mountain-side, I came once more
to overlook the upper surface of the fog; but it wore a
different appearance from what I had beheld at daybreak.

For, first, the sun now fell on it from high overhead, and its surface shone and undulated like a great nor'land moor country, sheeted with untrodden morning snow. And next the new level must have been a thousand or fifteen hundred feet higher than the old, so that only five or six points of all the broken country below me, still stood out. Napa valley was now one with Sonoma on the west. On the hither side, only a thin scattered fringe of bluffs was unsubmerged; and through all the gaps the fog was pouring over, like an ocean, into the blue clear sunny country on the east. There it was soon lost; for it fell instantly into the bottom of the valleys, following the water-shed; and the hilltops in that quarter were still clear cut upon the eastern sky.

Through the Toll House gap and over the near ridges on the other side, the deluge was immense. A spray of thin vapour was thrown high above it, rising and falling, and blown into fastastic shapes. The speed of its course was like a mountain torrent. Here and there a few treetops were discovered and then whelmed again; and for one second, the bough of a dead pine beckoned out of the spray like the arm of a drowning man. But still the imagination was dissatisfied, still the ear waited for something more. Had this indeed been water (as it seemed so, to the eye), with what a plunge of reverberating thunder would it have rolled upon its course, disembowelling mountains and deracinating pines! And yet water it was, and sea-water at that — true Pacific billows, only somewhat rarefied, rolling in mid air among the hilltops.

I climbed still higher, among the red rattling gravel and dwarf underwood of Mount Saint Helena, until I could look right down upon Silverado, and admire the favoured nook in which it lay. The sunny plain of fog was several hundred feet higher; behind the protecting spur a gigantic accumulation of cottony vapour threatened, with every second, to blow over and submerge our homestead; but the vortex setting past the Toll House was too strong; and there lay our little platform, in the arms of the deluge, but still enjoying its unbroken sunshine. About eleven, however, thin spray came flying over the friendly buttress, and I began to think the fog had hunted out its Jonah after all. But it was the last effort. The wind veered while we were at dinner, and began to blow squally from the mountain summit; and by half-past one, all that world of sea-fogs was utterly routed and flying here and there into the south in little rags of cloud. And instead of a lone sea-beach, we found ourselves once more inhabiting a high mountain-side, with the clear green country far below us, and the light smoke of Calistoga blowing in the air.

This was the great Russian campaign for that season. Now and then, in the early morning, a little white lakelet of fog would be seen far down in Napa Valley; but the heights were not again assailed, nor was the surrounding world again shut off from Silverado.

THE TOLL HOUSE

THE Toll House, standing alone by the wayside under nodding pines, with its streamlet and water-tank; its backwoods, toll-bar, and well trodden croquet ground; the ostler standing by the stable door, chewing a straw; a glimpse of the Chinese cook in the back parts; and Mr. Hoddy in the bar, gravely alert and serviceable, and equally anxious to lend or borrow books;— dozed all day in the dusty sunshine, more than half asleep. There were no neighbours, except the Hansons up the hill. The traffic on the road was infinitesimal; only, at rare intervals, a couple in a waggon, or a dusty farmer on a spring-board, toiling over "the grade" to that metropolitan hamlet, Calistoga; and, at the fixed hours, the passage of the stages.

The nearest building was the schoolhouse, down the road; and the school-ma'am boarded at the Toll House, walking thence in the morning to the little brown shanty, where she taught the young ones of the district, and returning thither pretty weary in the afternoon. She had chosen this outlying situation, I understood, for her health. Mr. Corwin was consumptive; so was Rufe; so was Mr. Jennings, the engineer. In short, the place was a kind of small Davos: consumptive folk consort-

ing on a hilltop in the most unbroken idleness. Jennings never did anything that I could see, except now
and then to fish, and generally to sit about in the bar
and the verandah, waiting for something to happen.
Corwin and Rufe did as little as possible; and if the
school-ma'am, poor lady, had to work pretty hard all
morning, she subsided when it was over into much the
same dazed beatitude as all the rest.

Her special corner was the parlour — a very genteel
room, with Bible prints, a crayon portrait of Mrs. Corwin in the height of fashion, a few years ago, another
of her son (Mr. Corwin was not represented), a mirror,
and a selection of dried grasses. A large book was laid
religiously on the table — "From Palace to Hovel," I
believe, its name — full of the raciest experiences in
England. The author had mingled freely with all
classes, the nobility particularly meeting him with open
arms; and I must say that traveller had ill requited his
reception. His book, in short, was a capital instance
of the Penny Messalina school of literature; and there
arose from it, in that cool parlour, in that silent, wayside, mountain inn, a rank atmosphere of gold and
blood and "Jenkins," and the "Mysteries of London,"
and sickening, inverted snobbery, fit to knock you
down. The mention of this book reminds me of another and far racier picture of our island life. The latter parts of *Rocambole* are surely too sparingly consulted in the country which they celebrate. No man's
education can be said to be complete, nor can he pronounce the world yet emptied of enjoyment, till he has
made the acquaintance of "the Reverend Patterson,
director of the Evangelical Society." To follow the

evolutions of that reverend gentleman, who goes through scenes in which even Mr. Duffield would hesitate to place a bishop, is to rise to new ideas. But, alas! there was no Patterson about the Toll House. Only, alongside of "From Palace to Hovel," a sixpenny "Ouida" figured. So literature, you see, was not unrepresented.

The school-ma'am had friends to stay with her, other school-ma'ams enjoying their holidays, quite a bevy of damsels. They seemed never to go out, or not beyond the verandah, but sat close in the little parlour, quietly talking or listening to the wind among the trees. Sleep dwelt in the Toll House, like a fixture: summer sleep, shallow, soft, and dreamless. A cuckoo-clock, a great rarity in such a place, hooted at intervals about the echoing house; and Mr. Jennings would open his eyes for a moment in the bar, and turn the leaf of a newspaper, and the resting school-ma'ams in the parlour would be recalled to the consciousness of their inaction. Busy Mrs. Corwin and her busy Chinaman might be heard indeed, in the penetralia, pounding dough or rattling dishes; or perhaps Rufe had called up some of the sleepers for a game of croquet, and the hollow strokes of the mallet sounded far away among the woods: but with these exceptions, it was sleep and sunshine and dust, and the wind in the pine trees, all day long.

A little before stage time, that castle of indolence awoke. The ostler threw his straw away and set to his preparations. Mr. Jennings rubbed his eyes; happy Mr. Jennings, the something he had been waiting for all day about to happen at last! The boarders gathered in the verandah, silently giving ear, and gazing down the

road with shaded eyes. And as yet there was no sign
for the senses, not a sound, not a tremor of the mountain road. The birds, to whom the secret of the hooting cuckoo is unknown, must have set down to instinct
this premonitory bustle.

And then the first of the two stages swooped upon the
Toll House with a roar and in a cloud of dust; and the
shock had not yet time to subside, before the second was
abreast of it. Huge concerns they were, well-horsed
and loaded, the men in their shirt-sleeves, the women
swathed in veils, the long whip cracking like a pistol;
and as they charged upon that slumbering hostelry, each
shepherding a dust storm, the dead place blossomed
into life and talk and clatter. This the Toll House?—
with its city throng, its jostling shoulders, its infinity
of instant business in the bar? The mind would not
receive it! The heartfelt bustle of that hour is hardly
credible; the thrill of the great shower of letters from
the post-bag, the childish hope and interest with which
one gazed in all these strangers' eyes. They paused
there but to pass: the blue-clad China-boy, the San
Francisco magnate, the mystery in the dust coat, the
secret memoirs in tweed, the ogling, well-shod lady
with her troop of girls; they did but flash and go; they
were hull-down for us behind life's ocean, and we but
hailed their topsails on the line. Yet, out of our great
solitude of four and twenty mountain hours, we thrilled
to their momentary presence; gauged and divined them,
loved and hated; and stood light-headed in that storm
of human electricity. Yes, like Piccadilly Circus, this
is also one of life's crossing-places. Here I beheld one
man, already famous or infamous, a centre of pistol-

shots: and another who, if not yet known to rumour, will fill a column of the Sunday paper when he comes to hang — a burly, thick-set, powerful Chinese desperado, six long bristles upon either lip; redolent of whiskey, playing cards, and pistols; swaggering in the bar with the lowest assumption of the lowest European manners; rapping out blackguard English oaths in his canorous oriental voice; and combining in one person the depravities of two races and two civilizations. For all his lust and vigour, he seemed to look cold upon me from the valley of the shadow of the gallows. He imagined a vain thing; and while he drained his cocktail, Holbein's death was at his elbow. Once, too, I fell in talk with another of these flitting strangers — like the rest, in his shirt-sleeves and all begrimed with dust — and the next minute we were discussing Paris and London, theatres and wines. To him, journeying from one human place to another, this was a trifle; but to me! No, Mr. Lillie, I have not forgotten it.

And presently the city-tide was at its flood and began to ebb. Life runs in Piccadilly Circus, say, from nine to one, and then, there also, ebbs into the small hours of the echoing policemen and the lamps and stars. But the Toll House is far up stream, and near its rural springs; the bubble of the tide but touches it. Before you had yet grasped your pleasure, the horses were put to, the loud whips volleyed, and the tide was gone. North and south had the two stages vanished, the towering dust subsided in the woods; but there was still an interval before the flush had fallen on your cheeks, before the ear became once more contented with the silence, or the seven sleepers of the Toll House dozed back to their accustomed corners. Yet a little, and the ostler would swing round the great barrier across the road; and in the golden evening, that dreamy inn begin to trim its lamps and spread the board for supper.

As I recall the place—the green dell below; the spires of pine; the sun-warm, scented air; that gray, gabled inn, with its faint stirrings of life amid the slumber of the mountains—I slowly awake to a sense of admiration, gratitude, and almost love. A fine place, after all, for a wasted life to doze away in—the cuckoo clock hooting of its far home country; the croquet mallets, eloquent of English lawns; the stages daily bringing news of the turbulent world away below there; and perhaps once in the summer, a salt fog pouring overhead with its tale of the Pacific.

A STARRY DRIVE

In our rule at Silverado, there was a melancholy inter-regnum. The queen and the crown prince with one accord fell sick; and, as I was sick to begin with, our lone position on Mount Saint Helena was no longer tenable, and we had to hurry back to Calistoga and a cottage on the green. By that time we had begun to realize the difficulties of our position. We had found what an amount of labour it cost to support life in our red cañon; and it was the dearest desire of our hearts to get a China-boy to go along with us when we re-turned. We could have given him a whole house to himself, self-contained, as they say in the advertise-ments; and on the money question we were prepared to go far. Kong Sam Kee, the Calistoga washerman, was entrusted with the affair; and from day to day it languished on, with protestations on our part and mel-lifluous excuses on the part of Kong Sam Kee.

At length, about half-past eight of our last evening, with the waggon ready harnessed to convey us up the grade, the washerman, with a somewhat sneering air, produced the boy. He was a handsome, gentlemanly lad, attired in rich dark blue, and shod with snowy white; but, alas! he had heard rumours of Silverado.

He knew it for a lone place on the mountain-side, with no friendly wash-house near by, where he might smoke a pipe of opium o' nights with other China-boys, and lose his little earnings at the game of tan; and he first backed out for more money; and then, when that demand was satisfied, refused to come point-blank. He was wedded to his wash-houses; he had no taste for the rural life; and we must go to our mountain servantless. It must have been near half an hour before we reached that conclusion, standing in the midst of Calistoga high street under the stars, and the China-boy and Kong Sam Kee singing their pigeon English in the sweetest voices and with the most musical inflections.

We were not, however, to return alone; for we brought with us Joe Strong, the painter, a most good-natured comrade and a capital hand at an omelette. I do not know in which capacity he was most valued — as a cook or a companion; and he did excellently well in both.

The Kong Sam Kee negociation had delayed us unduly; it must have been half-past nine before we left Calistoga, and night came fully ere we struck the bottom of the grade. I have never seen such a night. It seemed to throw calumny in the teeth of all the painters that ever dabbled in starlight. The sky itself was of a ruddy, powerful, nameless, changing colour, dark and glossy like a serpent's back. The stars, by innumerable millions, stuck boldly forth like lamps. The milky way was bright, like a moonlit cloud; half heaven seemed milky way. The greater luminaries shone each more clearly than a winter's moon. Their light was dyed in every sort of colour — red, like fire; blue, like steel; green, like the tracks of sunset; and so sharply did each stand forth in its own lustre that there was no appearance of that flat, star-spangled arch we know so well in pictures, but all the hollow of heaven was one chaos of contesting luminaries — a hurly-burly of stars. Against this the hills and rugged tree-tops stood out redly dark.

As we continued to advance, the lesser lights and milky ways first grew pale, and then vanished; the countless hosts of heaven dwindled in number by successive millions; those that still shone had tempered their exceeding brightness and fallen back into their customary wistful distance; and the sky declined from its first bewildering splendour into the appearance of a common night. Slowly this change proceeded, and still there was no sign of any cause. Then a whiteness like mist was thrown over the spurs of the mountain. Yet a while, and, as we turned a corner, a great leap of silver light and net of forest shadows fell across the road and upon our wondering waggonful; and, swimming low among the trees, we beheld a strange, misshapen, waning moon, half-tilted on her back.

"Where are ye when the moon appears?" so the old poet sang, half-taunting, to the stars, bent upon a courtly purpose.

"As the sunlight round the dim earth's midnight tower of shadow pours,
    Streaming past the dim, wide portals,
    Viewless to the eyes of mortals,
  Till it floods the moon's pale islet or the morning's golden shores."

So sings Mr. Trowbridge, with a noble inspiration. And so had the sunlight flooded that pale islet of the moon, and her lit face put out, one after another, that galaxy of stars. The wonder of the drive was over; but, by some nice conjunction of clearness in the air and fit shadow in the valley where we travelled, we had seen for a little while that brave display of the midnight heavens. It was gone, but it had been; nor shall I ever again behold the stars with the same mind. He who has seen the sea commoved with a great hurricane, thinks of it very differently from him who has seen it only in a calm. And the difference between a calm and a hurricane is not greatly more striking than that between the ordinary face of night and the splendour that shone upon us in that drive. Two in our waggon knew night as she shines upon the tropics, but even that bore no comparison. The nameless colour of the sky, the hues of the star-fire, and the incredible projection of the stars themselves, starting from their orbits, so that the eye seemed to distinguish their positions in the hollow of space — these were things that we had never seen before and shall never see again.

Meanwhile, in this altered night, we proceeded on our way among the scents and silence of the forest, reached the top of the grade, wound up by Hanson's, and came at last to a stand under the flying gargoyle of the chute. Sam, who had been lying back, fast asleep, with the moon on his face, got down, with the remark that it was pleasant "to be home." The waggon turned and drove away, the noise gently dying in the woods, and we clambered up the rough path, Caliban's great feat of engineering, and came home to Silverado.

The moon shone in at the eastern doors and windows, and over the lumber on the platform. The one tall pine

beside the ledge was steeped in silver. Away up the
cañon, a wild cat welcomed us with three discordant
squalls. But once we had lit a candle, and began to
review our improvements, homely in either sense, and
count our stores, it was wonderful what a feeling of
possession and permanence grew up in the hearts of
the lords of Silverado. A bed had still to be made up for
Strong, and the morning's water to be fetched, with clink-
ing pail; and as we set about these household duties,
and showed off our wealth and conveniences before the
stranger, and had a glass of wine, I think, in honour of
our return, and trooped at length one after another up
the flying bridge of plank, and lay down to sleep in our
shattered, moon-pierced barrack, we were among the
happiest sovereigns in the world, and certainly ruled
over the most contented people. Yet, in our absence,
the palace had been sacked. Wild cats, so the Hansons
said, had broken in and carried off a side of bacon, a
hatchet, and two knives.

EPISODES IN THE STORY OF A MINE

No one could live at Silverado and not be curious about the story of the mine. We were surrounded by so many evidences of expense and toil, we lived so entirely in the wreck of that great enterprise, like mites in the ruins of a cheese, that the idea of the old din and bustle haunted our repose. Our own house, the forge, the dump, the chutes, the rails, the windlass, the mass of broken plant; the two tunnels, one far below in the green dell, the other on the platform where we kept our wine; the deep shaft, with the sun-glints and the water-drops; above all, the ledge, that great gaping slice out of the mountain shoulder, propped apart by wooden wedges, on whose immediate margin, high above our heads, the one tall pine precariously nodded — these stood for its greatness; while, the dog-hutch, boot-jacks, old boots, old tavern bills, and the very beds that we inherited from bygone miners, put in human touches and realised for us the story of the past.

I have sat on an old sleeper, under the thick madronas near the forge, with just a look over the dump on the green world below, and seen the sun lying broad among the wreck, and heard the silence broken only by the tinkling water in the shaft, or a stir of the royal family about the battered palace, and my mind has gone back to the epoch of the Stanleys and the Chapmans, with a grand *tutti* of pick and drill, hammer and anvil, echoing about the cañon; the assayer hard at it in our dining-room; the carts below on the road, and their cargo of red mineral bounding and thundering down the iron chute. And now all gone — all fallen away into this sunny silence and desertion: a family of squatters dining in the assayer's office, making their beds in the big sleeping room erstwhile so crowded, keeping their wine in the tunnel that once rang with picks.

But Silverado itself, although now fallen in its turn into decay, was once but a mushroom, and had succeeded to other mines and other flitting cities. Twenty years ago, away down the glen on the Lake County side there was a place, Jonestown by name, with two thousand inhabitants dwelling under canvas, and one roofed house for the sale of whiskey. Round on the western side of Mount Saint Helena, there was at the same date, a second large encampment, its name, if it ever had one, lost for me. Both of these have perished, leaving not a stick and scarce a memory behind them. Tide after tide of hopeful miners have thus flowed and ebbed about the mountain, coming and going, now by lone prospectors, now with a rush. Last, in order of time came Silverado, reared the big mill, in the valley, founded the town which is now represented, monumentally, by Hanson's, pierced all these slaps and shafts and tunnels, and in turn declined and died away.

" Our noisy years seem moments in the wake
Of the eternal silence."

As to the success of Silverado in its time of being, two reports were current. According to the first, six hundred thousand dollars were taken out of that great upright seam, that still hung open above us on crazy wedges. Then the ledge pinched out, and there followed, in quest of the remainder, a great drifting and tunnelling in all directions, and a great consequent effusion of dollars, until, all parties being sick of the expense, the mine was deserted, and the town decamped. According to the second version, told me with much secrecy of manner, the whole affair, mine, mill, and town, were parts of one majestic swindle. There had never come any silver out of any portion of the mine; there was no silver to come. At midnight trains of packhorses might have been observed winding by devious tracks about the shoulder of the mountain. They came from far away, from Amador or Placer, laden with silver in "old cigar boxes." They discharged their load at Silverado, in the hour of sleep; and before the morning they were gone again with their mysterious drivers to their unknown source. In this way, twenty thousand pounds' worth of silver was smuggled in under cover of night, in these old cigar boxes; mixed with Silverado mineral; carted down to the mill; crushed, amalgamated, and refined, and despatched to the city as the proper product of the mine. Stock-jobbing, if it can cover such expenses, must be a profitable business in San Francisco.

I give these two versions as I got them. But I place little reliance on either, my belief in history having been greatly shaken. For it chanced that I had come to dwell in Silverado at a critical hour; great events in its history were about to happen—did happen, as I am led to believe; nay, and it will be seen that I played a part in that revolution myself. And yet from first to last I never had a glimmer of an idea what was going on; and even now, after full reflection, profess myself at sea. That there was some obscure intrigue of the cigar-box order, and that I, in the character of a wooden puppet, set pen to paper in the interest of somebody, so much, and no more, is certain.

Silverado, then under my immediate sway, belonged to one whom I will call a Mr. Ronalds. I only knew him through the extraordinarily distorting medium of local gossip, now as a momentous jobber; now as a dupe to point an adage; and again, and much more probably, as an ordinary Christian gentleman like you or me, who had opened a mine and worked it for a while with better and worse fortune. So, through a defective window-pane, you may see the passer-by shoot up into a hunch-backed giant, or dwindle into a pot-bellied dwarf.

To Ronalds, at least, the mine belonged; but the notice by which he held it would run out upon the 30th of June—or rather, as I suppose, it had run out already, and the month of grace would expire upon that day, after which any American citizen might post a notice of his own, and make Silverado his. This, with a sort of quiet slyness, Rufe told me at an early period of our acquaintance. There was no silver, of course; the mine "wasn't worth nothing, Mr. Stevens," but there was a deal of old iron and wood around, and to gain possession of this old wood and iron, and get a right to the water, Rufe proposed, if I had no objections, to "jump the claim."

Of course, I had no objection. But I was filled with wonder. If all he wanted was the wood and iron, what, in the name of fortune, was to prevent him taking them? "His right there was none to dispute." He might lay hands on all to-morrow, as the wild cats had laid hands upon our knives and hatchet. Besides, was this mass of heavy mining plant worth transportation? If it was, why had not the rightful owners carted it away? If it was, would they not preserve their title to these movables, even after they had lost their title to the mine? And if it were not, what the better was Rufe? Nothing would grow at Silverado; there was even no wood to cut; beyond a sense of property, there was nothing to be gained. Lastly, was it at all credible that Ronalds would forget what Rufe remembered? The days of grace were not yet over: any fine morning he might appear, paper in hand, and enter for another year on his inheritance. However, it was none of my business; all seemed legal; Rufe or Ronalds, all was one to me.

On the morning of the 27th, Mrs. Hanson appeared with the milk as usual, in her sun-bonnet. The time would be out on Tuesday, she reminded us, and bade me be in readiness to play my part, though I had no idea what it was to be. And suppose Ronalds came? we asked. She received the idea with derision, laughing aloud with all her fine teeth. He could not find the mine to save his life, it appeared, without Rufe to guide him. Last year, when he came, they heard him "up and down the road a hollerin' and a raisin' Cain." And at last he had to come to the Hansons in despair, and bid Rufe, "Jump into your pants and shoes, and show

407

me where this old mine is, anyway!" Seeing that
Ronalds had laid out so much money in the spot, and
that a beaten road led right up to the bottom of the dump,
I thought this a remarkable example. The sense of local-
ity must be singularly in abeyance in the case of Ronalds.

That same evening, supper comfortably over, Joe
Strong busy at work on a drawing of the dump and the
opposite hills, we were all out on the platform together,
sitting there, under the tented heavens, with the same
sense of privacy as if we had been cabined in a parlour,
when the sound of brisk footsteps came mounting up
the path. We pricked our ears at this, for the tread
seemed lighter and firmer than was usual with our
country neighbours. And presently, sure enough, two
town gentlemen, with cigars and kid gloves, came de-
bouching past the house. They looked in that place
like a blasphemy.

"Good evening," they said. For none of us had
stirred; we all sat stiff with wonder.

"Good evening," I returned; and then, to put them
at their ease, "A stiff climb," I added.

"Yes," replied the leader; "but we have to thank
you for this path."

I did not like the man's tone. None of us liked it.
He did not seem embarrassed by the meeting, but threw
us his remarks like favours, and strode magisterially by
us towards the shaft and tunnel.

Presently we heard his voice raised to his companion.
"We drifted every sort of way, but couldn't strike the
ledge." Then again: "It pinched out here." And
once more: "Every miner that ever worked upon it
says there's bound to be a ledge somewhere."

These were the snatches of his talk that reached us, and they had a damning significance. We, the lords of Silverado, had come face to face with our superior. It is the worst of all quaint and of all cheap ways of life that they bring us at last to the pinch of some humiliation. I liked well enough to be a squatter when there was none but Hanson by; before Ronalds, I will own, I somewhat quailed. I hastened to do him fealty, said I gathered he was the Squattee, and apologised. He threatened me with ejection, in a manner grimly pleasant — more pleasant to him, I fancy, than to me; and then he passed off into praises of the former state of Silverado. "It was the busiest little mining town you ever saw:" a population of between a thousand and fifteen hundred souls, the engine in full blast, the mill newly erected; nothing going but champagne, and hope the order of the day. Ninety thousand dollars came out; a hundred and forty thousand were put in, making a net loss of fifty thousand. The last days, I gathered, the days of John Stanley, were not so bright; the champagne had ceased to flow, the population was already moving elsewhere, and Silverado had begun to wither in the branch before it was cut at the root. The last shot that was fired knocked over the stove chimney, and made that hole in the roof of our barrack, through which the sun was wont to visit slug-a-beds towards afternoon. A noisy last shot, to inaugurate the days of silence.

Throughout this interview, my conscience was a good deal exercised; and I was moved to throw myself on my knees and own the intended treachery. But then I had Hanson to consider. I was in much the

409

same position as Old Rowley, that royal humourist, whom "the rogue had taken into his confidence." And again, here was Ronalds on the spot. He must know the day of the month as well as Hanson and I. If a broad hint were necessary, he had the broadest in the world. For a large board had been nailed by the crown prince on the very front of our house, between the door and window, painted in cinnabar — the pigment of the country — with doggrel rhymes and contumelious pictures, and announcing, in terms unnecessarily figurative, that the trick was already played, the claim already jumped, and Master Sam the legitimate successor of Mr. Ronalds. But no, nothing could save that man; *quem deus vult perdere, prius dementat.* As he came so he went, and left his rights depending.

Late at night, by Silverado reckoning, and after we were all abed, Mrs. Hanson returned to give us the newest of her news. It was like a scene in a ship's steerage: all of us abed in our different tiers, the single candle struggling with the darkness, and this plump, handsome woman, seated on an upturned valise beside the bunks, talking and showing her fine teeth, and laughing till the rafters rang. Any ship, to be sure, with a hundredth part as many holes in it as our barrack, must long ago have gone to her last port. Up to that time I had always imagined Mrs. Hanson's loquacity to be mere incontinence, that she said what was uppermost for the pleasure of speaking, and laughed and laughed again as a kind of musical accompaniment. But I now found there was an art in it. I found it less communicative than silence itself. I wished to know why Ronalds had come; how he had found his way without Rufe; and why, being on the spot, he had not refreshed his title. She talked interminably on, but her replies were never answers. She fled under a cloud of words; and when I had made sure that she was purposely eluding me, I dropped the subject in my turn, and let her rattle where she would.

She had come to tell us that, instead of waiting for Tuesday, the claim was to be jumped on the morrow. How? If the time were not out, it was impossible. Why? If Ronalds had come and gone, and done nothing, there was the less cause for hurry. But again I could reach no satisfaction. The claim was to be jumped next morning, that was all that she would condescend upon.

And yet it was not jumped the next morning, nor yet the next, and a whole week had come and gone before we heard more of this exploit. That day week, however, a day of great heat, Hanson, with a little roll of paper in his hand, and the eternal pipe alight; Breedlove, his large, dull friend, to act, I suppose, as witness; Mrs. Hanson, in her Sunday best; and all the children, from the oldest to the youngest;—arrived in a procession, tailing one behind another up the path. Caliban was absent, but he had been chary of his friendly visits since the row; and with that exception, the whole family was gathered together as for a marriage or a christening. Strong was sitting at work, in the shade of the dwarf madronas near the forge; and they planted themselves about him in a circle, one on a stone, another on the waggon rails, a third on a piece of plank. Gradually the children stole away up the cañon to where there was another chute, somewhat smaller than the

one across the dump; and down this chute, for the rest
of the afternoon, they poured one avalanche of stones
after another, waking the echoes of the glen. Meantime we elders sat together on the platform, Hanson
and his friend smoking in silence like Indian sachems,
Mrs. Hanson rattling on as usual with an adroit volu-
bility, saying nothing, but keeping the party at their
ease like a courtly hostess.

Not a word occurred about the business of the day.
Once, twice, and thrice I tried to slide the subject in,
but was discouraged by the stoic apathy of Rufe, and
beaten down before the pouring verbiage of his wife.
There is nothing of the Indian brave about me, and I
began to grill with impatience. At last, like a highway
robber, I cornered Hanson, and bade him stand and
deliver his business. Thereupon he gravely rose, as
though to hint that this was not a proper place, nor the
subject one suitable for squaws, and I, following his
example, led him up the plank into our barrack. There
he bestowed himself on a box, and unrolled his papers
with fastidious deliberation. There were two sheets
of note-paper, and an old mining notice, dated May
30th, 1879, part print, part manuscript, and the latter
much obliterated by the rains. It was by this identical
piece of paper that the mine had been held last year.
For thirteen months it had endured the weather and
the change of seasons on a cairn behind the shoulder
of the cañon; and it was now my business, spreading
it before me on the table, and sitting on a valise, to
copy its terms, with some necessary changes, twice
over on the two sheets of note-paper. One was then
to be placed on the same cairn—a "mound of rocks"

the notice put it; and the other to be lodged for registration.

Rufe watched me, silently smoking, till I came to the place for the locator's name at the end of the first copy; and when I proposed that he should sign, I thought I saw a scare in his eye. "I don't think that'll be necessary," he said slowly; "just you write it down." Perhaps this mighty hunter, who was the most active member of the local school board, could not write. There would be nothing strange in that. The constable of Calistoga is, and has been for years, a bed-ridden man, and, if I remember rightly, blind. He had more need of the emoluments than another, it was explained; and it was easy for him to "depytize," with a strong accent on the last. So friendly and so free are popular institutions.

When I had done my scrivening, Hanson strolled out, and addressed Breedlove, "Will you step up here a bit?" and after they had disappeared a little while into the chaparral and madrona thicket, they came back again, minus a notice, and the deed was done. The claim was jumped; a tract of mountain-side, fifteen hundred feet long by six hundred wide, with all the earth's precious bowels, had passed from Ronalds to Hanson, and, in the passage, changed its name from the "Mammoth" to the "Calistoga." I had tried to get Rufe to call it after his wife, after himself, and after Garfield, the Republican Presidential candidate of the hour — since then elected, and, alas! dead — but all was in vain. The claim had once been called the Calistoga before, and he seemed to feel safety in returning to that.

And so the history of that mine became once more

plunged in darkness, lit only by some monster pyro-technical displays of gossip.   And perhaps the most curious feature of the whole matter is this: that we should have dwelt in this quiet corner of the mountains, with not a dozen neighbours, and yet struggled all the while, like desperate swimmers, in this sea of falsities and contradictions.   Wherever a man is, there will be a lie.

TOILS AND PLEASURES

I MUST try to convey some notion of our life, of how the days passed and what pleasure we took in them, of what there was to do and how we set about doing it, in our mountain hermitage. The house, after we had repaired the worst of the damages, and filled in some of the doors and windows with white cotton cloth, became a healthy and a pleasant dwelling-place, always airy and dry, and haunted by the outdoor perfumes of the glen. Within, it had the look of habitation, the human look. You had only to go into the third room, which we did not use, and see its stones, its sifting earth, its tumbled litter; and then return to our lodging, with the beds made, the plates on the rack, the pail of bright water behind the door, the stove crackling in a corner, and perhaps the table roughly laid against a meal,— and man's order, the little clean spots that he creates to dwell in, were at once contrasted with the rich passivity of nature. And yet our house was everywhere so wrecked and shattered, the air came and went so freely, the sun found so many portholes, the golden outdoor glow shone in so many open chinks, that we enjoyed, at the same time, some of the comforts of a roof and much of the gaiety and

415

brightness of al fresco life. A single shower of rain, to be sure, and we should have been drowned out like mice. But ours was a Californian summer, and an earthquake was a far likelier accident than a shower of rain.

Trustful in this fine weather, we kept the house for kitchen and bedroom, and used the platform as our summer parlour. The sense of privacy, as I have said already, was complete. We could look over the dump on miles of forest and rough hilltop; our eyes commanded some of Napa Valley, where the train ran, and the little country townships sat so close together along the line of the rail. But here there was no man to intrude. None but the Hansons were our visitors. Even they came but at long intervals, or twice daily, at a stated hour, with milk. So our days, as they were never interrupted, drew out to the greater length; hour melted insensibly into hour; the household duties, though they were many, and some of them laborious, dwindled into mere islets of business in a sea of sunny day-time; and it appears to me, looking back, as though the far greater part of our life at Silverado had been passed, propped upon an elbow, or seated on a plank, listening to the silence that there is among the hills.

My work, it is true, was over early in the morning. I rose before any one else, lit the stove, put on the water to boil, and strolled forth upon the platform to wait till it was ready. Silverado would then be still in shadow, the sun shining on the mountain higher up. A clean smell of trees, a smell of the earth at morning, hung in the air. Regularly, every day, there was a single bird, not singing, but awkwardly chirruping among the green madronas, and the sound was cheerful, natural, and stirring. It did not hold the attention, nor interrupt the thread of meditation, like a blackbird or a nightingale; it was mere woodland prattle, of which the mind was conscious like a perfume. The freshness of these morning seasons remained with me far on into the day.

As soon as the kettle boiled, I made porridge and coffee; and that, beyond the literal drawing of water, and the preparation of kindling, which it would be hyperbolical to call the hewing of wood, ended my domestic duties for the day. Thenceforth my wife laboured single-handed in the palace, and I lay or wandered on the platform at my own sweet will. The little corner near the forge, where we found a refuge under the madronas from the unsparing early sun, is indeed connected in my mind with some nightmare encounters over Euclid, and the Latin Grammar. These were known as Sam's lessons. He was supposed to be the victim and the sufferer; but here there must have been some misconception, for whereas I generally retired to bed after one of these engagements, he was no sooner set free than he dashed up to the Chinaman's house, where he had installed a printing press, that great element of civilization, and the sound of his labours would be faintly audible about the cañon half the day.

To walk at all was a laborious business; the foot sank and slid, the boots were cut to pieces, among sharp, uneven, rolling stones. When we crossed the platform in any direction, it was usual to lay a course, following as much as possible the line of waggon rails. Thus, if water were to be drawn, the water-carrier left the house along some tilting planks that we had laid down, and not laid down very well. These carried him to that great highroad, the railway; and the railway served him as far as to the head of the shaft. But from thence to the spring and back again he made the best of his unaided way, staggering among the stones, and wading in low growth of the calycanthus, where the rattlesnakes lay hissing at his passage. Yet I liked to draw water. It was pleasant to dip the gray metal pail into the clean, colourless, cool water; pleasant to carry it back, with the water lipping at the edge, and a broken sunbeam quivering in the midst.

But the extreme roughness of the walking confined us in common practice to the platform, and indeed to those parts of it that were most easily accessible along the line of rails. The rails came straight forward from the shaft, here and there overgrown with little green bushes, but still entire, and still carrying a truck, which it was Sam's delight to trundle to and fro by the hour with various ladings. About midway down the platform, the railroad trended to the right, leaving our house and coasting along the far side within a few yards of the madronas and the forge, and not far off the latter, ended in a sort of platform on the edge of the dump. There, in old days, the trucks were tipped, and their load sent thundering down the chute. There, besides, was the only spot where we could approach the margin of the dump. Anywhere else, you took your life in your right hand when you came within a yard and a half to peer over. For at any moment the dump might begin to slide and carry you down and bury you below its ruins. Indeed, the neighbourhood of an old mine is a place beset with dangers. For as still as Silverado was, at any moment the report of rotten wood might tell us that the platform had fallen into the shaft; the dump might begin to pour into the road below; or a wedge slip in the great upright seam, and hundreds of tons of mountain bury the scene of our encampment.

I have already compared the dump to a rampart, built certainly by some rude people, and for prehistoric wars. It was likewise a frontier. All below was green and woodland, the tall pines soaring one above another, each with a firm outline and full spread of bough. All above was arid, rocky, and bald. The great spout of broken mineral, that had dammed the cañon up, was a creature of man's handiwork, its material dug out with a pick and powder, and spread by the service of the trucks. But nature herself, in that upper district, seemed to have had an eye to nothing besides mining; and even the natural hill-side was all sliding gravel and precarious boulder. Close at the margin of the well leaves would decay to skeletons and mummies, which at length some stronger gust would carry clear of the cañon and scatter in the subjacent woods. Even moisture and decaying vegetable matter could not, with all nature's alchemy, concoct enough soil to nourish a few poor grasses. It is the same, they say, in the neighbourhood of all silver mines; the nature of that precious rock being stubborn with quartz and poisonous with cinnabar. Both were plenty in our Silverado. The stones sparkled white in the sunshine with quartz; they were all stained red with cinnabar. Here, doubtless, came the Indians of yore to paint their faces for the war-path; and cinnabar, if I remember rightly, was one of the few articles of Indian commerce. Now, Sam had it in his undisturbed possession, to pound down and slake, and paint his rude designs with. But to me it had always a fine flavour of poetry, compounded out of Indian story and Hawthornden's allusion:

> "Desire, alas! desire a Zeuxis new,
> From Indies borrowing gold, from Eastern skies
> Most bright cinoper . . ."

Yet this is but half the picture; our Silverado platform has another side to it. Though there was no soil, and scarce a blade of grass, yet out of these tumbled gravel-heaps and broken boulders, a flower garden bloomed as at home in a conservatory. Calycanthus crept, like a hardy weed, all over our rough parlour, choking the railway, and pushing forth its rusty, aromatic cones from between two blocks of shattered mineral. Azaleas made a big snow-bed just above the well. The shoulder of the hill waved white with Mediterranean heath. In the crannies of the ledge and about the spurs of the tall pine, a red flowering stone-plant hung in clusters. Even the low, thorny chaparral was thick with pea-like blossom. Close at the foot of our path nutmegs prospered, delightful to the sight and smell. At sunrise, and again late at night, the scent of the sweet bay trees filled the cañon, and the down-blowing night wind must have borne it hundreds of feet into the outer air.

All this vegetation, to be sure, was stunted. The madrona was here no bigger than the manzanita; the bay was but a stripling shrub; the very pines, with four or five exceptions in all our upper cañon, were not so tall as myself, or but a little taller, and the most of them came lower than my waist. For a prosperous forest tree, we must look below, where the glen was crowded with green spires. But for flowers and ravishing perfume, we had none to envy: our heap of road-metal was thick with bloom, like a hawthorn in the front of June; our red, baking angle in the mountain, a laboratory of poignant scents. It was an endless wonder to my mind, as I dreamed about the platform, following the progress of the shadows, where the madrona with its leaves, the azalea and calycanthus with their blossoms, could find moisture to support such thick, wet, waxy growths, or the bay tree collect the ingredients of its perfume. But there they all grew together, healthy, happy, and happy-making, as though rooted in a fathom of black soil.

Nor was it only vegetable life that prospered. We had, indeed, few birds, and none that had much of a voice or anything worthy to be called a song. My morning comrade had a thin chirp, unmusical and monotonous, but friendly and pleasant to hear. He had but one rival: a fellow with an ostentatious cry of near an octave descending, not one note of which properly followed another. This is the only bird I ever knew with a wrong ear; but there was something enthralling about his performance. You listened and listened, thinking each time he must surely get it right; but no, it was always wrong, and always wrong the same way. Yet he seemed proud of his song, delivered it with execution and a manner of his own, and was charming to his mate. A very incorrect, incessant human whistler had thus a chance of knowing how his own music pleased the world. Two great birds — eagles, we thought —

dwelt at the top of the cañon, among the crags that were printed on the sky. Now and again, but very rarely, they wheeled high over our heads in silence, or with a distant, dying scream; and then, with a fresh impulse, winged fleetly forward, dipped over a hilltop, and were gone. They seemed solemn and ancient things, sailing the blue air: perhaps coeval with the mountain where they haunted, perhaps emigrants from Rome, where the glad legions may have shouted to behold them on the morn of battle.

But if birds were rare, the place abounded with rattlesnakes—the rattlesnakes' nest, it might have been named. Wherever we brushed among the bushes, our passage woke their angry buzz. One dwelt habitually in the wood-pile, and sometimes, when we came for firewood, thrust up his small head between two logs, and hissed at the intrusion. The rattle has a legendary credit; it is said to be awe-inspiring, and, once heard, to stamp itself forever in the memory. But the sound is not at all alarming; the hum of many insects, and the buzz of the wasp convince the ear of danger quite as readily. As a matter of fact, we lived for weeks in Silverado, coming and going, with rattles sprung on every side, and it never occurred to us to be afraid. I used to take sunbaths and do calisthenics in a certain pleasant nook among azalea and calycanthus, the rattles whizzing on every side like spinning-wheels, and the combined hiss or buzz rising louder and angrier at any sudden movement; but I was never in the least impressed, nor ever attacked. It was only towards the end of our stay, that a man down at Calistoga, who was expatiating on the terrifying nature of the sound, gave me at last a very good

imitation; and it burst on me at once that we dwelt
in the very metropolis of deadly snakes, and that the rattle was simply the commonest noise in Silverado. Immediately on our return, we attacked the Hansons on
the subject. They had formerly assured us that our
cañon was favoured, like Ireland, with an entire im-
munity from poisonous reptiles; but, with the perfect
inconsequence of the natural man, they were no sooner
found out than they went off at score in the contrary
direction, and we were told that in no part of the world
did rattlesnakes attain to such a monstrous bigness as
among the warm, flower-dotted rocks of Silverado.
This is a contribution rather to the natural history of
the Hansons, than to that of snakes.

One person, however, better served by his instinct,
had known the rattle from the first; and that was Chuchu, the dog. No rational creature has ever led an
existence more poisoned by terror than that dog's at
Silverado. Every whiz of the rattle made him bound.
His eyes rolled; he trembled; he would be often wet
with sweat. One of our great mysteries was his terror
of the mountain. A little away above our nook, the
azaleas and almost all the vegetation ceased. Dwarf
pines not big enough to be Christmas trees, grew thinly
among loose stone and gravel scaurs. Here and there
a big boulder sat quiescent on a knoll, having paused
there till the next rain in his long slide down the mountain. There was here no ambuscade for the snakes,
you could see clearly where you trod; and yet the
higher I went, the more abject and appealing became
Chuchu's terror. He was an excellent master of that
composite language in which dogs communicate with

men, and he would assure me, on his honour, that there was some peril on the mountain; appeal to me, by all that I held holy, to turn back; and at length, finding all was in vain, and that I still persisted, ignorantly foolhardy, he would suddenly whip round and make a bee-line down the slope for Silverado, the gravel showering after him. What was he afraid of? There were admittedly brown bears and California lions on the mountain; and a grizzly visited Rufe's poultry yard not long before, to the unspeakable alarm of Caliban, who dashed out to chastise the intruder, and found himself, by moonlight, face to face with such a tartar. Something at least there must have been: some hairy, dangerous brute lodged permanently among the rocks a little to the north-west of Silverado, spending his summer thereabout, with wife and family.

And there was, or there had been, another animal. Once, under the broad daylight, on that open stony hillside, where the baby pines were growing, scarcely tall enough to be a badge for a MacGregor's bonnet, I came suddenly upon his innocent body, lying mummified by the dry air and sun: a pigmy kangaroo. I am ingloriously ignorant of these subjects; had never heard of such a beast; thought myself face to face with some incomparable sport of nature ; and began to cherish hopes of immortality in science. Rarely have I been conscious of a stranger thrill than when I raised that singular creature from the stones, dry as a board, his innocent heart long quiet, and all warm with sunshine. His long hind legs were stiff, his tiny forepaws clutched upon his breast, as if to leap; his poor life cut short upon that mountain by some unknown accident. But the kangaroo rat, it proved, was no such unknown animal; and my discovery was nothing.

Crickets were not wanting. I thought I could make out exactly four of them, each with a corner of his own, who used to make night musical at Silverado. In the matter of voice, they far excelled the birds, and their ringing whistle sounded from rock to rock, calling and replying the same thing, as in a meaningless opera. Thus, children in full health and spirits shout together, to the dismay of neighbours; and their idle, happy, deafening vociferations rise and fall, like the song of the crickets. I used to sit at night on the platform, and wonder why these creatures were so happy; and what was wrong with man that he also did not wind up his days with an hour or two of shouting; but I suspect that all long-lived animals are solemn. The dogs alone are hardly used by nature; and it seems a manifest injustice for poor Chuchu to die in his teens, after a life so shadowed and troubled, continually shaken with alarm, and the tear of elegant sentiment permanently in his eye.

There was another neighbour of ours at Silverado, small but very active, a destructive fellow. This was a black, ugly fly — a bore, the Hansons called him — who lived by hundreds in the boarding of our house. He entered by a round hole, more neatly pierced than a man could do it with a gimlet, and he seems to have spent his life in cutting out the interior of the plank, but whether as a dwelling or a store-house, I could never find. When I used to lie in bed in the morning for a rest — we had no easy-chairs in Silverado — I would hear, hour after hour, the sharp cutting sound of his labours, and from time to time a dainty shower of sawdust would fall upon the blankets. There lives no more industrious creature than a bore.

And now that I have named to the reader all our animals and insects without exception — only I find I have forgotten the flies — he will be able to appreciate the singular privacy and silence of our days. It was not only man who was excluded: animals, the song of birds, the lowing of cattle, the bleating of sheep, clouds even, and the variations of the weather, were here also wanting; and as, day after day, the sky was one dome of blue, and the pines below us stood motionless in the still air, so the hours themselves were marked out from each other only by the series of our own affairs, and the sun's great period as he ranged westward through the heavens. The two birds cackled a while in the early morning; all day the water tinkled in the shaft, the bores ground sawdust in the planking of our crazy palace — infinitesimal sounds; and it was only with the return of night that any change would fall on our surroundings, or the four crickets begin to flute together in the dark.

Indeed, it would be hard to exaggerate the pleasure that we took in the approach of evening. Our day was not very long, but it was very tiring. To trip along unsteady planks or wade among shifting stones, to go to and fro for water, to clamber down the glen to the Toll House after meat and letters, to cook, to make fires and beds, were all exhausting to the body. Life out of doors, besides, under the fierce eye of day, draws largely on the animal spirits. There are certain hours in the afternoon when a man, unless he is in strong health or enjoys a vacant mind, would rather creep into a cool corner of a house and sit upon the chairs of civilization.

About that time, the sharp stones, the planks, the up-turned boxes of Silverado, began to grow irksome to my body; I set out on that hopeless, never-ending quest for a more comfortable posture; I would be fevered and weary of the staring sun; and just then he would begin courteously to withdraw his countenance, the shadows lengthened, the aromatic airs awoke, and an indescribable but happy change announced the coming of the night.

The hours of evening, when we were once curtained in the friendly dark, sped lightly. Even as with the crickets, night brought to us a certain spirit of rejoicing. It was good to taste the air; good to mark the dawning of the stars, as they increased their glittering company; good, too, to gather stones, and send them crashing down the chute, a wave of light. It seemed, in some way, the reward and the fulfilment of the day. So it is when men dwell in the open air; it is one of the simple pleasures that we lose by living cribbed and covered in a house, that, though the coming of the day is still the most inspiriting, yet day's departure, also, and the return of night refresh, renew, and quiet us; and in the pastures of the dusk we stand, like cattle, exulting in the absence of the load.

Our nights were never cold, and they were always still, but for one remarkable exception. Regularly, about nine o'clock, a warm wind sprang up, and blew for ten minutes, or maybe a quarter of an hour, right down the cañon, fanning it well out, airing it as a mother airs the night nursery before the children sleep. As far as I could judge, in the clear darkness of the night, this wind was purely local: perhaps dependent on the configuration of the glen. At least, it was very welcome to the hot and weary squatters; and if we were not abed already, the springing up of this lilliputian valley-wind would often be our signal to retire.

I was the last to go to bed, as I was still the first to rise. Many a night I have strolled about the platform, taking a bath of darkness before I slept. The rest would be in bed, and even from the forge I could hear them talking together from bunk to bunk. A single candle in the neck of a pint bottle was their only illumination; and yet the old cracked house seemed literally bursting with the light. It shone keen as a knife through all the vertical chinks; it struck upward through the broken shingles; and through the eastern door and window, it fell in a great splash upon the thicket and the over-hanging rock. You would have said a conflagration, or at the least a roaring forge; and behold, it was but a candle. Or perhaps it was yet more strange to see the procession moving bedwards round the corner of the house, and up the plank that brought us to the bed-room door; under the immense spread of the starry heavens, down in a crevice of the giant mountain, these few human shapes, with their unshielded taper, made so disproportionate a figure in the eye and mind. But the more he is alone with nature, the greater man and his doings bulk in the consideration of his fellow-men. Miles and miles away upon the opposite hilltops, if there were any hunter belated or any traveller who had lost his way, he must have stood, and watched and won-dered, from the time the candle issued from the door of the assayer's office till it had mounted the plank and disappeared again into the miners' dormitory.